A HISTORY OF POLICE IN ENGLAND

BY
Captain W. L. MELVILLE LEE
M.A. Oxon.

"Qu'on examine la cause de tous les reláchemens, on verra qu'elle vient de l'impunité des crimes et non pas de la modération des peines."—"L'Esprit des Lois-Bk. VI.," cap. xxii.

METHUEN & CO.
36 ESSEX STREET W.C.
LONDON
1901

CONTENTS

CHAP.		PAGE
I.	Anglo-Saxon and Norman Police	1
II.	Watch and Ward	21
III.	Justice and Constable	43
IV.	Forest Police and Police in the Fifteenth Century	60
V.	Commercial Police and Police under the Tudors	82
VI.	Ecclesiastical Police and Police under James I.	99
VII.	Military Police and Police under Charles II.	124
VIII.	Bow Street Police and Magisterial Reform	155
IX.	Parochial Police of the Eighteenth Century	176
X.	Police at the Dawn of the Nineteenth Century	196
XI.	Pioneer Reformers	217
XII.	"The New Police"	228
XIII.	"[ii]Public Opposition to the "New Police""	245
XIV.	Police Reform in Boroughs	262
XV.	Police Reform in Counties	279
XVI.	Co-operative Police and the Suppression of Riots	309
XVII.	Police Statistics and Penology	335
XVIII.	Detective Police and the Right of Public Meeting	366
XIX.	Conclusion	390

PREFACE

A title of convenient length, but one which shall exactly fit the subject-matter in hand, is a desideratum that seldom lies within an author's reach. The title selected for this book is open to the objection that, though consisting of as many as six words, it is, however, not quite explicit. The sense in which the word "police" is used is explained in the Introductory Chapter, but it here remains to be said that "England" must be taken to include the Principality of Wales, and, incidentally, that by the employment of the indefinite article an indication of the non-pretentious character of the work is intended.

References have been but sparingly given throughout, and, in answer to those critics who may possibly object that the array of authorities quoted is too meagre, the author can only plead in extenuation that opportunities for taking full advantage of good reference libraries are often denied to dwellers in camps and barracks. In general the plan adopted, or at least aimed at, has been to refer to all Acts of [iv]Parliament mentioned in the text, to acknowledge the source of *verbatim* quotations, and to give the authority relied on in support of any statement that may reasonably be held to verge on contentious, or even on debatable, ground.

In amplification of the Criminal Statistics tabulated on page 337, and in confirmation of the deductions there drawn, an encouraging fact may be mentioned. Although the Census Returns for 1901 shew that the population of England and Wales now exceeds thirty-two and a half millions, the Judicial Statistics recently published by the Home Office state that the number of persons brought to trial before the superior criminal courts during 1899 (the last year for which such statistics are available) was under eleven thousand, which is the lowest figure yet recorded.

Before concluding these prefatory remarks I must express my thanks to Lord Alverstone, who has been kind enough to find time to look through my proof-sheets and to allow me to dedicate the book to him; to H. W. Carless Davis, Esq., of All Souls' College, Oxford, who has so generously brought an expert knowledge of Anglo-Saxon history to bear upon my earlier chapters, and to those Chief Constables and other officials who have helped me with information and advice. In particular must I acknowledge my indebtedness to [v]D. W. Rannie, Esq., of Oriel College, Oxford, for it is not too much to say that without his invaluable assistance and encouragement the following pages would never have appeared.

Inner Temple Library
August 1901

INTRODUCTORY CHAPTER

Introducing himself to his readers at the close of the eighteenth century, Dr Colquhoun wrote: "Police in this country may be considered as a new science." A full generation later, or to be more precise, in the year of Queen Victoria's accession, one of the leading magazines of the day found occasion to remark as follows: "The art of preventing offences is unbeaten ground—has hardly had a scientific teacher. On laws and general legislation, on the theory of crimes and punishments, on prison discipline, on the execution of offenders, and all the ulterior proceedings of delinquency, we have treatises without number; but on the institutions of police we have not a single work, except perhaps the matter-of-fact publication of the late Dr Colquhoun."[1] Since this paragraph was first printed a period of unparalleled literary activity has been witnessed, a period so prolific of book-making that the thirty-nine miles of shelves with which the main building of the British Museum is furnished have not sufficed to contain the ever-increasing accumulation of volumes that must be housed. It is true [viii]that in modern melodrama the detective has been found an almost indispensable property, nor has he been altogether neglected by the modern novelist; there are scores of blue-books containing evidence collected by Parliamentary Committees on the subject of police, and there is no lack of excellent manuals wherein the constable's duty is defined and explained; but at the dawn of the twentieth century, and in spite of the over-crowded state of our public libraries, we are still waiting for the advent of the teacher who will investigate and expound for us the police sciences.

In the following pages some attempt will be made to approach this strangely neglected subject, not indeed by the avenue that a scientist would use, but simply to trace in outline the story of English police, keeping in view the underlying principles that have directed, as well as those political and other considerations that have controlled, its evolution. Previous neglect is not however the only reason why the institution of police calls for historical treatment. On three other grounds in particular can the subject claim recognition; it deserves notice on account of its interest, on account of its antiquity, and on account of its importance.

The history of any national institution should not be totally devoid of interest; and amongst all our institutions it would be hard to find one so eminently characteristic of our race, both in its origin and in its development, or one so little modified by foreign influences, as the combination of arrangements for maintaining the peace, which we call "police." Police [ix]questions touch each one of us so intimately in our daily life, in our personal liberty and in our self-respect; the character of a nation is so profoundly influenced by the nature of the control to which it is subjected, that a due appreciation of the scope of police functions, a proper knowledge of the origin and extent of the powers and duties delegated to our constabulary forces, must possess a more than academic interest. Continental gendarmeries, framed for the most part on the Latin model, have been imposed—often ready-made—on various nationalities, without heed to their racial peculiarities, and careless of local tradition or circumstance. Our English police system, on the other hand, rests on foundations designed with the full approval of the people, we know not how many hundreds of years before the Norman conquest, and has been slowly moulded by the careful hand of experience, developing as a rule along the line of least resistance, now in advance of the general intelligence of the country, now lagging far behind, but always in the long run adjusting itself to the popular temper, always consistent with local self-government, and even at its worst, always English.

When a people emerges from the savage state its first care is the institution of some form of civil government. To this there is no exception, it is, in the words of Macaulay, "as universal as the practice of cookery." Martial law may co-exist with, and at times obscure, the civil machinery; but depending essentially, as it does, on local and temporary causes, must in the end inevitably be superseded, and whenever there arises a conflict between the two, the civil [x]administration will invariably outstay the other by virtue of the inertia of its everlasting necessity. The penal department of any form of civil government must principally consist of two closely allied branches, the judiciary that interprets the law and exacts penalties for its infraction, and the police whose duty it is to enforce the legal code as laid down by the judges, it being in the nature of things that judicial functions cannot exist independently of police functions. Webster defines "police" as "the organized body of civil officers in a city, town or district, whose particular duties are the preservation of good order, the prevention and detection of crime, and the enforcement of the laws." Blackstone goes further when he says that "the public police and economy" must be considered as "the due regulation and domestic order of the kingdom, whereby the individuals of the State, like members of a well-governed family, are bound to conform to the rules of propriety, good neighbourhood and good manners, to be decent, industrious and inoffensive in their respective stations." As used in this book, the term "police" approximates to the definitions of both these authorities; in general merely a synonym for "constabulary," it also embraces all the various expedients employed by society to induce its members to acquiesce in the arrangements that tend to promote public security, including such measures as the compulsory education of children, the reformation of criminals, the observance of sanitary and hygienic conditions, the control of the liquor traffic, and the prevention of cruelty to children and animals. In this latter sense the object of police [xi]is not only to enforce compliance with the definite law of the land, but also to encourage a general recognition of the unwritten code of manners which makes for social progress and good citizenship.

Police, therefore, occupies a position of vital importance in the commonwealth; it is not too much to assert that the restraining influence exerted by a good police system is as necessary to the welfare of society as are self-imposed moral and physical restraints to the health of the individual. To the superior judges fall the duties of solving abstruse legal problems, and of determining the weightiest legal issues, but it is the police magistrate who is in daily contact with the criminal and with the aggrieved person, it is he who applies the law in the first instance, and to him the large majority of the people look for decisions upon which their liberty or their property may depend. "There is scarcely a conceivable case," said a London magistrate in 1834,[2] "arising particularly among the lower orders, which may not immediately or indirectly come under the notice of the Police Offices. It is most important, therefore, that every means should be adopted for upholding their reputation, and so extending and increasing their moral influence." Only second in importance to the magistracy comes the constabulary, "the primary constitutional force for the protection of individuals in the enjoyment of their legal rights,"[3] designed to stand between the powerful and the [xii]weak, to prevent oppression, disaster and crime, and to represent the cause of law and order at all times and in all places. In every court and alley the policeman stands for good citizenship, he is a reality that the most ignorant can comprehend, and upon his impartiality, efficiency, and intelligence depends the estimation in which the law is held by the masses.

There is no doubt that this country is well policed, and fortunately for us, there is equally no doubt that we are not over-policed. However numerous and outrageous may be the theoretical imperfections of our method for maintaining the peace, its practical superior has yet to be discovered. A police system does not only need to be efficient, it must be popular; that is to say, it must conduct its operations with so scrupulous a regard to the susceptibilities of the people that public sympathy and approval are not alienated. The problem of devising an engine of sufficient power and mechanical ability to compel subjection to a rigid standard of uniformity is not a matter of great difficulty, but there is little credit and no comfort in the indiscriminate tyranny of a Juggernaut that mangles its suicidal votaries. Government cannot be exercised without coercion, but the coercion employed ought to be reduced to the lowest possible limit consistent with safety, the ideal police force being the one which affords a maximum of protection at the cost of a minimum of interference with the lawful liberty of the subject. The real difficulty of the police problem is therefore to fix the limits where non-interference should end, [xiii]and where coercion should begin. Mill enunciated the maxim that "all restraint qua restraint is an evil," and Bentham taught that only those preventive measures are sound the application of which involves no injury to the innocent; but there is one limit which cannot be disregarded if police is to be a blessing rather than a curse, and that is, that the plan adopted for the prevention of crime must never become more intolerable than the effect of the crime itself.

English police, however, is not the creation of any theorist nor the product of any speculative school, it is the child of centuries of conflict and experiment. Simple pecuniary compensation to the injured, sumptuary laws for the removal of temptation, torture in lieu of legal process, the payment of blood-money to informers, martial law enforced by puritan zealots, an amateur constabulary spasmodically supported by soldiery, the wholesale execution or banishment of offenders, these and many other expedients have all in their turn been grafted on the parent stock, tried, and found wanting. Are our present methods for the maintenance of the peace, for the suppression of crime, and for the encouragement of social virtue, perfect or nearly so? We can hardly suppose that posterity will answer these questions in the affirmative, but we can at least congratulate ourselves that the people of England, no longer living under a barbarous criminal code, enjoy to-day no small measure of security for their property and persons, without having to submit to a host of meddlesome restrictions and unreasonable formalities.

CHAPTER I
ANGLO-SAXON AND NORMAN POLICE

In the days before the attainment of English unity, the maintenance of the peace was the care of certain local institutions and bodies, the nature of which need not here be specified. The Anglo-Saxon period of our history being one of continual change and gradual development, the maintenance of the peace cannot be treated as a homogeneous whole before the various arrangements which secured it had been consolidated, and, for the first time reduced to a system, by Edgar. From this time onwards, however, the whole of the now united England may be said to have enjoyed a general guarantee for public order under the name of the "King's Peace," so called because the king guaranteed, or at least promised, to his subjects, a state of peace and security in return for the allegiance which he demanded from them.[4]

As "the highest maintainer of the peace," the king claimed an actual police supremacy, and was not content with a mere title. Moreover, by virtue of his position as Commander-in-Chief, he had the power of enforcing compliance with the rules of the peace, of which he was the chief guardian and [2]exponent. An English king was not only the hereditary ruler of his people, he was their chosen chief magistrate also. The idea that the peace and orderliness of the kingdom intimately depended upon the personality of its ruler was so deeply rooted that, at his death, the "King's Peace" was held to have lapsed, and, on their accession, English sovereigns were wont to make proclamation afresh of "general peace orders," an example which was followed by William the Conqueror and his successors.[5] Referring to the death of Henry I., a chronicler writes: "The king died on the following day after St Andrew's mass day, in Normandy, then there was tribulation in the land, for every man that could, forthwith robbed another ... a good man he was, and there was great awe of him. No man durst misdo against another in his time. He made peace for man and beast."[6]

The King's Peace was of two kinds: there was the public peace of the realm, common to all men; and there was the private peace proper to the king himself, designed to safeguard his person, to uphold his dignity, and to secure his interests in every way. This royal peace, as it may be called, was especially concerned with certain places, seasons, and individuals; a special measure of protection was accordingly extended to the king and his nobles, to nuns, widows and clergy; whilst breaches of the peace [3]which occurred on Coronation days, on Fast days, and the like, or which were committed in the vicinity of the royal palaces or upon the "King's Highway," received exemplary punishment from the royal judges. The public peace, on the other hand, afforded protection to all alike, to the exclusion only of the "unfrith," as those men were called whose crimes placed them without the pale of society, or who, holding no land, yet failed to enrol themselves in a "tything."

The police system which, under the king, maintained the peace was partly organised on the basis of land tenure. As in the Sudan to-day the Omdah is held responsible for the robberies committed in his district, and as in China the head of a family may legally be called upon to answer for the transgressions of his kinsfolk, so King Alfred looked to the thane[7] to produce the culprit or satisfy the claim. The plan adopted counted on the assistance of self-interest for its complete success; the thane being a landed proprietor and consequently unable to dispose of his property secretly, was security to the king for all the members of his household—if any of them broke the law, his over-lord the thane was careful to bring him to justice. Yet poverty brought no exemption to the landless freeman. He too had to find a guarantee for his good behaviour; if he was unable to attach himself to some thane, he was compelled to combine with others in the same position as himself, in order that their joint goods or aggregate credit [4]should provide sufficient bail for the shortcomings of any member of the society: the penalty incurred by those who could not, or would not, thus find the required security was that they were forbidden to possess cattle, and were no longer under the protection of the law. Freemen, therefore, who had no freehold, banded themselves together into "tythings": a tything consisted of the inhabitants of ten homesteads, and the members elected one of their number to be their "headborough,"[8] who thus became their representative, and was responsible for the community.

The police organisation which we are considering is generally spoken of as the "Frankpledge system," frankpledge signifying the guarantee for peace maintenance demanded by the king from all free Englishmen, the essential properties of this responsibility being, that it should be local, and that it should be mutual. As we trace the history of police in England we shall see that these two qualities have survived through the successive stages of its evolution, and seem to be inseparable from our national conception of police functions.

The development of this system led to the institution of the Hundred,[9] which, as its name implies, was [5]a group of ten tythings, under a responsible head. Hundreds as well as tythings had definite police functions to perform: when a crime was committed, information had to be at once given to the hundred-men and tythingmen of the district, and it was their duty to pursue, arrest, and bring to justice all peace-breakers. In the event of the non-appearance of a culprit at the court of justice to which he was summoned, his nine fellow-pledges were allowed one month in which to produce him, when, if he was not forthcoming, a fine was exacted, the liability falling, in the first place, on any property of the fugitive that might be available, in the second place, on the tything, and,—should both these sources prove insufficient to satisfy the claim,—on the Hundred.[10] Furthermore the headboroughs were required to purge themselves on oath, that they were not privy to the flight of the offender, and to swear that they would bring him to justice if possible. On the other hand, if any member of a tything was imprisoned for an offence, it was not customary to release him without the consent of his fellow-pledges, even though the fine had been paid.[11]

The practice of levying police fines from hundreds and tythings was an old one, and the limits of its application were clearly defined by Edgar: "and let every man so order that he have a surety, and let the surety then bring and hold him to every justice: and if anyone do wrong and run away, let the surety bear that which he ought to bear. But if it be a thief, and if he can get hold of him within twelve months, let him deliver him up to justice, and let be rendered unto him what he before has paid."[12]

The fines[13] that were exacted, called respectively fightwitt, grithbryce, and frithbrec, differed in character, and varied in amount. When several persons had participated in a common crime the fine was payable by all who had a hand in it; an infraction of the peace by seven associates constituted a riot, and if thirty-five persons were concerned, the breach amounted to a rebellion.

Distinct from the official police societies, created by the central government for the general security, there also existed certain private and voluntary associations called peace-guilds, entered into by the inhabitants of London and other towns for their own protection. Each guild consisted of members arranged in ten groups under ten headmen, one [7]of whom acted as chief of the guild and treasurer, the remainder forming a kind of consulting committee to discuss and advise upon the various interests of the associations at their monthly gatherings.

The object of these guilds was simply mutual assurance, and each member had to pay fourpence to a common fund, out of which subscribers were compensated for any loss they might sustain through theft, the treasurer being authorised further to contribute a sum not exceeding one shilling towards the apprehension of delinquents.

The military and police systems were closely allied: the national militia was organised in tythings and hundreds, and had a place to fill in the complete design of peace maintenance; its embodiment was not only resorted to in time of war, it was also liable to be called out by "summons of the array" if disturbances were feared, or even for the pursuit of a single fugitive from justice, but its members could not be called upon to serve beyond the limits of their respective shires except to repel invasion. Every free Englishman between the ages of fifteen and sixty (the clergy and infirm only excepted) was liable to be called upon to perform three public services[14] for the peace of the commonwealth; he was bound to assist in repelling invasions, in crushing rebellions, and in suppressing riots. The Sheriffs therefore who were responsible for the conservancy of the peace in the hundreds were enabled to muster [8]the *posse comitatus*, or whole available police force of the shire, in case of emergency. All men went armed in those days, and since the members of a tything were obliged on the summons of a headborough to join in the pursuit, the cry of "Stop thief" was a formidable weapon in the hands of the local executive.

The Anglo-Saxon conception of police functions is thus clearly intelligible: the internal peace of the country was held by them to be of the first importance, and every free man had to bear his part in maintaining it; theoretically all men were policemen, and it was only for the sake of convenience that the headborough (or tythingman as he came to be more generally called) answered for those of his neighbours, on whom he had to rely in case of necessity. The word "peace" was used in its widest possible meaning, and a breach of the peace was understood to include all crimes, disorders, and even public nuisances. The principle on which the police system was based was primarily preventive. "The conservancy of the peace," says Lambard, "standeth in three things: that is to say, first, in foreseeing that nothing be done that tendeth either directly or by means to the breach of the peace; secondly, in quieting and pacifying those that are occupied in the breach of the peace; and thirdly, in punishing such as have already broken the peace." Our Saxon ancestors did not spend much time in "quieting" or "pacifying"—a lawbreaker was at war with the community and received no quarter—but in other respects Lambard's definition applies.

[9]

It was assumed that all but a small minority of the king's subjects were, to use a modern phrase—good citizens—and personally interested in keeping the king's peace inviolate; and that they might therefore safely be trusted to do everything in their power to preserve it, without any necessity arising for the use of coercion. Had all men been equally trustworthy in this respect no police measures would have been required and none devised; but there existed on the fringe of Anglo-Saxon society, as will occur with all societies, a certain number of delinquents perpetually on the look-out for opportunities of preying on their fellows, and the decennary system of police, as it may be called, was an attempt to hold in check this lawless minority without having to raise and permanently support an expensive or elaborate force for its suppression.

The design was to group all honest men into convenient companies, excluding therefrom and from the benefits that civil government could then confer, not only those men who were living in open defiance of the rules laid down by society for its protection, but those men also, whose reputation for honesty and fair dealing did not stand high enough in the estimation of their neighbours to induce a sufficient number to accept a share of responsibility for their defaults. By this means a fence was set up which divided with a fair degree of accuracy the law-breaking section of society from the law-abiding, the problem of peace-maintenance being much simplified thereby; it was not the declared enemy nor the recognised outcast that was feared; the former might be met with [10]superior force, and the latter could be kept down like vermin, it was the danger of the wolf within the fold that alarmed our ancestors. The dread of secret crime is a deeply-seated national characteristic, and accounts for the savage treatment served out to witches and Egyptians (as gypsies used to be called) through the middle ages and almost up to our own times. Alfred the Great reflected this feeling when he drew a distinction between cutting down a neighbour's tree with an axe and burning it with fire, the latter offence being declared the more heinous of the two, not as one might suppose, because of the danger of the fire spreading to other trees, but because of the clandestine character of the deed, it being open to the offender if detected to declare the burning to be accidental, a plea that he could not advance if the axe was used.

A detected criminal was either fined, mutilated, or killed, but punishment, as we now understand the term, was seldom inflicted; that is to say, the dominant idea was neither to reform the culprit nor to deter others from following in his footsteps. If a man was killed it was either to satisfy the blood-feud or to remove him out of the way as a wild beast would be destroyed; if a man was mutilated by having his forefinger cut off, or branded with a red-hot iron on the brow, it was done, not so much to give him pain, as to make him less expert in his trade of thieving, and to put upon him an indelible mark by which all men should know that he was no longer a man to be trusted; if fines were levied, it was more with a view to the satisfaction of the recipients of the money or [11]cattle or what not, than with the intention of causing discomfort or loss to the offender.

The distinction that we now make between remedial and legal justice was theoretically held by the Anglo-Saxons, that is to say, repayment in money or kind for a civil offence, and death or some less punishment for an offence against the criminal code was recognised in their penal administration; but at the same time fines to expiate criminal injuries were also allowed, both in the shape of amercements to the Crown and of compensation to the injured. Homicides rendered themselves liable to a triple penalty, which, it appears, was the same whether the killing was wilful or whether it was accidental—one third part, called "Maegbote," being assigned to the next-of-kin to compensate him for the death of a relative; a second portion, or "Manbote," reconciling the thane to the loss of his vassal; and the remaining share, known as "Wite," passing to the king on account of the violence done to his peace.[15] Only offences of a particularly heinous description were "bootless" (bote-less), as those crimes for which no compensation was permitted were called—of such a nature were murder when committed in a church, and the slaying of a man asleep.

The fines payable by the aggressor in cases where minor personal injuries had been inflicted were carefully graduated; thus, for a cut one inch long on the face, the sum of two shillings had to be paid; if the wound was underneath the hair only half that sum was exacted; but should the victim have suf[12]fered the loss of an ear, he was compensated to the extent of thirty shillings, and so on.[16]

It would offend our modern ideas of justice if a murderer were allowed to go free on payment of a sum of money to the relatives of his victim, still more so if a portion of the fine went to the Sovereign; but the practice is common amongst semi-civilised communities, to whom the complex and costly methods we now employ would be at once unintelligible and impracticable.

When it came to a question of proof, reliance was placed, in the absence of any surer method of discovering the truth, upon the oath of the interested party or parties; and just as the security of a thane was sufficient, where that of a landless freeman had to be supplemented by the contributions of his neighbours, so would the oath of a man of fortune and position prevail in cases where that of a common man had to be fortified by the corroborating oaths of his fellows.[17]

No matter what his station in life might be a man could always strengthen his case in this way: the more numerous the oath-helpers the greater the value of their evidence, and this held good even if it was clear that none of them were acquainted with the circumstances under consideration, because it was commonly believed that divine interference would prevent any considerable number of persons from perjuring themselves *en bloc*. The various ordeals, by combat, by fire, by water and many others, were conceived in the same spirit.

The principle of making every man responsible for his own actions, and to some extent answerable for the doings of his neighbour, has much to commend it, and its application would produce an almost ideal state of social security if its practical employment was not marred by two inherent weaknesses; in the first place it can only be applied with success to an agricultural community that is content to live always in the same spot, or whose migratory instincts the authorities are prepared to suppress; and, in the second place, such a system puts a premium both on the concealment of crime, and on the commission of perjury, since a tything had every inducement to forswear itself in order to escape the infliction of a fine or to save one of its members from punishment.

That the system above described was effectual in dealing with any crime that may have existed in England at the time cannot be doubted, and Gneist,[18] in his review of the period, says, "The insular position of the country, and the pre-eminently peaceable character of the later Anglo-Saxon times, developed the maintenance of the peace to such a perfection, that the chroniclers give an almost Arcadian picture of the peacefulness and security of the land in the time of Alfred the Great, and at some subsequent periods." Lord Coke[19] too declares that before the Conquest, whilst this ancient constitution remained entire, a man might ride through England with much money about him and run no risk of molestation, [14]though armed with no other weapon than a white wand.[20]

If it is allowable to estimate the efficiency of a police system by the measure of the security enjoyed by those under its protection (nor is it easy to conceive of a fairer or more comprehensive test), it may then be asserted with confidence that the Anglo-Saxon model, crude as it undoubtedly was in many respects, compares not unfavourably with the various preventive agencies which the wisdom of succeeding generations has been able to produce. This comparative superiority survived, as we shall see, until the advent of the admirable system of police, not yet a century old, under which we have the good fortune to live to-day.

After the Conquest, the national police organisation was retained by the Normans, the headborough becoming the "præpositus," and the joint guarantee being known as "mutual security"; but the old forms which had weighed lightly on the people hitherto, were now harshly administered by the conquerors, whose officials, unaccustomed to the system, and indifferent to the susceptibilities of the native population, arbitrarily exacted the police fines, and did so in a manner that whilst proper investigation was rare, violence was common.

Of these officials the worst offender was the "vicecomes," the successor to the shire-reeve (*i.e.* sheriff), who under the Anglo-Saxon régime had controlled the police administration of the county.[21] [15]The Vicecomes went on circuit each Michaelmas, to hold an ambulatory police court, called the Court of the Tourn, to deal with petty offences in the provinces, to bring capital crimes to the cognisance of the superior courts, and to make an annual revision of the frankpledge, *i.e.* an inspection of the police societies, with the object of ensuring that all the tythings were full. The visit of the Norman sheriff generally resolved itself into a demand for the payment of heavy fines, that might, or might not, be legally due, and which too often were heavier than the people could bear, for whereas the English shilling had been worth about fivepence, the Norman shilling was equivalent to twelve pence, and yet amercements were still calculated on the old scale without any allowance being made for the change in the value of the coin. Even in the rare cases where extortion was not practised the local character of the police administration, which had always been one of its most prominent features, was to a certain extent destroyed by the interference of the alien Tourn.

The object of the Vicecomes being to collect as many fines as possible, and to return to the king with some substantial evidence of his zeal, he was not over particular as to details, but fined a whole township or borough, and left the community to settle the incidence of the burden amongst the individuals composing it.

A representative and well-known example of the harsh control that then obtained, may be instanced; an enactment of William the Conqueror ordained [16]that any hundred within whose boundaries a Norman was found murdered, should pay forty-six marks[22] unless the murderer was delivered up within five days; and the sheriffs threw the burden of proof of the victim's nationality on the hundred; in other words, the corpse was assumed to be Norman and had to be paid as such, unless the contrary was proved to their satisfaction; it is almost unnecessary to add that in nine cases out of ten, acceptable proof could not be produced in the specified period of time.

Another unpopular institution was that of Curfew Bell, introduced by the Conqueror ostensibly as a protection against fire, but in reality intended as a check upon the Saxons, to prevent them from meeting after dark, and discussing the shortcomings of their oppressors, or for other political purposes. The Anglo-Saxon Chronicle gives a pathetic account of the severity and injustice meted out by the Normans. "A.D. 1124. This same year after St Andrew's Mass, and before Christmas, held Ralph Basset and the King's thanes a 'géwitenemote' in Leicestershire, at Huncothoe, and there hanged more thieves than ever were known before, that is, in a little while, four and forty men altogether: and despoiled six men of their eyes and mutilated them. Many true men said that there were several who suffered very unjustly; but our Lord God Almighty, who seeth and knoweth every secret, seeth also that the wretched people are oppressed with all unrighteousness. First they are bereaved of their property and then they are slain. Full heavy year [17]was this." And again, "then was corn dear, and cheese, and butter, for there was none in the land: wretched men starved with hunger: some lived on alms who had been erewhile rich: some fled the country, never was there more misery, and never heathen acted worse than these. The earth bare no corn, you might as well have tilled the sea, for the land was all ruined by such deeds."

If we may accept this as a true version of the condition of England and the English, it is abundantly clear that the system of police by decennary societies was inevitably doomed to failure after the Conquest. The two nations, who had little in common, who were in fact animated by bitter racial animosity, could not combine for any common purpose; and it is obvious that the "mutual security" plan can only be successful amongst a community bound together by the ties of family or friendship.

The sheriff's court never won the confidence of the people, and gradually certain neighbourhoods, or, more correctly speaking, certain lords more favoured than the rest, obtained the royal consent to the substitution of local police courts, under a steward nominated by the Lord of the Manor. These "courts of the leet" not only had the power to "inquire of and punish all things that may hurt or grieve the people in general, in their health, quiet, and welfare," but were authorised to abate or remove public nuisances.[23]

Courts Leet became so popular, and proved so successful, that we soon find them established, not [18]merely in a few privileged places, but all over the country; before long the Sheriff's Tourn became the exception and the Court Leet the rule, the struggle for survival only coming to an end when the sheriff altogether ceased to trouble the village communities with his annual visit of inspection.

The rise of the Court Leet marks an important stage in the development of English police. The decennary system could only be of value as long as its strictly local character could be preserved, and the power of interference possessed by the Vicecomes was foreign to the national idea of police administration. Although the creation of the sheriff's court must only be considered as an ill-advised and novel attempt at centralisation, and its discontinuance a return to first principles, it was not to be expected that the Tourn, when once established, would be allowed to disappear until there was an alternative institution ready and able to take its place. On this account the appearance of the Court Leet was well timed, for the moment and indispensable for the future, to act as a link between ancient principles and modern practice.

When Henry II. returned from the Continent in 1170 he found it necessary to investigate the complaints that were persistently made against the sheriffs, who were said to have been guilty of oppression and extortion. The charges were well founded, and the result of his inquiry was that several were dismissed from their office, whilst a few years later the Assize of Northampton considerably [19]reduced the authority of the remainder. In the years that follow we find evidence, over and over again, of the abuse of their power by the sheriffs, whose importance steadily declined in consequence; the decay of their office was gradual at first, but proceeded more rapidly, as we shall see, after the institution of "Conservators of the Peace" by Richard I. At the Council of Northampton provision was also made for holding assizes in the different counties of England. For this purpose the kingdom was divided into six circuits, and three judges, subsequently known under the title of "justices itinerant," were assigned to each circuit.

Notwithstanding the recent friction between the two nationalities (now happily on the wane), and all the evils which had accompanied it, hundreds and tythings continued to perform their executive functions as best they could, and not altogether without success; but the levying of amercements, which was essential to the system, was so liable to abuse at the hands of royal officers, and the fines grew so out of proportion to the offences for which they were exacted, that advantage was very properly taken of King John's humiliation in 1215 to insist that they should only be enforced in future "on oath being made by the worthy men of the district," and steps were taken to confine amercements to their proper limits. By Magna Carta police fines were henceforward to correspond in amount to the magnitude of the crime for which they were incurred, and might not be enforced except with *beneficium competentiæ i.e.* every man had a right [20]to his bare living, the merchant to his merchandise, and the villein to his agricultural implements.[24]

In the following reign an attempt was made to put fresh life into the police administration that for more than a hundred years had been deteriorating; it was therefore ordained[25] that a view of frankpledge should be made every Michaelmas, and tything be kept as in the old days; the effort, however, was not a success, and before long the prestige of the institution was irrevocably damaged by the relief granted to the Baronage and Clergy by the Statute of Marlborough, which excused them from attendance at the Court, unless they received special orders to be present. In any case a return to the past was impossible, the country had outgrown the method of control that had once been efficacious, and altered conditions had completed the wreck of the decennary system that racial differences had commenced. From this time onwards, when frankpledge is spoken of, it must be understood to mean only the general principle that was the basis of the indigenous system; that is to say, a recognition of the bounden responsibility of every citizen to take his part in the duty of maintaining peace in the state; or, in other words, the liability that all men share to render police services when called upon to do so.

---

[21]

CHAPTER II
WATCH AND WARD

The intimate bond which linked together the Kingly Office and the general police organisation invested the latter with a certain concrete dignity that was beneficial. The people were impressed by the fact that police was the special province of the highest personage in the land, at a time when they were incapable of appreciating the abstract importance of the subject. The responsibility for peace-maintenance was in this way definitely fixed on the one individual, who besides being best able to enforce compliance with his commands, had also the greatest stake in the continued preservation of the public peace; a kingdom without order being a kingdom in name only. This was so well recognised that, overbearing or indifferent as too many of our English sovereigns proved themselves, not one of them ever repudiated this responsibility, or failed to lay claim to be considered as the champion of order.

The benefits that resulted from this royal pre-eminence were, it must be confessed, often counter-balanced and sometimes outweighed by corresponding disadvantages—good kings were rare—the hand of a king who was inclined to oppress his people became the more grievous by reason of his police [22]supremacy—whilst under a weak king the burden of oppression grew intolerable on account of the numberless oppressors who immediately arose to take advantage of his supineness. The reign of Henry III., externally brilliant, internally miserable, is a case in point; for fifty-six long years peace gave place to chaos—the king robbed, and the barons plundered, whenever and whomsoever they could—shoals of needy foreigners invaded England—the clergy swindled their congregations first on one pretext then on another, and remitted the bulk of their spoil to the pope's nominees in far-off Italy—"crimes," we are told, "escaped with impunity because the ministers themselves were in confederacy with the robbers." Men had cause to be dissatisfied and an excuse for taking the law into their own hands, with the result that violence from above was answered by violence from below. The lawlessness which followed took several forms and infected all classes of the community—the half-starved peasantry, hitherto patient, now scoured the country, and regained by force a portion of the spoil amassed at their expense by foreigners and others who had traded on the ignorant superstitions of the native English. The outbreak which at first was directed against the Italian clergy soon degenerated into a general campaign of license, until, as we learn, "men were never secure in their houses, and whole villages were often plundered by bands of robbers."[26] The king adopted a capricious policy of repression, but his action, never vigorous, came [23]too late to be effectual, and failed to pacify the disturbed districts.

The obvious, if still unconfessed, inability of Henry III. to cope with the disorders which infested the realm served as a pretext to the barons to usurp the royal functions of peace-maintenance, and keeping the king a virtual prisoner in their hands, they caused the so-called Mad Parliament holden at Oxford in 1258 to create a Committee of Reform armed with authority to formulate new regulations for the preservation of the peace. This committee appointed that four knights should be chosen by the freeholders of each county with power to inquire into and present to Parliament the police shortcomings of their respective shires, enacting as a further safeguard that the freeholders concerned should annually elect a new sheriff, and that the sheriff should be called upon to render to Parliament an account of his stewardship on relinquishing office.

These regulations, which formed part of the "Provisions of Oxford," were well conceived, and for the moment proved extremely popular. But they left little permanent impress on the future life of the nation because they were fraudulently put forth by the barons, who, as it soon appeared, were only scheming to win the populace over to their side in the struggle for power, and who were far more anxious for their own aggrandisement than they were for any object connected with the mitigation of the troubles that afflicted the people. The whole attitude of the nobles was so lawless, supporting, as they did, bands of adherents to prey on each other's lands and on [24]the chattels of the defenceless commonalty, that no lasting good could be expected to follow upon their most specious actions, their very gifts were presumptive evidence of premeditated guilt, and their evil disposition was a matter of common knowledge. "Knights and Esquires," says the Dictum of Kenilworth,[27] "who were robbers, if they have no land, shall pay the half of their goods, and find sufficient security to keep henceforth the peace of the kingdom." Well might Hume exclaim, "Such were the manners of the times!"

The practical disappearance of the decennary societies, followed by the failure of the Provisions of Oxford to restore peace to the State, necessitated the creation of some more effectual agency for the re-establishment of good order. Such a substitute was fortunately provided by the famous Statute of Winchester, which was passed in the thirteenth year of Edward I., of whom it has been said that he did more for the preservation of the peace in the first thirteen years of his reign than was collectively accomplished by the thirteen monarchs next succeeding.

This Winchester statute is especially important to our inquiry, because it sums up and gives permanency to those expedients introduced in former reigns, which were considered worthy of retention for the protection of society; and because it presents to us a complete picture of that police system of the middle ages which continued with but little alteration for more than five hundred years, and which [25]even now, though greatly changed in its outward appearance, is still the foundation upon which our present police structure is built.

The Statute of Winchester is not here presented as a brand-new system of police extemporised in the year 1285, but rather as the definite product of a long series of experiments all tending in the same direction. Legislation hastily conceived seldom survives; and however the case may stand in other lands, or in other departments of government, every police measure which has won a permanent place in English history has had a gradual growth, now retarded, now accelerated—here something removed as old fallacies were exposed, there something added as new knowledge was acquired. A few well-known and representative examples of the process at this stage of its development may be enumerated.

First in importance comes the "Assize of Clarendon," issued in 1166, which describes how notorious and reputed felons are to be 'presented' to the Courts of the Justices or to the sheriffs, which commands one sheriff to assist another in the pursuit and capture of fugitives, and which deals with the restrictions to be enforced against the entertainers of strangers and the harbourers of vagabonds. The Assize of Northampton, which was issued three years after the rebellion of 1173, prescribes severer punishments, provides for the registration of outlaws, and reduces the powers of sheriffs. A writ for the conservation of the peace issued in 1233 is referred to by Dr Stubbs in these words: "This is a valuable illustration of the permanence of the old English [26]regulations for the security of peace in the country.... The principle thus expanded is here developed into a separate system of Watch and Ward, which a few years later is brought into conjunction with the Assize of Arms, and completed by Edward I. in the Statute of Winchester, and by the assignment of Justices of the Peace under Edward III." Finally, Writs for enforcing Watch and Ward and the Assize of Arms, issued in 1252 and in 1253, may be instanced as the immediate precursors of the Statute of Winchester.

Few legislative measures have stood so long or so prominently as this Act of 1285. Its vitality has been remarkable; we find it periodically referred to, and its provisions re-enforced whenever an increase of lawlessness afflicted the State, as the universal and proper remedy to apply to all distempers of the sort; we find it cited as the standard authority on Watch and Ward, even in the eighteenth century, when two Acts of Parliament[28] quote it to prove that the protection of a district is a constitutional duty compulsorily incumbent on its inhabitants; nor was it until 1793, in which year a Committee of the House of Commons appointed to inquire into the state of the nightly watch of the city of Westminster stated that "the Statute of Winchester being very obsolete is a very improper regulation," that people began to talk of it as old-fashioned.

After stating that, "robberies, murders, burnings and thefts, be more often used than heretofore," the statute confirms the ancient responsibility of the [27]hundred for offences committed within its boundaries, "so that the whole hundred, where the robbery shall be done, with the franchises being within the precinct of the same hundred, shall be answerable for the robberies," and ordains that "cries shall be made in all counties, markets, hundreds, fairs and all other places, where great resort of people is, so that none shall excuse himself by ignorance."

Another paragraph defines the law with regard to "Watch and Ward"—the gates of walled towns are to be shut between sunset and daybreak, men are forbidden to live in the suburbs, except under the guarantee of a responsible householder, and it is enacted that in every city "from the day of the Ascension until the day of St Michael," a watch of six men is to be stationed at each gate: every borough has to provide a watch of twelve persons, whilst the number of watchmen insisted upon by law for the protection of the smaller towns, varies from four to six, according to the number of inhabitants in each. Strangers must not pass the gates during the hours of darkness, any attempting to do so are to be arrested by the Watch, and detained until morning, when, "if they find cause of suspicion, they shall forthwith deliver him to the sheriff," but if no such cause is found, "he shall go quit." The affiliated institutions "Hue and Cry" and the "Assize of Arms" are next considered. Both had previously existed in some form or other, but had been allowed to fall into disuse, so it is now laid down afresh that in case strangers do not obey the arrest of the Watch, "hue and cry shall be levied upon them, [28]and such as keep the watch shall follow with hue and cry, with all the towns near." Sheriffs are reminded that it is their duty to follow the cry with the country-side, in pursuit of law-breakers: and that if they are neglectful, a report will be made by the constables to the judges, who will inform the king of the default.

The clauses relating to the Assize of Arms command every male between the ages of fifteen and sixty to have harness in his house, "for to keep the peace"; the nature of the arms to be provided depends upon the man's rank, and on the value of his property, and varies from "an hauberke, an helme of iron, a sword, a knife and a horse" for a knight, down to bows and arrows, which were the only weapons that the poorest class had to furnish. In each hundred two constables were appointed to make a half-yearly inspection of arms, and "such defaults as they may find" shall be notified through the judges to the king, and the king "shall find remedy therein."

The Assize of Arms was something more than a mere police regulation. Sheriffs and constables were royal officers, and the powers entrusted to them, which included the liberty to make domiciliary visits for the purpose of viewing the armour, together with the general supervision they exercised over an armed population, placed at the king's disposal a force that could on occasion be employed for political ends unconnected with the professed motive of the Assize, that of peace maintenance.

The only other part of the statute that need now [29]be noticed deals with the regulating of highways: it is directed that roads leading from one market town to another "shall be enlarged so that there be neither dyke, tree nor bush whereby a man may lurk to do hurt, within two hundred foot on the one side and two hundred foot on the other side of the way": this, however, is not to apply to oaks or great trees, but if a park march with the roadway, the lord must "minish his park the space of two hundred foot from the highways, as before is said, or that he make such a wall, dyke or hedge, that offenders may not pass, nor return to do evil."

The declared object of the Statute of Winchester, was, in the words of the preamble, "for to abate the power of felons," and the highway clause is said to have been designed against the depredations of bands of robbers called Drawlatches and Roberdsmen, who, concealing themselves in the thick undergrowth by the roadside, had been a terror to travellers for the last hundred years or more.

If the law could have been enforced in this particular, so as to leave a clear two hundred feet both sides of the road, the result would have been admirable, but the regulation was framed on too ambitious a scale, with the result that it was generally disregarded, or at the best only partially carried out, and it is extremely unlikely that many lords minished their parks as they were ordered.

It was, of course, extremely difficult to give effect to the new police system throughout England; conditions and customs varied in different districts; before the introduction of newspapers ideas spread [30]but slowly; and people did not readily comprehend strange institutions, nor accept them, when understood, without protest. This was especially the case in the north-westerly provinces; the men of Cheshire, amongst others, were dissatisfied with the new arrangements, and petitioned the king to relieve them of the burden of maintaining so many peace officers; but Edward was not to be influenced against his judgment, by these entreaties, and answered in an abrupt manner that he would not change the law, nor revoke his statutes. The men of Shropshire and Westmoreland also, who, as it appears, had successfully evaded their obligations under the decennary system, now took it upon themselves to ignore the provisions of the Statute of Winchester; with the result that some fifteen years later, on it being brought to his notice that the regulations which he had laid down were not being properly carried out, the king ordained that "the same statute be sent again into every county to be read and proclaimed four times a year, and kept in every particular as strictly as the great charters, upon pain of incurring the penalties therein limited."

It is worthy of notice, that as early as the thirteenth century, the police of the capital city was placed on a different footing from that of the rest of the kingdom, a distinction which, to some extent, has been retained until the present day. The Statute of Winchester did not apply to London, but in its stead a local Act[29] was passed in the same year, having special reference to the government of the [31]metropolis. From this and from other sources, a comprehensive reconstruction might be made of the police arrangements that controlled London at the time of Edward I., the principal features of which may here be briefly indicated.

The city was divided into twenty-four wards, and in each ward there were six watchmen supervised by an alderman, who was expected to acquaint himself with the personal characters of the residents of his ward, and was ordered to secure any malefactors that he might find; the aldermen, therefore, were executive as well as judicial officers, and might have to adjudicate in the morning upon the evidence they themselves had collected overnight.

In addition to the ward-watchmen there was a separate force called the "marching watch" (the germ of the patrols of later days), whose duty it was to exercise a general vigilance for the maintenance of peace in the city, and to give their assistance to the stationary watchmen as occasion demanded. Foreigners, who were not freemen of the city, might not be innkeepers, and lepers were forbidden to leave their houses under the severest penalties; regulations were made against the rearing of oxen or swine within the city walls, and against the establishment of schools of arms where fencing with the buckler was taught. By day the gates were open, but even then care was taken to exclude undesirable visitors, for two sergeants "skillful men and fluent of speech" were placed at each gate to scrutinise all those who passed in or out.

One hour after sunset, curfew was rung simultaneously [32]from the Church of St Martin's Le Grand and in the other parishes, the gates were then shut, taverns were closed, and men might not go about the streets armed till the morning, "unless he be a great man, or other lawful person of good repute, or their certain messengers, having their warrants to go from one to another with lanthorn in hand."

The peace officers were authorised to arrest anyone who broke these regulations, and to bring him the following day before the Warden, Mayor, or Aldermen of the city, for punishment; officers were secured against all penalties for acts done in the execution of their office, and no complaints were permitted to be made against them with regard to the imprisonment or punishment of offenders, "unless it be that an officer should do so of open malice, and for his own revenge, or for the revenge of another that maliciously procureth the same, and not for the keeping of the peace."

It will be observed that the intention both of the Statute of Winchester and of these regulations for the government of London is in the main a preventive one, that whilst every care is taken to place obstructions in the way of transgressors, and every caution exercised to render a criminal career difficult, we hear but little of the penalties that follow upon detection. This tendency is in marked contrast to the custom of subsequent legislation, which increasingly insisted on the infliction of punishment as the only effectual means of diminishing crime. The earliest English police known to us, relied almost entirely, as has already been pointed out, on the [33]efficacy of the preventive principle. The system inaugurated by the Statute of Winchester which took the place of the ancient institutions, may be considered as the connecting link between the two extreme conceptions of police functions, between the policy of prevention and the policy of repression. Watch and Ward was the civil equivalent of the sentry who, in time of war is posted outside the camp, and whose functions are purely preventive, whilst Hue and Cry was partly preventive and partly repressive. Although the main object of the latter institution was the apprehension of offenders, quite half its value depended on the effect produced on the minds of intending criminals by the fear that any illegal act on their part might raise the whole county in arms against them, and by the knowledge that escape was well-nigh impossible.

The law against vagrancy was conceived in the same spirit, the Statute in question requiring Bailiffs of towns to make enquiry every week of all persons lodging in the suburbs, in order that neither vagrants, nor "people against the peace" might find shelter, a regulation designed on the lines of the universal police maxim "Allow the thief no rest." The custom was to make the householder responsible for the deeds of those whom he harboured, and to punish the indiscriminate giver of alms.[30]

This method was not only more humane, but it also proved more effectual than the everlasting imprisonment, whipping, and branding of vagrants, that Tudor legislation enjoined.

[34]

Neglect of the Hue and Cry, failure to make "fresh and quick pursuit," and sometimes want of success when pursuit was duly made, were visited by the imposition of fines upon the neglectful or unfortunate inhabitants as the case might be: many examples of this are on record, *e.g.* (Exchequer Rolls, vol. i. sect. 14).

"Item. The citizens of Lincoln fined fifty marks for suffering a robber to escape, etc.: and the men of Colchester for the like.

Item. (Sussex: 16 Edward I.) Homicide committed in a fray: the offender who had stabbed his adversary, a butcher, takes refuge in the Church of Crawley and abjures the realm: townships of Crawley and Hurst amerced because they did not make suit.

Item. A quarrel in an alehouse at Hodley, in which a man is struck on the head and dies four days afterwards. The offender escapes, and all the persons present in the alehouse amerced, because they did not secure him."[31]

When Hue and Cry had been raised against a fugitive, every man had to lay aside his work and join in the pursuit to the best of his ability, anyone failing to do so, or withdrawing himself without permission, was considered to have taken the part of the person who was fleeing from justice, and the two might be hunted down together, and when apprehended, delivered to the Sheriffs, "not to be set at liberty, but by the King, or by his chief justice."[32] [35]Once levied, Hue and Cry recognised no boundaries, the pursuit spread from hundred to hundred, and from county to county, "till they come to the seaside," or until the man surrendered himself. "The life of Hue and Cry," says Coke, "is fresh suit," and in order that valuable time should not be lost in preliminary enquiries, no liability for malfeasance attached to those who followed the chase; if therefore an innocent man was hunted down, he had no remedy against his pursuers, but, to obtain satisfaction, had first to discover the author of the false report. If the fugitive sought refuge in a house, and refused to open the door, the peace officer might break it open, and in the event of a man grievously wounding another, it was held that killing was no murder, provided that Hue and Cry had been duly levied, and provided also, that the offender could not otherwise be taken.[33]

The best, and as a rule, the only practicable chance of escape open to the pursued, lay in the possibility of his reaching a sanctuary before the hunters came up with him. If a man took sanctuary, his life was safe, but he remained a close prisoner within the precincts of the asylum in which he had found refuge until he received the King's pardon, or until he purchased his freedom by "abjuring the realm," an undertaking which entailed upon him perpetual banishment, besides the forfeiture of all his belongings.

These sacred asylums, within whose precincts the [36]law was powerless, were often made use of in a manner never contemplated when the privilege of affording protection to fugitives was first extended to them. If an offender was unpopular his chance of reaching sanctuary was very remote, it was easy enough to head him off, or to surround the place in such a manner that approach meant certain capture; on the other hand, if the country folk were disposed to favour the escape of the hunted man, there was little difficulty in managing the pursuit in such a way that he should reach his goal in safety. Hue and Cry was therefore not as effectual as it ought to have been, especially against men who for one reason or another enjoyed the goodwill of their neighbours, and its efficacy was still further reduced by the freedom with which Charters of Pardon were granted by the King to powerful nobles and others, who were prepared to pay for the concession.[34]

In addition to the Statute of Winchester upon which his reputation as a police reformer mainly rests, Edward I. was the author of other valuable measures designed to produce and conserve a state of public tranquillity. Under former rulers Sheriffs had been allowed a dangerous amount of freedom, which they had abused for their own advantage, both by improperly admitting to bail offenders who ought not to have been permitted to remain at large, and by exacting bail from others on trivial or trumped-up charges. This practice Edward combated, and forbade sheriffs, under severe penalties, to hold to bail any who were not strictly bailable. Mindful [37]also of the disturbances wrought by idle rumour, he set himself to put a stop to the dissemination of scandal by irresponsible tale-bearers, and decreed that henceforth those "who be so hardy as to tell or publish any false news or tales whereby discord may arise" should be "taken and kept in prison until he is brought into the Court which was the first author of the tale."[35]

Of greater practical value, however, were his enactments dealing with Coroners[36] (so-called because they were principally concerned with pleas of the Crown). With the intention that these most important officers should stand high in the estimation of all men, Edward, in 1275, ordained that no one under the degree of knight should be chosen to the office, and in the year following he defined the powers of Coroners, setting forth what steps they were called upon to take for the better preservation of the peace, and in what manner their functions ought to be carried out. It was enacted[37] that, in the event of any person meeting with an unnatural or violent death, the township concerned had to immediately give notice to the nearest Coroner, who was thereupon bound to issue a precept to the constables of the neighbouring vills, requiring them to cause to appear before him a competent number of good and lawful men in order that the matter might forthwith be investigated at the place where the [38]corpse had been found. If, upon inquiry, and upon the oath of the jurymen, it should appear that foul play had been the cause of death, the Coroner was, by the same statute, further instructed to use his best endeavour to discover the guilty party, and if the murderer was known, the Coroner was authorised to deliver him to the Sheriff and to proceed to his house, and there to cause a valuation of all his belongings to be made, the amount thereof being notified and secured to the township or hundred, which was then answerable to the judges for any amercement that might subsequently be imposed. Nor was the business of holding inquisitions in cases of sudden death the only duty of the Coroner; he was also expected to make enquiry, in like manner, of every reported case of housebreaking, and was required to keep a watchful eye on any of the King's subjects who seemed to live riotously, haunting taverns and the like, and to attach them by four or more pledges on the not unreasonable suspicion that the funds which supported such extravagances proceeded either from some illegal practice, or from a secret store of treasure trove. Though answerable to the King, Coroners were chosen by the county, and sworn by the sheriff; any holder of the office concealing felonies, or failing in his duty through favour to the misdoers, was liable to be fined at the King's pleasure and to be imprisoned for a year.

Much of the good work done for the internal peace of the kingdom by Edward I. was undone by his successor, whose predilection for evil counsellors [39]led to much Baronial resistance, and threw the country back into that state of lawlessness from which it had been delivered by the wise police regulations of the Statute of Winchester.

Organised bands of robbers harried the country, setting at defiance sheriffs, judges, and even the King himself, who was stopped near Norwich by a freebooting knight called Sir Gosseline Denville, and stripped of his money and other valuables. With such an example of reckless disregard of the King's peace before them, it is not wonderful that the lower orders of the people ignored the restrictions that the law imposed; the weak had no protectors, so the hand that was strong enough to take and to hold fast was seldom empty. These predatory rovers waxed so powerful, and grew so numerous as the result of the impunity they enjoyed, that nothing short of a regular military campaign sufficed to free the land from their ravages. The end of this same Denville illustrates the extensive nature of these operations. After years spent in successful plundering, and after an unprecedented reward had been put on his head, he was at length brought to bay by the sheriff of Yorkshire, who, with five hundred men surrounded the inn where the robber slept, and in the course of the desperate fight which followed between the *posse comitatus* of the peace officer and the banditti, it is said that two hundred men were killed before the knight and his brother were captured.[38]

Indolent and incapable as Edward II. proved, [40]his police administration was not altogether without merit, and an important Statute passed in the eighteenth year of his reign is worthy of more than passing notice. In order that the value of this Act may be fully appreciated a few words of preliminary explanation are necessary. One of the principal functions of the Norman Sheriff at his annual visit of inspection or Tourn, was to inform himself (by making inquiry from the chief frankpledges) as to the nature and extent of the crime existing in his district, and to make a report thereof to the King, if, in his opinion, any particular offence or class of offences was unduly prevalent. The exercise of this function, which was known as "presentment," to some extent secured the trial and punishment of criminals, by bringing their offences to the knowledge of the central authority, and the officer who made the report may, in a sense, be considered to have acted the part of a public prosecutor. When the Court Leet took the place of the Sheriff's Tourn this function was partially lost, and the object of the Statute in question was to increase the value of the Court Leet as a preventive agency, by reaffirming and clearly defining its responsibility with regard to the important duty of presentment, which it had inherited along with the other functions of the Sheriff's Tourn. To this end Courts Leet were now (1325) ordered to certify that all the chief-pledges were present at the sitting of the Court to which they were summoned, and that they duly brought to the notice of the same Court all offences committed within their knowledge. For their guidance [41]a list of the matters which concerned them, arranged under thirty-four headings, was added, of which the most important were the following:—

- (*a*) Of damages done to walls, houses, ditches and hedges set up or beaten down to annoyance.
- (*b*) Of Bounds withdrawn or taken away.
- (*c*) Of breakers of houses.
- (*d*) Of petty larrons, and their receivers (*i.e.* harbourers).
- (*e*) Of such as go messages for thieves.
- (*f*) Of cries levied and not pursued.
- (*g*) Of bloodshed and of frays made.
- (*h*) Of escape of thieves and felons.
- (*i*) Of clippers and forgers of money.
- (*j*) Of persons outlawed returned, not having the King's warrant.
- (*k*) Of women ravished not presented before the Coroner.
- (*l*) Of false balances, measures, and weights.
- (*m*) Of such as continually haunt taverns, and no man knoweth whereon they do live.
- (*n*) Of such as sleep by day, and watch by night, and eat and drink well, and have nothing.
- (*o*) Of persons imprisoned and let go without mainprize.
- (*p*) Of the Assize of Ale and Bread broken.

A glance at the subjects enumerated in this schedule is sufficient to illustrate the comprehensive nature of the part assigned to Courts Leet in the general scheme of peace maintenance, and to show how in addition to their primary duty of bringing to light all breaches of the peace, these [42]local police courts were furthermore charged with the supervision of everything that tends to promote good order and good citizenship, such as, for example, the regulating of weights and measures and the abatement of public nuisances.

This Statute is entitled "A Statute for View of Frankpledge," but it was not put forward with any intention of reverting to the old system of police by decennary societies, nor with any idea of superseding or even modifying the Statute of Winchester, but rather as an auxiliary measure to enlarge the sphere of usefulness of that Statute, and to render its administration more effectual, by ensuring that no violations of its provisions should go undetected and unpunished.

[43]

CHAPTER III
JUSTICE AND CONSTABLE

The accession of Edward III. marked the beginning of a new police era, that of the petty constable acting under the direction of the Justice of the Peace. The Statute of Winchester continued to be the guide in matters of police, but the executive which carried out its provisions underwent a change.

Any attempt to follow in detail the history of the Justices of the Peace, and the powers resident in them, is beyond the scope of the present work; this task has already been often and ably performed.[39] It is impossible, however, to divorce the functions of the Justice from those of the Constable; the story of the evolution of the latter is so dovetailed into the history of the former, the two are so closely allied in their mutual relationship of master and servant, that some reference must here and elsewhere be made to the office of the Justice, a functionary who claims a considerable share of attention in any enquiry that deals with police in the full interpretation of the word, because the executive power vested in a Justice as Peace Officer is antecedent to, and on the whole more important than, the judicial [44]authority attaching to him as Magistrate: in other words, he must be considered as a policeman first, and as a judge afterwards.

The origin of the Justice's office is by no means obscure. Towards the close of the twelfth century (1195), by a proclamation of Richard I.,[40] Knights were appointed to see that all males over the age of fifteen years were "sworn to the King" by taking a solemn oath to maintain the peace: after fifty years or so had elapsed (1253) these Knights had become Peace Wardens or Conservators, who again, continually undergoing a process of development as the importance of the Sheriffs dwindled, were eventually invested with judicial powers, and were then known as Justices of the Peace.

When the office of Justice was first created, it was not intended that the Sheriff should be altogether superseded, but rather that the new officer should become an auxiliary agent for the preservation of the peace, to co-operate, as the Conservator had formerly done, with the Sheriff, who still retained the primary responsibility for the policing of his shire. It would appear that the supremacy of the royal officer in matters of police was generally recognised throughout the thirteenth century; for when, in 1285, Edward I. had occasion to rebuke the men of Kent for the prevalence of crime in their county, he made no mention of the Conservator, but ordered the inhabitants to afford in future every assistance in their power to the Sheriff, whose especial province it was (so the King declared) to keep the peace, not [45]only by his own power, but also by means of the "posse comitatus," or power of the county.[41] On the other hand, even at this time, the Sheriff was not always given a free hand. In Warwickshire, for example, all arrangements for the preservation of the peace had first to be submitted to the Conservator for his approval;[42] it cannot, however, be supposed that the supervision exercised by the Conservators over the police administration was more than nominal, because, as a rule, they were great noblemen, holding a plurality of offices, and because the districts within their wardenship were usually too large to be effectively controlled by any one man. We learn, for instance, that in 1281 the Earl of Cornwall was Peace Warden for the counties of Middlesex, Essex, Herts, Cambs, Hunts, Norfolk, Suffolk, Kent, Surrey, Oxon, Beds, Bucks, Berks, Northants, Lincoln, and Rutland.

When both population and trade increased, and when offenders and offences grew more varied and numerous, it became necessary to augment to a proportionate degree the staff of officers answerable to the King for the internal peace of the kingdom: it was no good making more Sheriffs, who had seldom proved a success in the past (whose misconduct, in fact, had led to the restricting of their power to do harm on more than one occasion), and so it came about that the Justice gradually superseded the Conservator, and in the end not only deprived the Sheriff of his judicial powers, but to a large extent took his place as director of the police also.

[46]

The Sheriff did not submit to this curtailment of his authority without a struggle. After he was no longer allowed to act in his old capacity, he sometimes managed to get made a Justice, and to hold both offices in the same county at one time, to the great oppression of the people, who bitterly complained of the heavy fines that were inflicted, and of the outrageous bail that was exacted by these pluralists, until in 1378, at the request of Parliament, Richard II. put an end to such practices. Nevertheless, the Sheriff still remained the responsible person for the levying of Hue and Cry, for the pursuit and apprehension of felons, for the due execution of the sentences pronounced by the law-courts, and was answerable for the persons of prisoners handed over to him for punishment. He also had to perform various duties connected with elections, and until the reign of Edward VI. retained certain military functions.

Before 1328, the so-called justices were executive officers only, "they were little more than constables on a large scale";[43] but in this year, Edward the Third, who had recently come to the throne, considerably extended their powers by entrusting to them the examination and punishment of law-breakers.

The King reserved to himself the right of nominating those who should hold the office, and, throughout his long reign, continued to take the liveliest interest in his Justices of the Peace. He ordered that they should be connected with the county for which they [47]were appointed, by holding therein a certain amount of landed property, a qualification which has been retained for many centuries. He made it a condition that they should be *bons gentz et loiaulx*; and for fear lest the granting of judicial powers to local officials should open the door to extortion on the one hand, and to ignorant maladministration on the other, was very careful as to the class of man he selected. For this reason, the pleadings of Parliament notwithstanding, he could not be induced to give up the privilege of appointing his own nominees, and even the democratic tendencies of modern times have left the appointment of Justices of the Peace in the hands of the Crown. Another Statute[44] (also passed in 1328) ordained that no man should "go offensively" or "ride armed" before the new magistrates—a wise enactment designed to protect them from being brow-beaten and intimidated by those great nobles who sought to obtain their own ends through the awe inspired by the display of a large armed retinue.

In 1333[45] Edward informed the Commons that one of his principal reasons for calling them together was to take counsel with them concerning the means that should be adopted for preserving the peace, and to this end charged them to assist him to the best of their ability. The Commons readily accepted the invitation, and subsequently lost no opportunity of expressing the interest they took in the Justices of the Peace, whose office was the constant theme of suggestions and petitions, which, however, the [48]King, who preferred to take his own line, usually disregarded.

Of the several Statutes that were successively passed dealing with the office in question, the most important became law in 1360.[46] "In every county in England, there shall be assigned for the keeping of the peace, one lord, and with him three or four of the most worthy men in the county, together with some learned in the law, and they shall have power to restrain offenders, rioters, and other barretors, and to pursue, arrest, take, and chastise them, according to their trespass or offence; and to cause them to be arrested and duly punished according to the law and custom of the realm, and according to that which to them shall seem best to do by their discretions and good advisement; ... and to take of all them that be not of good fame, where they shall be found, sufficient surety and mainprise of their good behaviour toward the King and his people ... and also to hear and determine at the King's suit all manner of felonies and trespasses done in the same county according to the laws and customs aforesaid."

Two years after the Statute above quoted had been enacted, the Justices were empowered to sit quarterly for the transaction of business,[47] and before long Quarter Sessions absorbed the major portion of the executive and administrative government of the county.[48]

[49]

When Richard II. ascended the throne, the Justice of the Peace was thus firmly established as one of the permanent institutions of the kingdom. Since that time, the office has passed through many vicissitudes, experiencing many a rise and many a fall; but through all these changes, the Statute quoted above, which first defined his position, has always been referred to when any doubt arose as to the powers a Justice may exercise by virtue of his commission, and its meaning has been stretched and extended by degrees until, as Burn says, "there is scarcely any other Statute which hath received such a largeness of interpretation."[49]

It will be observed that in addition to the powers given to Justices for the punishment of offences against the peace, express authority was also conferred upon them by the same instrument for the prevention of such offences, for they were specially ordered to "take sufficient surety and mainprise of all them that be not of good fame." We have seen how under the decennary or tything system, all freemen were bound to find sureties for the preservation of the peace, and we have watched the decay of that system after the Norman invasion; in the provisions of this Act of Parliament, however, we may discover at least a partial revival of the ancient plan of demanding guarantees against any contingent infraction of the public peace, and of associating in a joint pecuniary responsibility the actual or potential peacebreaker with his immediate neighbours.[50] The "sufficient security" which Justices were authorised [50]to take might be of two kinds—"Surety of the Good Behaviour" and "Surety of the Peace," and the security might be by Bail or by Mainprise, the difference between the two being "that mainpernors are only surety, but bail is a custody; and therefore the bail may retake the prisoner, if they doubt he may fly, and detain him."[51] ... Sureties of the Good Behaviour and Sureties of the Peace were granted on suspicion or on the flimsiest sort of evidence; for instance, "any suspected person who lives idly, and yet fares well, or is well apparelled, having nothing whereon to live," any common gamester, or the reputed father of a bastard child, or an eaves-dropper even, might be called upon to find mainpernors or bail; and so great discretion was required on the part of the Justices, who had to decide such knotty points; it was consequently of the highest importance that these officers should be familiar with the districts in which their duties were performed, and legal erudition was a consideration subordinate to personal character and local knowledge. When the Law was young evidence was received for what it was held to be worth, without distinction as to whether it might be hearsay, circumstantial, or direct; the word of a thane would prevail against the evidence of six ceorls; in fact the credibility of every witness was appraised in proportion to his social position, just as a man's life had formerly been estimated at a distinct valuation, and scheduled according to a recognised scale.[52]

[51]

The feudal system had taught the retainer to look to the Lord of the Manor for the redress of any grievance that he might have against his neighbour. To the tribunal of the Manor, also, he was wont to bring family differences for settlement; here the father would recount the follies of his son, and the wife complain of the habits of her husband: for, just as the priest was the spiritual adviser to his congregation, so, in many instances, was the Lord of the Manor the lay-counsellor to the dwellers on his estate. It was essential, therefore, that the Justice, who had to perform many of the duties formerly attaching to the feudal lord, should be a local man and a man of position; people would have nothing to do with a stranger, or with one who, in their opinion, was a man of no account, however great a lawyer he might be.

The status of the Justice of the Peace at the time of Edward IV. was not very different from that held by the same functionary at the present day. His powers and duties are not now quite the same as they once were, but the history of the office has been remarkable for its steady persistence in one groove: the Justices of five hundred years ago might be defined as a select number of country gentlemen deriving their authority from the Crown, primarily responsible to the Crown for the preservation of the peace, and exercising judicial functions of a simple kind within the limits of the county for which they were appointed—and such a definition would still apply.

The rise of the Justice of the Peace at the [52]expense of his rivals was due to some extent to political causes. Sovereigns were favourable to the growing importance of an estate that promised to act as a counterpoise to the arrogant claims of the nobles, and although Parliament had nothing to do with the appointment of the new magistrates it was generally in sympathy with them, because they did not abuse their powers as the sheriffs had done, nor neglect their duties like the conservators; and also because the House of Commons, which was almost entirely composed of country gentlemen, recognised in the Justices, members of the same social class to which they themselves belonged. The mass of the people, too, were inclined to view them with favour, choosing to place themselves and their fortunes in the hands of men they knew something about, who were on the spot and likely to execute justice speedily, rather than in the hands of strange judges whose visits were few and far between, and who, when they came, were likely to be deficient in local knowledge.

The first Justices therefore were in the enviable position of enjoying at one and the same time the hearty support of King, Commons, and People; but unfortunately such a healthy state was not destined to be permanent, and before long the symptoms of internal disease presented themselves.

As the attractions of town life increased it became more and more difficult to obtain the services of the best kind of country gentlemen for a post that was often arduous, that brought no emolument to the holder, and that was incompatible with absenteeism. [53]An inferior type of man was glad enough to take the place for the sake of the patronage and the social position he thereby acquired, and a corresponding depreciation in the police administration was at once apparent. Richard II. endeavoured to counteract this tendency by ordaining that Justices should be possessed of property in their own county of a minimum annual value of twenty pounds, and at the same time relieved them of some of their routine duties by appointing Clerks of the Peace to assist them. He fixed the number of Justices for each county at eight, two of whom only had to be in attendance at each Sessions.

These remedial measures served their purpose for the time, but in after years we find the danger resulting from the admission of inferior men into the ranks of the Justices constantly recurring, necessitating a more rigid enforcement of the property qualification.

In the city of London the duties that in the country would have fallen to the Justices of the Peace were performed instead by the Mayor and Aldermen, a custom that has been continued ever since, and with good results.[53]

All that remains to be said on the subject of Justices of the Peace in this place must be compressed into a few lines. Various Statutes, passed between 1389 and 1399, multiplied their powers exceedingly by giving them authority to settle the [54]wages of labourers and servants, to punish unlawful huntings, false weights in the staple, and the unlawful wearing of liveries. In the reign of Henry IV. they were directed by statute to suppress riots with the help of the Sheriff and his "posse," and Henry V. ordained that, in future, Justices should only be appointed from "the most sufficient men of the counties, resident respectively therein," and that they should thenceforward be nominated by the King's Council.[54]

The Yorkist period saw Justices of the Peace at the zenith of their power; for, although the importance of the office tended to increase rather than to diminish, Tudor sovereigns, always masters in their own house, refused to allow them the same measure of independence that they had before enjoyed—in fact, one of the first acts of Henry VII.[55] was to rate them soundly for their past negligence, and to threaten unpleasant consequences if an improvement was not quickly manifest.

Subordinate to the Justices were the petty constables; "the lowe and lay ministers of the peace" as Lambard calls them; these officers were appointed annually by the jury of the Court Leet, but their control was vested almost entirely in the hands of the magistrates who swore them in, and who afterwards directed their actions.

Careful investigation into the origin and precise nature of the petty constable's office has failed to set finally at rest the many discussions that have arisen from time to time, and has left some minor points still obscure; the essentials, however, are [55]sufficiently clear for the purposes of the present inquiry.

The word "constable" was imported by the Normans, but its etymology is not quite certain; formerly it was said to be derived from "Conning," a king,[56] and "Stapel," a stay or prop, and to signify "the king's right-hand man," but this is an unlikely solution, because the invaders despised the Anglo-Saxon language, and would not use a word which was partly derived from that tongue. Latterly the derivation "Comes-stabuli," meaning an Equerry or Master of the Horse, has been generally accepted as correct. In England the title has been applied to a variety of functionaries, some high and some low, who had little in common beyond the fact that they all owed their authority to the Crown.

The first mention of petty constables occurs in 1252, in a writ of Henry III. for enforcing watch and ward. This writ provides for the employment of these officers in parish and township, but it is more than likely that the office was not then a new one, because the word "constable" is there used without any explanation being added, and it may therefore be assumed that its meaning was a matter of common knowledge.

The Statute of Winchester, it will be remembered, ordained that there should be two constables in each hundred, to carry out the inspection of arms; these officers were probably connected with the Militia, and were closely allied to, if not identical with, the High Constables of later date; in any case they [56]must not be confused with the petty constables, who, according to Blackstone, were so called when they added the duties of assistants to the High Constable, to their ancient business of keeping the peace, and who, as Lambard explains, were modified tythingmen; "when there be many tythingmen in one parish, there only one of them is a constable for the king, and the rest do serve but as the ancient tythingmen did."

The transition from the Anglo-Saxon tythingman to the petty constable, that is to say, from the chief frankpledge to the Justice's assistant was very gradual, and it is impossible to determine a rigid boundary line between the two. All we can say is that the term "constable" was introduced as early as the year 1252, and that the term "tything man" continued to be occasionally made use of down to the beginning of the nineteenth century: that first and last the offices were in effect the same does not admit of doubt, both were primarily *ex officio* guardians of the peace, and when the tything man came to be commonly called "constable," it does not follow that the change marked the creation of a new office.

The Normans naturally substituted French or Latin names for Anglo-Saxon ones; headborough became præpositus, and shire-reeve or sheriff became vicecomes. Of these foreign titles, the former is now never used, and the latter[57] has acquired a new meaning totally distinct from its original sense. "Constable," on the other hand, survived, although at first [57]it was used only by the Normans, and in official documents, the people continuing to employ the native words according to the custom of the different parts of the country; thus in Middlesex there were Headboroughs, in Kent Borsholders, and in the West of England tythingmen.

It is not necessary to pursue the matter further except to say, that when the Justices of the Peace, owing to the increased amount of work thrown upon them, were in want of subordinate officers, advantage was taken of the staff of tythingmen already existing, some of whom were given new functions, *e.g.* the execution of the Justices' warrants and the service of summonses, but without prejudice to their duties in connection with peace-maintenance; in short, the titles of tythingman, petty-constable, parish-constable, and finally police-constable, are the various names applied to the same office from the time of Alfred the Great to that of King Edward the Seventh.

We do not know enough about the social distinctions of the period to say what the precise status of the early constable was. His position was without doubt an honourable one, superior in every way to that of the parish constable of later years, who only served because he could not help it, or because he was poor enough to bear another man's burden for a paltry pecuniary consideration.

The local competence of the officer has always been insisted upon, and his incapacity to exercise any powers outside a particular area was one of the causes that contributed to make him the useless nonentity that he at one time became. So close was the [58]connection between constable and parish that the Court of King's Bench decided, in 1734, that a place that did not employ one constable at least must be considered merely as a hamlet, and was not entitled to the privileges that belonged to an independent township; and whenever similar questions arose, the decision invariably turned on the existence or the non-existence of a parish constable.

The qualifications that a constable ought to possess are thus tabulated by Coke:—

- i. Honesty: to execute his office truly without malice, affection, or partiality.
- ii. Knowledge: to understand his duty, what he ought to do.
- iii. Ability: as well in estate as in body, that so he may attend and execute his office diligently, and not neglect the same through want or impotency.[58]

It would be tedious to recount the multifarious duties that from time to time have fallen to the constable, especially as many of the most important are noticed in subsequent chapters; it will here be sufficient to state, in a general way, a few of the main directions by which he was expected to act: these may shortly be summarized as follows:—

- i. His duties with regard to watch and ward were, to keep a roster of the watchmen, to see that they were vigilant and alert during the hours of watching, to receive into custody any guilty or reasonably suspected person handed over to him by the watch, and to keep such [59] person in safety, until he should give bail or be brought before a Justice of the Peace.
- ii. With regard to Hue and Cry, and generally with regard to the pursuit and arrest of felons, peacebreakers and suspected persons, his duty was to obey the sheriff, to follow with the Hue and Cry, and to keep in safe custody any prisoner delivered to him, until relieved of further responsibility by the orders of Justice or Sheriff.
- iii. With regard to inquiring into, and prosecuting offences: he was bound to make presentment at the assizes, sessions of the peace or leet, and in some cases before the coroner, "of all bloodsheddings, affrays, outcries, rescues, and other offences committed or done against the King's Majesty's Peace."
- iv. Finally he had to serve precepts, warrants and summonses, and obey all the lawful commands of the High Constable and Justice of the Peace.

The subordination of petty constables to Justices was from the first generally understood and acted upon, but the custom did not receive definite official sanction until the seventeenth century, when it was tardily recognised by statute.[59] The true relationship between the two has found apt expression in an old simile which likens constables to the eyes and hands of the Justices, "eyes to see through the medium of presentments, and hands to act by virtue of warrants or process."

CHAPTER IV
FOREST POLICE AND POLICE IN THE FIFTEENTH CENTURY

Just as the state of public tranquillity brought about by the wise government of Edward I. had been disturbed by the irresponsible and childish behaviour of his pleasure-loving successor, so was the admirable domestic policy of Edward III. robbed of its due reward by the lack of judgment and the want of administrative capacity exhibited by Richard II., whose unhappy reign is thus described by Froissart. "The State generally of all men in England began to murmur and to rise one against another, and ministering of justice was clear stopped up in all courts of England, whereof the valiant men and prelates, who loved rest and peace, and were glad to pay their duties, were greatly abashed; for there rose in the realm companies in divers routs, keeping the fields and highways, so that merchants durst not ride abroad to exercise their merchandise for doubt of robbing; and no man knew to whom to complain to do them right, reason, and justice; which things were right prejudicial and displeasant to the good people of England, for it was contrary to their accustomable usage."

It would be unjust, however, to attribute the state of affairs as above portrayed solely to Richard's incapacity: he was still a minor when his grandfather died, and many circumstances conspired to render his task an extremely difficult one. A latent discontent had smouldered amongst the peasantry ever since the oppressive Statute of Labourers had been passed some thirty years before, and the universal poll-tax of one shilling a head, imposed in 1379 to meet the expenses incurred in the interminable wars with France and Scotland, suddenly caused the flame of rebellion to blaze forth with unexampled violence. It has been said that if anything like an adequate police force had been available in 1381, Wat Tyler's movement might have been arrested before the riots in the Southern Counties had attained the dimensions of a general insurrection. Such may, or may not, be true of this particular rising; but happily for English liberty there has never existed in this country any police force at the disposal of the central government, powerful enough to coerce the nation at large. Our national police has always been of the people and for the people, and obviously at no time could long be used to oppress those from whom its strength was derived, provided only that one and the same sentiment pervaded a majority of the oppressed.

The attack on villenage was too reasonable to be fruitless, and resistance to the popular demands could be but temporary. The death of Tyler, and the consequent suppression of the insurrectionary movement which he led, caused the concessions wrung from the King to be revoked, and so delayed the cause of agrarian freedom; but the ultimate triumph of free tenure and labour was already assured from the moment that unanimity was achieved.

The constitution of the general police of the country being of such a nature that it was powerless to enforce any universally unpopular measure, a distinct and separate organisation was required to administer the well-hated code of law which had to do with the royal prerogative of hunting. The whole subject of forest law and forest police is of sufficient interest and importance to warrant an account of its main characteristics in some detail.

The King's Peace, as we have already seen, was of two kinds—there was the public peace of the realm, and there was the royal or private peace, enjoyed by the Sovereign, and by those closely connected with him. If we examine further these main divisions, we shall find that each is composed of certain sub-divisions, with their own particular laws and customs: thus under the general heading of public peace must be included—(1) the peace and privacy to which every man is entitled at his own fireside, securing him against all intrusion as long as he commits no felonious action—(2) the "peace of the church" as kept by the Ecclesiastical Courts—and (3) the "peace of the sea" with its court (afterwards known as the Court of Admiralty) "to maintain peace and justice amongst the people of every nation passing through the sea of England."[60]

[63]

The private peace of the King, besides protecting his person and the precincts of his palaces, extended also over all the Royal Forest land, that is to say, over about a third part of the whole area of England: Canute's law was "I will that every man be entitled to his hunting in wood and field, on his own possession. And let everyone forego my hunting";[61] but there is no evidence to prove that the Danish King enforced his forest law otherwise than by the ordinary law of the land. The system of game preservation that grew up under the Normans, however, was so rigid that it necessitated the creation of special laws, special courts of law, and a special police for the prevention and punishment of illegal hunting. The Norman code was modified somewhat by Magna Carta,[62] and again in 1217; but it continued to oppress the nation through many generations, for wherever the peace of the forest was well maintained, there did the peace of the people suffer.

The amount of afforested land varied considerably from time to time. Henry II. possessed 68 forests, 13 chaces and 781 parks,[63] but it was not necessarily those monarchs who were particularly devoted to sport that were the most exacting, a strict enforcement of the forest laws brought much money to the [64]royal exchequer in the shape of fines levied on trespassers and others who were tempted to offend against the arbitrary restrictions imposed.

"A Forest," says Manwood,[64] "is a certain territory of woody grounds and fruitful pastures, privileged for wild beasts and fowls of forest, chase and warren to rest, and abide there in the safe protection of the King, for his delight and pleasure: which territory of ground so privileged is mered and bounded with irremovable marks, meres and boundaries, either known by matter of record or by prescription: and also replenished with wild beasts of venery and chase, and with great coverts of vert, for the succour of the said beasts (to have their abode in): for the continuance and preservation of the said place, together with the vert and venison,[65] there are particular officers, laws and privileges belonging to the same, requisite for the purpose, and proper only to a Forest and no other place."

In connection with every forest there were four Courts, called respectively the Woodmote Court, the Court of Regard, the Court of Swanimote, and the Court of the Justice Seat. Of these the first was only competent to inquire of offences, and [65]could not proceed to conviction. The Verderers, as the judicial officers of this Court were called, met once in every forty days, and could acquit accused persons, or hold them to bail—in the latter case the attachment had to be by the goods of the offender, unless he was "taken with the Mayneer," *i.e. in flagrante delicto*,[66] when the attachment might be by his body. "If any Forester shall find any man attachable for Vert in the Forest, first he shall attach him by two pledges, if they be to be found: and if he be afterwards found, he shall attach him by four pledges: and if the third time, he shall be presented before the Verderers, and be put by eight pledges: after the third attachment, his body shall be attached and retained, that he may remember what thing Vert is."[67]

Coke tells us that there were four degrees of "Mayneer," viz.:—

- (i.) Dog-draw, or tracking a wounded deer.
- (ii.) Stable-Stand, that is, standing ready to shoot or course, with weapon in hand, or greyhounds in leash.
- (iii.) Back-bear, or carrying away the venison; and
- (iv.) Bloody-Hand, or being found in the forest stained with blood.[68]

[66]

The second Court, that of "Regard," was held once in three years, and had for its object the prevention of unlawful hunting. For this purpose all dogs belonging to dwellers near the forest were registered and divided into three classes; that is to say (1) greyhounds, including spaniels and lurchers; (2) mastiffs, including the various kinds of large dogs; and (3) dogs of the smaller breeds. No restriction was placed on the possession of the last-mentioned class, but whilst greyhounds were not allowed on any pretence, mastiffs might be kept by a man for his own protection, provided that he had them mutilated in such a way that they could not pursue and pull down the game. This operation, called "lawing" or "expeditation," consisted in removing the claws of the fore-feet, and was performed in the following manner—One of the dog's fore-feet was placed upon a piece of wood eight inches thick and twelve inches square, and then the three claws were struck off at one blow with a two-inch chisel; if a mastiff was found "unlawed" near a forest, a fine of five shillings was imposed on its reputed master.

The "Court of Swanimote" met three times a year, and had the power not only of inquiring into all alleged offences against the forest laws, but, unlike the Woodmote, might also convict. Finally, judgment was given and sentences passed by the chief Justice of the Forest, at the triennial meeting of the Court of the Justice Seat.[69]

Each forest was surrounded by its "purlieu," or belt of pasturage, for the deer to graze in. The [67]jurisdiction of the Courts above enumerated extended over both forest and purlieu, and since the two together covered a third part of the kingdom, it will be seen that the police regulations that secured the peace of the forest profoundly affected the daily life of the nation. Many of these regulations pressed very hardly on the people, especially on folk who had the misfortune to live in the purlieu: for instance, a man found trespassing by night could be imprisoned, even if he was only in search of strayed cattle, and his beasts might be confiscated. In times of drought, or when grazing was scarce, foresters might lop trees and cut fodder for their charges on the land of any man, whilst tanners and dealers in horn were not permitted to live anywhere in the neighbourhood of a forest, for fear lest their trade should tempt them to become receivers of stolen property.

When an offence had been committed Hue and Cry might be made by any of the King's ministers of the forest, but the pursuit had to be "fresh"; that is to say, the offender had to be detected in the act, and the fugitive kept always in sight. Pursuit, on suspicion, was illegal, and Hue and Cry was applicable to Trespass in Venison only, not to Trespass in Vert. If any township or village failed to follow the Hue and Cry they were liable to be amerced at the Justice Seat for the default.[70]

From the "Carta de foresta"[71] we learn that the [68]officers originally appointed to each forest were fifty-two in number, and consisted of four Primarii or Chiefs of the forest, sixteen Mediocres homines, or Yoongmen, and thirty-two Minuti homines, or Tine-men. This organization did not long continue, however, and was quite extinct at the accession of Henry II. The four Primarii were superseded by four Verderers; the sixteen Yoongmen gave place to twelve Regarders; and instead of thirty-two Tine-men we find a staff of Foresters, with their underlings, called Walkers or Rangers.[72] The number of Foresters and Rangers employed was not arbitrarily fixed, but varied with the size of the forest, and in accordance with the exigencies of time and place. The ministers of the forest appear to have been very numerous in the days of the Plantagenets, and the functions of the different grades were clearly defined: thus, the Verderers were judicial officers, roughly corresponding to Justices of the Peace; the Agisters were officers whose business it was to look after the pasturage of the purlieu; the Regarders were responsible for the lawing of dogs; whilst the Foresters and Rangers were sworn to preserve the wild beasts and timber respectively in their several bailiwicks. The precautions taken to preserve the peace of the forest were doubled during the Month of Fence, or breeding season, at which time the officers were ordered to be more than usually vigilant, and offences were punished with increased severity.

[69]

In the last chapter reference was made to the oath which every male over fifteen years of age had to take in furtherance of the general scheme of peace-maintenance. Similarly, under forest law, an oath was required from all the inhabitants of the forest, that they would not disturb the peace of the wild beasts therein. Manwood says that this oath was anciently administered in doggerel verse, in some such words as these:

"You shall true Liege-man be,

Unto the King's Majestie:

Unto the beasts of the Forest you shall no hurt do,

Nor anything that doth belong thereunto:

The offences of others you shall not conceal,

But to the utmost of your power you shall them reveal,

Unto the officers of the Forest,

Or to them who may see them redrest:

All these things you shall see done,

So help you GOD at his Holy Doom."[73]

Such then in brief were the salient features of the police arrangements by which the prerogative of hunting was secured to the Sovereign, arrangements which, it will be seen, were closely allied to the general scheme of peace maintenance then in vogue throughout the realm. A fuller description of Forest Law, together with an interesting map of the Forest lands, may be found in Mr Inderwick's "The King's Peace": the present enquiry, however, must not extend beyond this slight survey of the machinery by which the laws in question were enforced, and may conclude with a glance at the [70]influence that such legislation exerted over the country at large. The severity of the law coupled with the inadequacy of the executive government produced their natural result. The people resented the harsh treatment they were subjected to, and broke the unpopular regulations or evaded the irksome restrictions whenever they could, which was not seldom. Many who under a wiser régime would have remained good citizens became outlaws merely out of a spirit of opposition, and in consequence, these huge tracts of forest, whose recesses were hardly ever visited even by the forest officers, and whose boundaries were hardly known to anyone else, became the stronghold of the lawless and disaffected, as well as the refuge of the unfortunate.[74]

In the opinion of many, our existing game laws, are harsh and tyrannical: it is often said that all men have an inalienable right to chase or snare any animal that is not domesticated, because, in the nature of things, a wild beast cannot have an owner. All this may be perfectly true, but if such a common right existed, it has not been enjoyed for a very long time, not since the days, perhaps, when our [71]forefathers performed their Druidical rites at the monoliths of Stonehenge, apparelled only in woad and mistletoe. It is unprofitable to argue about the rights of prehistoric man: what was best for him is not always applicable to a twentieth century community, and we may be thankful that whilst a few beasts of warren and chase still remain to us, we are no longer oppressed, as men used to be, by a relentless "lex foresta" for their protection.

To return, however, from the digression into which the consideration of forest law has led, to the more general theme of the police system of the Statute of Winchester, it is to be observed that the terms "Watch" and "Ward," though commonly used in conjunction to express a single idea, are not really synonymous. Blackstone says that the ward was set by day, and the watch by night, and that the one begins only when the other ends. Without making too much of the distinction between the two, we must remember that the population was almost entirely an agricultural one, and was occupied throughout the day in the fields; consequently every man could protect his own property and, if necessary, raise the hue and cry against any who came to despoil him. Household belongings were few, and apparently of such little account that not only were they always left unprotected in the daytime, but it was even thought unnecessary to employ a nightly police except during the summer and autumn months, when the crops were ripening in the fields, the Statute only requiring the watch to be set "from the day of the Ascension until the day of St Michael."

[72]

The method of setting the watch was by house-row, that is to say, a list of the dwellings in every parish and township was prepared, and as his turn came round each householder or some one lodging under his roof was required to keep a watch: if any such "contemptuously refused" to obey the summons of the constable, that officer might set him in the stocks for his contempt. The liability to watch by roster attached equally to all the male inhabitants; when, however, it happened that it came to a woman's turn, she was allowed to find a substitute, but there is no evidence to show whether the substituted service was rendered gratuitously or whether she had to pay for the accommodation. Watchmen were expected to be able-bodied and sufficiently armed, a pitchfork was not held to be an adequate weapon,[75] but within reasonable limits a man might arm and accoutre himself as he pleased, and it was not until comparatively recent times that the watch were provided with arms at the parish expense.

Generally speaking, the house-row arrangement worked smoothly enough, but that friction occasionally arose, when the constables came to call upon unwilling citizens to perform the police duties incumbent on them, the following extract from "Town Life in the Fifteenth Century" bears witness: "In Aylesbury" according to the constables' report, "one Reygg kept a house all the year until the watch time came, and when he was summoned to the watch there came Edward Chalkyll 'fasesying' and said he [73]would not watch for no man and thus bare him up, and that caused the other to be bolder for to bar the King's watch.... He said and threatened us with his master," add the constables, "and thus we be over crakyd' that we dare not go, for when they be 'mayten' they be the bolder. John Bossey said the same wise that he would not watch for us, and three others lacked each of them a night."[76]

The police regulations for the government of London, as introduced in 1285, had become very minute and exacting by the latter half of the fifteenth century, many restrictions being placed on the enjoyment of personal liberty. The use of coal was prohibited, Sunday trading was forbidden, and, amongst other rules for the control of the wheeled traffic, a maximum width between wheels for vehicles was laid down which might on no account be exceeded. Ordinances also were promulgated against tradesmen who should attempt to advertise their callings in an objectionable manner, such as, for instance, the display of a basin of blood by barbers anxious to let people know that phlebotomy was included in the list of their accomplishments. The provisions of the before-quoted Statuta Civitatis (London), touching the control of leprous persons continued in force, and about this time special officers were appointed to prevent such as were infected with the plague from associating with those who were whole.

The employment of a "police des mœurs" was a [74]novel feature of the administration. A register containing the names of all women of ill-fame was kept by the police, and such women were not allowed to reside within the city walls; a certain promenade, known as the "Stews of Southwark," was assigned to them, where they were kept under the vigilant eyes of the City Sergeants, who, in consideration of the extra work thus thrown upon them, might confiscate and retain as a perquisite any "minever fur or cendale silk" that a courtesan might presume to wear. The inhabitants of the Surrey suburb were probably not consulted as to the desirability or otherwise of this arrangement, Edward III. having granted the town and borough of Southwark *in perpetuo* to the citizens of London. This he did in answer to their complaint that the peace of the city was continually being placed in jeopardy by the facility with which thieves and felons could make good their escape over the river and take refuge in Southwark, a place with no recognised privilege of sheltering runaways. The official sanctuaries were of course on a different footing, and in the fifteenth century were rendered less dangerous to society, than had formerly been the case, by an ordinance which required those who lived hard by the sanctuary to watch all avenues of escape by day and night until the refugee surrendered himself, a fine of five pounds being levied against the responsible ward if he succeeded in getting away.

The general scope of the responsibilities and powers proper to these old-time city constables is clearly defined in the oath that they were required [75]to take before entering upon the duties of their office. "You shall swear, that you shall keep the Peace of our Lord the King well and lawfully according to your power, and shall arrest all those who shall make any contest, riot, debate or affray, in breaking of the said peace, and shall bring them unto the house or Compter of one of the Sheriffs. And if you shall be withstood by strength of such misdoers, you shall raise upon them hue and cry (and) shall follow them from street to street, and from ward to ward until they are arrested. And also you shall search at all times when you shall be required by Scavenger or Bedel, for the common nuisances of the ward; until they are arrested. And also if there be anything done within your bailiwick contrary to the Ordinances of the City. And the faults you shall find, you shall present them unto the Mayor and to the Officers of the said City. And if you should be withstood by any person, or persons, that you cannot duly do your office, you shall certify unto the Mayor and Council of the said City the name and names of such person or persons who trouble you. And this you shall not fail to do. So God you help and the Saints."[77]

When the decennary societies ceased to exist, the connection between the peace officer and the particular group which he represented underwent a change, but the alteration was one of degree rather than one of kind. The fifteenth century constable was taught to look for the support of his fellow-citizens in case of need, though not to the same [76]extent, perhaps, as the headborough was wont to rely on the members of his tything. The great principle of mutual responsibility remained, and was kept alive by insisting that all freemen should enter into a solemn obligation to keep the peace, a compact which, modified to suit more modern requirements, had its origin in the ancient oath of allegiance. The form of oath varied in different places; in London it was as follows—"You shall swear that you shall be good and true unto the King of England and to his heirs, Kings and the King's Peace you shall keep; and unto the Officers of the city you shall be obedient, and at all times that shall be needful, you shall be ready to aid the officers in arresting misdoers, and those disobedient to the King's Peace, as well denizens as strangers. And you shall be ready, at the warning of the Constables and Bedels, to make the watches and (to bear) the other charges for the safeguard of the peace, and all the points in this wardmote shown, according to your power you shall well and lawfully keep—and if you know any evil covin within the ward or the city, you shall withstand the same, or to your alderman make it known. So help you God and the Saints."[78]

An examination of the oaths administered to constables and freemen respectively reveals to us in a concise form the motives which directed the mediæval machinery for maintaining the peace. We see how a compromise was arrived at between the ancient system of frankpledge and the more [77]modern plan of employing a professional class of peace officers, and how, by means of the combined action of police and public, domestic tranquillity was assured. Had it been possible to have made this co-operation complete and thorough, the resulting security would have left little to be desired; but, as was only to be expected, discord not infrequently took the place of harmony, and freemen sometimes forgot what was due to the oath they had taken. Let the events of a certain night in Canterbury serve as an illustration. Some watchmen, it appears, challenged a man whom they found abroad "out of due time" and inquired his business, but (to continue the story verbatim) "the suspect person gave none answer, but ran from thence into St Austin's liberty, and before the door of one John Short they took him. And the same John Short came out of his house with other misknown persons and took from the said watchmen their weapons, and there menaced them for to beat, contrary to the oath of a true and faithful freeman."[79]

According to the strict letter of the law it was a constable's duty, immediately after making an arrest, to deliver his prisoner to the sheriff; but, as a matter of fact, this was seldom done, and the sheriff had little or nothing to do with accused persons until after their conviction. In the absence of proper lock-ups the village stocks were commonly used by the parish constable to secure his man until he could conveniently bring him before a magistrate [78]but, as time went on, confinement in the stocks became the normal mode of punishment for minor offences, and it was no rare thing for a constable to keep a troublesome parishioner in this uncomfortable custody for a space, on his own initiative and responsibility.

Prisons had existed in some form or other from the earliest times. The first dungeon was doubtless coeval with the first fortress, and London's great jail at Newgate dated back to the twelfth century. But it was not then a penal establishment in our sense of the term, in so far that imprisonment was hardly as yet the recognised punishment for the ordinary run of criminals; such places were rather convenient strongholds in which to confine debtors till they paid their dues, suspected persons till they confessed their crimes, Jews till they disgorged their wealth, and generally for the safe-guarding of political opponents or private enemies whom it was desirable to keep under lock and key. It was not until the fifteenth century that we find a regularly graduated connection between punishment by imprisonment and punishment by fine; the penalty for drawing a sword in the City of London, for example, was then half a mark or fifteen days, for inflicting a wound with the same, twenty shillings or forty days, and so on.

The pillory was a more serious affair, and its pains were beyond the power of a constable to inflict; it was generally resorted to in cases where the offender had been guilty of practices which rendered him particularly obnoxious to the people, so [79]that the punishment he received at their hands was nicely proportioned to the degree of unpopularity he had earned for himself. The baker who gave short weight, or the dairyman who watered his milk, received such a lesson at the hands of his customers that he was little likely to repeat his offence. It was customary, moreover, in sentencing a man to the pillory, to make the punishment fit the crime as much as possible, and to compel the culprit to advertise his guilt in some personally unpleasant fashion; thus, the man who had stolen a cart was forced to pull it through the streets to the place of punishment, and an offending vintner had to drink a full draught of the sour wine that had disagreed with the frequenters of his shop.

Englishmen are proverbially interested in what they eat and drink, and this public concern for good victualling explains why, when life and property were as yet but moderately secure, safeguards against the adulteration of human food were notably complete. The chief legislative authority upon which police action, directed against dishonest purveyors, rested, was the "Judicium Pillorie," or, as it is commonly called, "The Statute of the Pillory and Tumbrel."[80] This Act belonged to the same period as the Statute of Winchester (both dating from the latter half of the thirteenth century), and like its more famous contemporary had a long career of practical usefulness in the public service. From 1266, the year of its enactment, until 1710, the date of its repeal, the Judicium Pillorie did much [80]for English food, by maintaining a high standard in the quality of our meat and bread, and in the soundness of our ale. The Statute requires that "they have in the town a pillory of convenient strength as apperteineth to the liberty of their market, which they may use (if need be) without bodily peril either of man or woman." Provision is made for the sending of six "lawful men" to collect all the measures of the town, care being taken that the owner's name is legibly inscribed on each measure, "after which thing done" a jury of twelve lawful men have to make oath that they will truly answer concerning such things as may be demanded of them on the King's behalf, "and such things as be secret, they shall utter secretly and answer privately," also, "if any butcher do sell contagious flesh, or that died of the murren, or flesh that hath been kept so long that it loseth its natural wholesomeness, or meat bought from Jews and then sold to Christians"—for these and similar offences the penalty is the same, viz.: "If a baker or a brewer be convict ... then he shall suffer punishment of the body—that is to wit—a baker to the pillory and a brewer to the tumbrel."

From "Liber Albus" we get a more detailed account of the fashion in which these exemplary punishments were carried out in London, we learn that "if any default be found in the bread of a baker in the city, the first time, let him be drawn upon a hurdle from the Guildhall to his own house through the great street where there be most people assembled, and through the great streets which are most dirty, with [81]the faulty loaf hanging from his neck: if a second time he shall be found committing the same offence, let him be drawn from the Guildhall through the great street of Cheepe, in the manner aforesaid, to the pillory, and let him be put upon the pillory, and remain there at least one hour in the day; and the third time that such default shall be found, he shall be drawn, and the oven shall be pulled down, and the baker made to forswear the trade in the city for ever."

Before leaving this part of the subject, it may be worth mentioning, that as long ago as the year 1318[81] all public officers in city and borough were debarred from selling wine or victual during their term of office, a prohibition which some people think might with advantage be applied at the present day to such modern officials as the members of Borough Watch Committees.[82]

---

[82]

CHAPTER V
COMMERCIAL POLICE AND POLICE UNDER THE TUDORS

The growth of the royal power that was so well defined a characteristic of the sixteenth century was accompanied by a general re-establishment of good order throughout the kingdom. As long as the reins of government were slackly held by feeble monarchs, the king's peace was reckoned of but little account, and in the words of the Anglo-Saxon writer already quoted, "every man that could, forthwith robbed another." Nobles surrounded by their retainers, broke the peace whenever they chose, and laid their hands on any property that they felt strong enough to hold. As long as punishment overtook the man who had offended against a great noble with more precision and with greater celerity than it did the offender who had broken the law of the land, guardians of the peace were despised, whilst peace-breakers were admired by the multitude, if not respected.

When Henry VII. came to the throne he resolutely set himself to put an end to this state of affairs, and to re-assert the personal ascendancy of the sovereign, especially with regard to the maintenance of the [83]peace. He was obviously unable to achieve this object single-handed, for he had no army with which to enforce his commands, and the mass of the people were not yet thoroughly emancipated. Something of course might be done by dividing the nobles into separate factions, and then pitting one faction against another, and these tactics he pursued with some success; the class however to which in the end the king had to look for assistance was the middle-class, which was chiefly occupied with money-making, which was inclined to resent any interference with a pursuit at once so novel and so absorbing, and which, at the same time, was beginning to cry out for increased protection for its newly acquired wealth. As it seemed worth while to purchase the goodwill of the spokesmen of this powerful class, at the cost of complying with their not unreasonable requirements, the king was ready to meet them halfway, and the police administration was modified accordingly.

The compulsory duty of serving as a constable, argued the middle-class, was not only unprofitable but a wicked waste of good time that might be devoted to objects that paid better; and so the system of deputy constable crept in. Hue and cry was all very well, they said, for the agriculturist or the villein; he could lay down his spade to join in the pursuit with little detriment to himself; but it was different in the case of the weaver or the merchant, the former could not afford to leave his loom nor the latter to lose a bargain; and so hue and cry fell into desuetude. When property consisted only of timber, cattle, and land, difficult things [84]for a thief to remove, little protection was demanded, but when valuable articles, all more or less portable, became common, and when many kinds of fraud, all more or less subtle, menaced both consumer and producer, a better guarantee for security was asked: and so the old-established trade-guilds adapted themselves to the changed conditions, and introduced new protective measures. These modifications must now be examined in more detail.

It is doubtful at what date the custom first arose of discharging the office of constable by proxy, but certain it is that, in the Tudor period, instead of one headborough responsible to the Crown for the maintenance of the peace in Tything and Hundred, which, as we have seen, was anciently the system, we find two or more constables answerable to the Justices, nominally employed by the year, but practically as permanent deputies, performing duties delegated to them in parish and township, and their services paid for, not by the public at large, but by the individuals whose deputies they were.

In some respects the change, which in all probability was a gradual one, contributed to the deterioration of the police administration, because unfortunately a very indifferent sort of man was almost invariably selected as deputy. Speaking of constables, Bacon says they are "of inferior, yea, of base condition, which is a mere abuse or degenerating from the first institution, for the petty constables in towns ought to be the better sort of residents in the same, save that they be not aged or sickly, but of able bodies in respect of their keeping watch and [85]toil of their place"; and Blackstone says that considering the class of man that commonly acts as constable, it is just as well that he should remain in ignorance of the powers that are entrusted to him by law.

Despite the fact that the employment of deputies was mischievous in its immediate consequences, the rise of the custom marked a distinct stage in the development that resulted in the freedom from personal liability which, without prejudice to the police administration, we now enjoy; it began to be felt that the onerous and thankless position of constable deserved remuneration, and that it was more economical to delegate constabulary duties to experts, than that every man should be compelled to serve his turn in an office that interfered with his normal activity, and for which, perhaps, he had no special aptitude. England, as we have seen, was rapidly becoming a commercial country, and all were eager to take advantage of every chance of money-making that offered itself, and finding that the duties of citizenship absorbed more of their time than they were willing to spare, peace-officers were no sooner elected than they hastened to hire any proxies whom they could persuade to undertake the burden of office. This reluctance of busy men to devote their valuable time to an unpaid public service was reasonable enough, and the practice of employing substitutes was winked at by the authorities; yet centuries passed before a way was found to organize with intelligence, and officially recognize a system, that whilst freeing the mass of the people from an unnecessary conscription, should yet retain the [86]essential principle that every man shares in, and cannot divest himself of, a definite responsibility for the maintenance of good order in the commonwealth.

The decay of the feudal system and the gradual abolition of villenage went hand in hand, as we have seen, with the rise of the merchant and the artisan; as trade increased and as the skilled workman became a recognized power in the state, the police horizon widened, new interests needed protection, new laws and regulations had to be made and enforced. The supreme direction of commercial police rested with the Crown; and, as long as the sovereign's prerogative was confined to the control of fairs and ports, to the granting or withholding of monopolies, and to the regulating of weights and measures, the services of the Justices of the Peace, assisted by their constables, had been found sufficient for all practical purposes. But when questions arose, touching our trade with foreign merchants or demanding a technical knowledge of native manufactures, it became necessary to submit these difficult problems to some more expert authority than the ordinary executive officer. This want was supplied, to a great extent, by the above-mentioned police development of the Trade-Guilds or Livery Companies, which, recently deprived of much of their former political influence, now for the first time seriously began to devote themselves to the special interests of their several trades, by properly confining their energies to channels more legitimate than state-craft, such as the protection [87]and control of the various markets, manufactures, and handicrafts.

In the early stages of its development in this country, commerce stood on a very different footing from that upon which it rests to-day: skilled artizans came and settled in England from all parts of the continent, bringing their laws and customs with them; arrived here, they not only competed with the native manufacturer, but beat him at all points of the game. In the absence of any preventive police worth mentioning, the position of these aliens would have been an impossible one, except for two considerations; in the first place they thoroughly recognised the value of combination and acted upon it, and in the second place the very considerable revenue that their activities brought to the royal coffers, secured for them the king's protection and support.[83]

This incursion of foreigners was not without its effect on our craftsmen, who saw, that to command success, they too must combine, organize, and regulate. The result was that nearly every trade and industry soon had its guild organized on the continental model, the object of which (unlike the modern trades-unions that exist mainly to prevent the power of the capitalist over his employées from becoming absolute), was to create a monopoly, and hedge it round so that no outsider could enter the exclusive circle without being properly initiated and regularly admitted to craft-membership.

[88]

The Livery Company punished the fraudulent workman, corrected the idle apprentice, and also prosecuted the would-be interloper who attempted to infringe upon its rights and privileges.

We are indebted to these trade-guilds for introducing to our shores in the first instance, many mechanical arts which, greatly to our advantage, subsequently became naturalized, and afterwards for keeping them alive through times of difficulty and danger, when the central government was not strong enough to afford much protection; the high character that English goods have earned throughout the world's markets is, to a great extent, owing to this system of commercial police, which compelled every workman to serve a long apprenticeship in a technical school, and which punished the producer of fraudulent and worthless articles. On the other hand whole fields of industry were arbitrarily closed to honest and capable folk by the absurd restrictions imposed for the sole benefit of corporations, which, when full allowance has been made for the good they did, and when full credit has been given for the service they rendered by standing in the breach at the critical moment, were, after all, thoroughly reactionary in their tendency, bent, as they were, upon stifling healthy competition whenever possible, and inclined to look upon any new invention as a crime against their craft mysteries.

A serious defect in the constitution of our mediæval police consisted in the numerous privileges enjoyed by favoured communities. No police regulation was of universal application; we have [89]seen how in Anglo-Saxon times the king's peace afforded especial protection to certain classes, and how various limitations were imposed according to locality and according to season; subsequently charters were freely given to monasteries, guilds, boroughs and cities, carrying rights and conferring favours that were not shared by the nation at large. The consequence was that every rule bristled with exceptions, and legislation grew proportionally more complicated and difficult of application than would have been the case had all men been equal in the eye of the law. Many a useful measure was rendered largely inoperative by reason of the numbers of persons who could plead privilege against its enforcement in their particular case. Hue and Cry could avail nothing against the baron who had bought a charter of pardon for felonies committed in the past or contemplated in the future, and the pursuit of the sheriff was stayed when the fugitive took refuge in sanctuary. First the clergy, and afterwards persons not in orders who could prove their ability to read a word or two in the Gothic character,[84] were entitled to plead "benefit of clergy," and thereby escape perhaps well-merited punishment. In the reign of Henry VII. this privilege was wisely restricted, by ordaining that those who had pleaded "clergy" once, should be branded on the brawn of the thumb with a hot iron (M for a Murderer, T for a Thief), so as to prevent their cheating justice a second time by means of the [90]same plea. Gradually benefit of clergy was taken away from one offence after another, until at last[85] no serious crime was left to which this exemption from punishment attached. Again, the scholars of Oxford and Cambridge were not subject to many regulations that applied elsewhere, the members of these universities being allowed to beg, under certain restrictions, without incurring the penalties that ordinary "vagabonds and sturdy beggars" were liable to; on the other hand Jews and gypsies were subject to pains that did not attach to the native population.

The confusion of the illiterate constable, called upon to act when confronted with a medley of contradictory charters, passports and privileges, can well be imagined, and, needless to say, personation and forged certificates were largely resorted to both by the habitual criminal and by the professional beggar.

A very necessary reform introduced in this reign was that which, in cases of homicide, made the trial of the accused follow immediately upon the discovery of the offence. By long-established usage, originating from the time when the blood-feud was the recognised agency for avenging murder, the custom had arisen of postponing royal interference until the relatives or friends of the deceased had been allowed ample time in which to bring the criminal to justice, and, by ancient consent, those parties who were interested acted the rôle that our [91]police detectives are now charged with, and, so to speak, had to "get up" the case against the alleged offender. An "Appeal," as it was called, was then made before the Coroner and by him publicly declared at five consecutive county-courts. It had been laid down in

1277,[86] that homicides should not be proceeded against at the King's suit until a year and a day had elapsed since the commission of the murder, and in 1482,[87] twelve months was declared to be the privileged period in which appellors alone might formulate an accusation. The natural result (to quote the Statute,[88] which did away with these out-of-date restrictions) was, that "the party is oftentimes slow, and also agreed with, and by the end of the year all is forgotten, which is another occasion of murder."

The anxiety to make money that pervaded all classes, but which was especially observable in the middle class, besides influencing the status of the constable and making the guild such a prominent feature of the time, was to a large extent responsible for the increasing rigour of the criminal law. The claims of property were urged to the uttermost, and people who had anything to lose pressed for the infliction of exemplary punishment in all cases where the rights of ownership were threatened. The result of this attitude was, that the war of extermination against those who had no visible means of subsistence was waged more relentlessly than ever before. The dissolution of the religious houses, following upon the civil commotions of the [92]previous century, had multiplied the number of vagrants until the country was full of homeless and starving wanderers, many of whom, needless to say, maintained themselves by robbery. Bad government first created this dangerous class, and then attempted to exterminate it by wholesale hanging: it is said that more than 70,000 persons were put to death during the thirty-eight years of Henry the Eighth's reign; from this number a considerable reduction may be made for exaggeration, and of the remainder a large proportion suffered on religious and political grounds. But the general government was rigorous in the extreme, and, the value of human life being but little accounted of, a penal system grew up which exacted the death penalty for offences of a comparatively trivial nature, thus laying the foundations of the barbarous code which continued to disgrace our Statute book for centuries, vainly endeavouring to supply the place of preventive police by repressive measures that were expected to deter by virtue of their extreme severity. Sir Thomas More saw the uselessness of such a policy, and pointed out in his "Utopia," that as robbers often killed their victims on the principle that dead men tell no tales, it would be desirable, therefore, to reduce the punishment for theft in order to check the frequency with which murders were committed.

Wales and the Welsh borderland had long been the refuge of the outlaw, and the fastness of the robber; for whilst the natural features of the country favoured the escape of the fugitive from justice, the [93]division of the principality into independent lordships, from which the king's writ was excluded, still further increased the difficulty of arrest. At one time there were 141 of these lordships, under as many petty chieftains known as Lords-Marchers, who indiscriminately sold charters, and harboured any lawbreaker who would pay for his footing. This kind of home-rule in Wales was incompatible with the maintenance of order in the West of England, and the counties near the border suffered severely for their proximity to this Alsatia. Accordingly in 1536 it was decided to extinguish the separate jurisdiction of the Lords-Marchers, and the whole of Wales was incorporated into England by an Act passed in the 27th year of Henry the Eighth, which provided Justices-of-the-Peace, Justices-of-the-Quorum, and Justices-of-Gaol-delivery for the Welsh counties, armed with the same power and authority that the corresponding Justices in England were possessed of; shortly afterwards (1543)[89] these newly-appointed Justices of the Peace were authorised to select two "substantiall gentlemen, or yeomen, to be chiefe constables of the hundred wherein they inhabite, which two constables in every hundred shall haue a speciall regard to the conseruation of the King's Peace."

A somewhat similar state of unrest existed in the neighbourhood of the Scottish border. Here the simple expedient of incorporation by Act of Parliament was of course impossible, so in the following year Henry instituted a Court, called the President [94]and the Council of the North, and empowered it to preserve the peace, in that part of the realm, in the king's name; so that "his true subjects ... have undelayed justice daily administered."

Nearer home, Thomas Cromwell, acting for the king, overhauled the administration of police, and amongst other improvements established parochial registers of births, marriages and deaths,[90] but he was too fond of thrusting petty and vexatious regulations down the throats of a people, who, recently freed from their old bondage, were now for the first time beginning to think for themselves; his whole system moreover was vitiated by the frequency with which he employed spies and informers, a method of police control always peculiarly abhorrent to the English.

The law against vagrancy, which, as we have seen, was extremely severe during the preceding reigns, reached its most barbarous stage soon after the accession of Edward the Sixth. It is the irony of circumstance which associates the name of so mild a prince with one of the most atrocious measures ever imposed upon Englishmen, for Edward was but a child when the Statute in question was passed, and can have had no hand either in the inception or application of its provisions.[91] The responsibility belongs to [95]the Protector, Somerset, yet it will always remain a mystery how he could sanction such a measure, for he is well known to have felt much sympathy for the masses of his countrymen, and was ever anxious to please. After remarking in the preamble that "idle and vagabond persons are worthy of death, whipping, imprisonment, and other corporal pain," the Statute proceeds to enact that "the offender there described to be an idle person shall be taken before a Justice of the Peace, who shall cause him to be marked with a hot iron in the breast, the mark "V," and adjudge him to be a slave to the person presenting him for two years, to be fed with bread and water, and be put to work (how vile soever it be) by beating, chaining, etc.: and if he runs away, the Justice, on conviction, shall cause such slave to be marked on the forehead or ball of the cheek with the sign of an "S," and shall further adjudge him to be his master's slave for ever:[92] and if he again run away, he shall suffer death as a felon."[93] No record tells how many unfortunates suffered the pains above recited, but the number is not likely to have been considerable, because vagabondage was by no means stamped out: the conclusion is forced upon one, however, that whilst law-making of such a type was in vogue, the infirmity of the police, whose business it was to enforce its enactments, cannot be considered as an unmitigated evil.

The grandmotherly domestic policy of the time, [96]which told people what they were to eat, how they were to dress, and the number of hours they must labour, resulted, as all such attempts to interfere with the natural laws of supply and demand must result, in serious conflict between the authorities and the people, who sooner or later are sure to resent coercion, and have recourse to violent resistance to obtain economic freedom for themselves and their descendants. Dissatisfaction had long been dormant, but matters came to a head early in the reign of Edward VI.; popular risings took place simultaneously all over the country, the most serious outbreaks occurring in counties as far remote from each other as Cornwall in the West, and Norfolk in the East. There was no machinery in existence for the suppression of riots, no standing army, and no civil power in any way adequate to meet force with force: the executive was well-nigh powerless. Under these circumstances a penal statute[94] against unlawful assemblies was passed, much of which survives in our present Riot Act now in force. It became high treason for twelve or more persons, being assembled together, to attempt to alter any laws, etc., or to continue together for the space of an hour after being commanded by a Justice of the Peace to depart. It was made felony for twelve or more persons to "practice to destroy a park, conduit, or dovehouse," to pull down houses, barns, or mills, to burn any stack of corn, or to abate the price of victuals; or being assembled, to continue together an hour, after being ordered in like manner to depart.

[97]

To make this statute effectual, it was necessary to devise some new executive to enforce its provisions; accordingly in each county a high official called the Lord-Lieutenant was appointed, who was authorized to levy men and lead them against the enemies of the king, to which category rioters, as being guilty of High Treason, were now specifically declared to belong. With the appointment of Lords-Lieutenant, the last of the military functions exercised by the Sheriff passed out of his hands into those of the new official, who to this day retains a remnant of authority over the regiments of Yeomanry and Militia of his county.[95]

Until the middle of the sixteenth century any person so inclined[96] could keep an alehouse—there were no licensing laws and no excise-duty leviable on alcoholic beverages, which indeed, remained untaxed until 1643. Police control was therefore both difficult and unpopular. A first attempt to grapple seriously with this rapidly increasing mischief was made in 1552,[97] when Justices of the Peace and Constables were given powers, which, it was hoped, would do something to "remedy the intolerable hurt and trouble to the Commonwealth of the Realm" by "common alehouses and other houses called Tipling-houses." To this end Justices [98]were authorized "to remove and put away ... the common selling of Ale and Beer" as they might see fit. Henceforward only houses "admitted and allowed in the open Sessions of the Peace" were to be used for the sale of liquor, and Justices were furthermore instructed to take bond and surety of the occupiers; "for which recognizance, the party so bound shall pay but 12 pence." Alehouse keepers who should fail to comply with these conditions might be committed to gaol by the Justices of the Peace.

---

[99]

CHAPTER VI
ECCLESIASTICAL POLICE AND POLICE UNDER JAMES I

The accession of Queen Elizabeth inaugurated a period of great activity for the police departments. Her rule was masterful and her control maternal. Magistrates and constables were kept busy in administering the statutes dealing with apprentices, wages, disputes in service, hours of labour, the regulation of industrial trades, laws for the suppression of rogues and vagabonds, and other enactments too numerous to mention, which followed each other in quick succession. Of the many statutes, public and private, passed in this reign, having for their object the enforcement of government by police, amongst the most important were those which referred to the City and Borough of Westminster, "for the suppressing and rooting out of vice there used." The police administration of the city had from time immemorial rested with the ecclesiastical authorities, and in 1559 the Queen gave a charter to the Dean and Chapter, carrying the same privileges, immunities and powers, that the Abbot and Convent used to enjoy. The Dean and Chapter delegated their authority to a functionary [100]called the High Steward, and made him responsible for the preservation of the peace, but they conferred upon him no power of levying money on the inhabitants for that purpose, and made no provision for the appointing of assistants to help him in his duties. The result of this policy was continued disorder, and after twenty-five years of failure, a change of system was decided upon. In 1584[98] Westminster was divided into twelve wards, each under a Burgess, who was nominated by the Dean or High Steward, and these twelve Burgesses, as well as the superior officers, were authorized to punish "incontinences, common scolds, inmates, and common annoyances" in accordance with the laws and the customs of London. They had the power, also, to commit to prison peace-breakers, but they were bound to give notice of such committals to a Justice of the Peace for Middlesex within twenty-four hours. It was hereby further enacted that "if any person or persons, after he or they shall happen to be punished and banished from this city for any incontinency of life or such like, and shall return again to the city or borough, to the intent there to inhabit and dwell, that then every such person and persons shall be whipped naked at the cart's tayle throughout the said city, for every time so offending, contrary to this order."[98]

Lord Burleigh was the first High Steward appointed under this Act, and on his initiative certain ordinances[99] for the better government of the people [101]of Westminster were added in the course of the same year. These regulations were as minute as they were varied. Not more than one hundred ale-houses were allowed, which taverns were bound to display a lantern with candle complete at their street-doors "every night, nightly (except those nights as the moon shall then and at that time shine and give light) upon paine to forfeit and pay for every time offending herein fourpence." Fourpence was in like manner the fine imposed on those burgesses and their assistants who failed to attend Divine Service at the Abbey on Sunday, but the owner of any hogs found wandering in Tuthill were mulcted in the sum of twelve pence. It would be interesting to learn the basis of these computations, and why a wandering hog cost the owner as much as three absences from morning prayer. More valuable, however, were the regulations introduced with the object of preventing the sale of bad and unwholesome food. Special officers, called Searchers, "discreet men having a knowledge of the trade," were appointed to look after the butchers, poulterers, and provision purveyors, with power to seize and burn bad meat, and to commit the owners (or their agents exposing food unfit for consumption), to prison, for a period of twenty-four hours. The licensing of ale-houses still rested with Justices of the Peace, and constables who neglected to apprehend "sturdy beggars" were liable to a fine of six shillings and eightpence.

In addition to the extra work thrown on their shoulders in connection with the Acts above mentioned, the jurisdiction of the Justice of the Peace [102]was extended so as to encroach upon territory that had hitherto been the province of the Justice of Assize. Courts Leet, moreover, having by this time become quite unimportant, the appointment and control of the constabulary was centred almost entirely in the hands of the county magistrates. They held office under the Crown direct, and on their Commission took an oath to do equal right between rich and poor, to accept nothing beyond the customary fees for the performance of their duties, and to pay all fines inflicted by them into the Queen's Exchequer without embezzlement or delay. "The Justices of the Peace," writes Sir Thomas Smith, "be those in whom, at this time, for the repressing of robbers, thieves, and vagabonds, of privy complots and conspiracies, of riots and violences and all other misdemeanours in the commonwealth, the prince putteth his special trust ... and generally, as I have said, for the good government of the shire, the prince putteth his confidence in them."[100]

Amongst the duties laid upon the rural police for the control of agriculture, we find that before a labourer "retained in husbandry" could leave his parish or township, he had to obtain a testimonial from the constable, and to get two householders to declare his lawful departure.[101] This system of passports for the suppression of vagrancy never worked smoothly, and its development in later times as enforced against beggars by parish constables, led to serious abuses that will demand our attention [103]further on.[102] The 15th section of the same Act empowered Justices and constables, upon request being made during harvest time, to compel labourers to work on farms where labour was scarce, and to put those who obstinately refused in the stocks for two days and one night.

The treatment served out to rogues, vagabonds, and sturdy beggars was more severe. Persons taken begging or "misordering themselves" were to be committed to the common gaol, and if convicted of the offence at the next sessions of the peace or gaol-delivery—"grievously whipped, and burnt through the gristle of the right ear with a hot iron of the compass of an inch about."[103] The burning was repealed, and open whipping "until his or her body be bloody" was afterwards substituted.[104] Although the severity of the punishment was thus mitigated, it was now apparently inflicted in a more summary fashion, for offenders were no longer to be committed to gaol, but were to be whipped on apprehension, probably by the constables at the instance of a Justice.

Up to this point the history of the constable is one long record of new duties undertaken, and fresh responsibilities incurred (though perhaps unwillingly), by that officer. This tendency, as we shall see, becomes more pronounced as time goes on, though in one particular, the contrary may be noticed. In 1601, the famous Poor Law of Elizabeth[105] sensibly relieved the parish officer of much irksome responsi[104]bility by associating with him churchwardens to help in assessing the poor-rate, and to assist in the general duty of supervising the needy. From this date until 1849 (when the Essex Rural Constabulary were first employed as assistant relieving officers for casuals) the care of the impotent poor was entrusted to overseers specially appointed for the purpose, with the result that constables had more leisure to make things unpleasant for the vagrant man and the sturdy beggar.

Hue and Cry remained the only practical agency for the pursuit and capture of delinquents. The method of its application, by whom it was to be made, and the penalties that followed upon its neglect, are fully dealt with in an Act passed during the 27th year of this reign,[106] which declares that Hue and Cry is to be deemed lawful only when made by Horsemen and Footmen, "any usage or custom to the contrary notwithstanding." It is not clear what is meant by this restriction, but it is probable that the prohibition of man-hunting with the aid of dogs was intended. In cases where the fugitive was not apprehended, and where the inhabitants responsible for the capture refused to pay the amercement, the constables and headboroughs were authorised to distrain upon the goods and chattels of the obstinate parishioners, and to hand over the money realized by the sale thereof to the Justices.[106]

The system pressed hardly on certain Hundreds, which owing to their situation and local circum[105]stances, were unable to apprehend all the peace-breakers of the neighbourhood, and which were often so poor that a heavy fine meant ruin to one or more families in the group. We find in consequence that petitions against amercements were not uncommon: in 1597, for instance, the poor inhabitants of Benhurst in Berkshire had to appeal to the clemency of the Queen on account of the constant penalties imposed on them, some at least of which they thought should be borne by the neighbouring town of Maidenhead. The language in which this appeal is couched is so quaint and pitiful that their own words are given. "That whereas the said Hundred doth consist only of five small villages and three small Quillets or Hamlets, and hath lying through it two great highways: the one leading from London to Henley-on-Thames and the other from London to Reading: and either of them at the least three miles in length within the Great Woody Ground called the 'Thicket'—and no-one of the same villages standeth upon or adjoining to either of the said ways, but lie dispersedly far from the same: neither have the inhabitants of the same Hundred any open or common fields, either arable or other, adjoining or lying near to such parts of the same ways (within the said Thicket) as are most apt for robberies to be done, whereby they may have their servants or workmen labouring within the view of the said ways, to take notice of the robberies done: and therefore the said inhabitants cannot well have any speedy notice or intelligence of any robbery which shall be there committed unless the Party or Parties robbed should [106]give the same unto them."[107] It is to the Queen's credit that the inhabitants of Benhurst in Berkshire did not appeal in vain to the royal clemency.

When in 1595 the civil arm was found insufficient to put down the riotous proceedings that disturbed the peace of the Home Counties, its shortcomings were made good by the supplemental employment of the military power. Elizabeth has been accused of proclaiming Martial Law when its application was not warranted by the exigencies of the case.[108] It is difficult for us at the present day to determine how grave were the disturbances that induced the Proclamation in question, or how far the ordinary methods of control had been tried and found wanting; but it is certain that no adequate police existed to quell anything in the nature of a serious riot. It was no doubt discreditable to the Government that such should be the case, but it was a discredit that it shared with all preceding Governments, and one that attached with a greater degree of culpableness to all subsequent Governments down to the year 1829. Given an unlawful and violent assembly of riotous persons, and the lack of any civil force strong enough to disperse them, it is difficult to see the practicability of any alternative measure to that of calling out the troops. The Commission given to Sir Thomas Willford in 1595 did not amount to Martial Law in the usual acceptation of the term, that is to say, the ordinary Law was not to be entirely superseded, the Provost Marshal was [107]only to "speedily execute" those offenders whom the Justices of the Peace signified as deserving of death, and such sentence was to be carried out in the presence of the Justices who had had judicial cognisance of the offence. The only additional powers granted to Sir Thomas Willford were those by which he was authorized to "repair with a convenient company," and "calling to your assistance some convenient number of our justices and constables abiding about the said places, to apprehend all such vagrant and suspected persons, and them to deliver to the said justices, by them to be committed,"[109] etc., etc. The powers, in fact, given to the soldiers on this occasion were solely executive; no one was to be tried by Court-Martial; the verdict lay with the civil power; and only the carrying out of the sentence rested with the military authorities.

At no time of our history have the duties of the Justice and the tasks of the constable been more varied and onerous than they were at the period we are considering. The jurisdiction and control of these officers reached to the furthest corners of the social edifice; they had to see that the labourers rose betimes and did not take too long over their meals, nor might the country parson marry without "the advice and allowance"[110] of two Justices of the shire. All these multifarious duties they performed for the most part without pecuniary reward, the only fee to which they were entitled being the sum of five shillings for each day they sat in the execution of the [108]Statute of Labourers. On the whole it must be allowed that they carried out the duties entrusted to them both with credit to themselves, and to the public advantage; for whilst Sheriffs, Under-Sheriffs, and Bailiffs were for ever giving cause for complaint on account of their "misdemeanour and evil behaviour," it was a rare occurrence for a Justice to be accused of extortion or injustice, and crime was far less common at this time than it afterwards became. Contemporary writers, however, criticise the county magistracy with some severity. Freak, the Bishop of Worcester, for example, writes to the Lord Treasurer in 1587, giving his opinion of the Justices of the Peace: "I do observe some weakness in that number: divers of them being but superficial, either for advice or for execution of any weighty affaires of the county," whilst Shakespeare is very hard upon all police functionaries as he knew them. Mr Justice Shallow, representing the Bench, Dogberry and Verges of the Watch, as well as Elbow and Dull of the Constabulary, are all treated with good-humoured contempt. The dramatist's account of the interview between Escalus and Elbow is of particular interest because it illustrates the evils of the system of deputy which clung to the office of parish-constable until forty or fifty years ago.[111]

The sort of difficulties that magistrates had to contend with, owing to the slackness of the constabulary, are graphically described in a letter dated 1596 in the course of which, Mr Hext, then a Justice of the Peace for Somersetshire, complains officially to [109]the Lord Treasurer that thieves and robbers had grown so cunning, through having often been in gaol, that these old hands could seldom be laid hold of. "Others," he writes, "are delivered to simple constables and tything-men, that sometimes wilfully, and other times negligently suffer them to escape." After suggesting that steps should be taken to punish all keepers of ale-houses who harbour suspicious persons, and all constables and tything-men who suffer them to be at large, he goes on to explain how difficult it is to get the country people to prosecute in cases of theft, "for most commonly the most simple country man and woman, looking no further than to the loss of their own goods, are of opinion, that they would not procure any man's death for all the goods in the world." This same reluctance to prosecute, as we shall see, hindered the administration of justice for many generations, and the question of how best to remove it, is to this day a police problem, that has only been partially solved by the comparatively recent institution of the office of Public Prosecutor. Mr Hext was either very credulous, or thieves' appetites must have been prodigious in the sixteenth century, for in the same letter he describes how "within this three months I took a thief, that was executed this last assizes, that confessed unto me, that he and two more lay in an ale-house three weeks: in which time they eat twenty fat sheep: whereof they stole every night one." Finally he gives a woeful account of the Egyptians (*i.e.* Gypsies) that infested his county. "The inhabitants," declares the [110]magistrate, "being wonderfully grieved by their rapines, made complaint at our Easter Sessions, after my Lord Chief Justice's departure: precepts were made to the tythings adjoining for the apprehending of them. They made answer, but (the Gypsies) were so strong that they durst not adventure of them: whereupon precepts were made to the constables of the shire: but not apprehended, for they have intelligence of all things intended against them.... And they grow the more dangerous in that they find they have bred that fear in Justices, and other inferior officers, that no man dares call them in question."[112]

From all this it is clear that the police organization left much to be desired. The country, in fact, was not yet ripe for a good police. With the central government corrupt, the superior courts venal, the upper classes of society prone to violence, and the masses for the most part unacquainted with justice, the sixteenth century would have found a good police force according to our standard, about as useful and as easy of comprehension as they would an Edison's phonograph or a modern treatise on the Spectrum Analysis.

The police administration of the seventeenth century differed but little from that which had gone before, no real advance being discoverable either in the theory or practice of peace-maintenance. Certain changes were indeed taking place from year to year, as old customs fell into disuse and as ancient words acquired new meanings; but, on the whole, growth [111]and decay were almost evenly balanced. If it is admitted that the duties of a constable, and the matters that fell within his province, were now more clearly defined than heretofore, it must also be confessed that he was permitted to shirk his work more than ever. This slackness of performance may be clearly demonstrated by a comparison between the oaths taken by High and Petty Constables respectively, on their appointment, and the copious evidences of neglect that are everywhere apparent. Before his admission to office an oath was administered to the High-Constable-elect in these words:—"You shall swear, That you shall well and truly serve our Sovereign Lord the King in the Office of Constable. You shall see and cause His Majestie's Peace to be well and truly kept and preserved according to your power. You shall arrest all such persons as in your sight and presence shall ride or go armed offensively, or shall commit or make any Riot, Affray, or other Breach of His Majestie's Peace. You shall do your best endeavour (upon complaint to you made) to apprehend all Felons, Barretors, and Rioters, or persons riotously assembled: and if any such offenders shall make resistance (with force) you shall levy Hue and Cry, and shall pursue them until they be taken. You shall do your best endeavour that the watch in and about your Hundred be duly kept, for the Apprehending of Rogues, Vagabonds, night-walkers, Evesdroppers, Scouts, and other suspected persons, and of such as go armed, and the like: and that Hue and Cry be duly raised and pursued according [112]to the Statute of Winchester, against Murderers, Thieves, and other felons: and that the Statutes made for the punishment of Rogues and Vagabonds, and such other idle persons as come within your bounds and limits be duly put in execution. You shall have a watchful eye to such persons as shall maintain or keep any common house or place, where any unlawful game is or shall be used: as also to such as shall frequent or use such places, or shall use or exercise any unlawful games there or elsewhere, contrary to the Statutes.

"At your Assizes, Sessions of the Peace, or Leet, you shall present all and every the offences done contrary to the Statutes made 1 Jacobi, 4 Jacobi, and 21 Jacobi Regis, to restrain the inordinate haunting and tippling in Inns, Alehouses, and other Victually Houses, and for repressing of drunkeness: you shall there likewise true presentment make of all Bloudsheddings, affrays, outcries, Rescous, and other offences committed or done against the King's Majestie's Peace within your limits: You shall once every year during your office present at the Quarter Sessions all Popish Recusants within your liberty, and their Children above 9, and their servants, (*scil* their monthly absence from the Church).[113] You shall well and duly execute all precepts and Warrants to you directed, from the Justices of the Peace of the County or higher Officers: you shall be aiding to your neighbours against unlawful purveyances: in time of Hay or Corn Harvest, upon request, you shall cause all [113]persons meet to serve by the day for the mowing, reaping, or getting in of Corn or Hay: You shall in Easter week cause your Parishioners to chuse Surveyors for the mending of the Highways in your parish or Liberty; and you shall well and duly, according to your Knowledge, Power, and Ability, do and execute all other things belonging to the Office of Constable, so long as you continue in the said Office. So help you God."

If the obligations here enumerated had been effectually carried out, the King's Peace might have been a reality instead of the meaningless formula it had become; but High Constables were not professional police-officers like our Chief Constables, nor were they county magnates like the High Constables who once had superintended the police of the shire. The status of the office had steadily declined: instead of the great noblemen who, as we have seen, occupied similar posts under the Plantagenet Kings, and instead of the "Yeomen of the better class" spoken of by Lord Bacon, we find ale-house keepers and petty tradesmen, hardly less ignorant than the petty constables they were supposed to instruct, undertaking the office for the sake of profit, without any special aptitude, knowledge, or experience of their important duties, and without any serious intention of learning their work; for as no inducement or encouragement was held out to tempt or stimulate them to exertion, they were as inefficient when they relinquished their task as they were when they undertook it.

The form of oath required of petty constables, [114]or Tything men, as they were still called, was as follows—"You shall swear that you shall well and truly execute the office of a Tythingman of the Tything of H. (or headborough, etc.). His Majestie's Peace in your own person you shall keep, and see it kept in all others, as much as in you lieth. In the presence of the High Constable you shall be aiding and assisting unto him: and in his absence you shall execute his office, and do all other things belonging to your office, according to your knowledge and Power, untill another be chosen in your room, or you shall be legally discharged thereof.—So help you God."

It is immaterial whether these police officers deliberately took the required oath, meaning not to be bound by it, or whether they were so ignorant as not to understand the nature of a solemn affirmation; but be this as it may, High Constables neglected their oath and their office, and petty constables followed suit, rarely acting at all except under compulsion, or unless an opportunity offered for some petty tyranny or extortion, whilst anything like professional activity was quite unknown. Nor was the prevailing stagnation the worst feature of the times. The moral character, as well as the social position of peace officers, Justice and constable alike, deteriorated under Stuart misgovernment. The King of course remained *ex officio* the "highest maintainer of the peace," and his weaknesses, illegalities, and extortions were not only repeated but multiplied in the descending links of the chain of responsibility.

[115]

It was in the reign of James I. that corrupt magistrates first earned for themselves the nickname of "Basket Justices," as the predecessors of the "Trading Justices" of later days were called; and even the higher judges were not altogether above suspicion. With such a degenerate personnel to carry out its provisions, small wonder that the law frequently became a dead letter. Let one instance suffice. During this reign the right of sanctuary was abolished by law; but custom, which was far more powerful than the police, having decided that sanctuaries should continue, not only was no attempt made to deprive these asylums of their ancient privileges, but certain of them, notably Whitefriars, secured for themselves additional immunities. The country, in fact, too often had to witness the ridiculous spectacle of a Legislature solemnly filling the Statute Book with elaborate enactments, whilst the constables whose duty it was to see the law enforced, were quietly going about their own business, following the plough, or minding the shop. English police was in truth at a low ebb, and the inevitable consequences of such a feeble executive quickly followed; bullies and blackguards of every kind overran the realm, and the weak had no rights except such as the strong chose to leave them. "Private quarrels were nourished" (writes the historian of the period) "... and duels in every street maintained: divers sects and peculiar titles passed unpunished and unregarded, as the sect of the Roaring Boys, Bonaventors, Bravadors, Quarterors, and such like, [116]being persons prodigal, and of great expense, who, having run themselves into debt, were constrained to run next into factions, to defend themselves from danger of the law. These received countenance from divers of nobility: and the citizens, through lasciviousness consuming their estates, it was like that the number (of these desperadoes) would rather increase than diminish: and under these pretences, they entered into many desperate enterprises, and scarce any durst walk in the Street after nine at night.... Alehouses, dicing houses, taverns and places of iniquity, beyond manner abounding in most places."[114]

Slack as the police were in other directions, the campaign against vagrants continued to be conducted with vigour. All men, whatever their station, were ordered to apprehend such rogues or vagabonds as they might see begging, and to convey them to the nearest constable or tythingman, at whose hands they were liable to be branded with the letter "R," should they be found incorrigible.[115] Nor was this all. Justices of the Peace were instructed to summon the constables together some four or five days before the half-yearly sessions, and to command them "to make a general privy search one night for the finding out of such rogues and idle persons, and such as they find they shall bring to the Justices, and if for punishment (cause them to be) conveyed to the house of correction, there to be set to labour."[116] In order, moreover, [117]that this privy search might be the more effectual, constables were empowered to claim the assistance of as many neighbours as they might find sufficient for their purpose.

Such persistent persecution of the vagrant class does not argue that the police were efficient, for if the vagrants had been organized or able to stand up for themselves, there is little doubt that they would have been left alone just as the Roaring Boys and the Bonaventors were. This is also true, to some extent, of those unfortunate persons who were suspected of being afflicted with the plague, and who were, in consequence, treated with as little consideration as are pariah dogs in an Indian cantonment. Fear of the plague aroused an unwonted display of energy amongst police officers, and caused extraordinary powers to be given to the Justices, who were authorised to appoint Searchers, Watchmen, Examiners, and others to see that no person suspected of being infected left their houses. If any such person, having been duly warned, "contemptuously went abroad," the Watchmen might, with violence, enforce him to keep his house, but if he was caught in the public streets having any infectious sore upon him uncured, he was adjudged "*ipso facto*" guilty of felony, and might be sentenced to death. Furthermore, if any man was discovered abroad "conversing with company" after being cautioned to keep house, even if there was no sore found about him, it was ordained that he should be punished as a vagabond, and be subject to all penalties for vagabondage (including whipping) be[118]sides being bound to his good behaviour for the space of one year.[117] In remote country districts similar powers were conferred, not only on Justices of the Peace, but also on constables and headboroughs.[118]

The following police regulations, which were in force during an outbreak of the plague in the City of Oxford, are from a Proclamation by Charles I. in the year 1644, and are far milder and more reasonable than those considered necessary in the previous reign, as a few extracts will shew. It is ordained—"That a Watchman (be) set at the Fore door of the house, to keep in the persons within the house, and also to fetch them such necessaries as they want, to be delivered to them so discretely and warily as may not endanger themselves, or those to whom they may resort.

"That when a house shall be known to be infected with the plague, forthwith a Red Crosse be set on the outward doore of the house, with an inscription in Capital Letters, with these words LORD HAVE MERCY UPON US.

"That every such Watchman, when he sitteth or goeth in the streets, carry a white stick in his hand, so that others may be admonished not to presse too neare into his company.

"That all burialls of persons dying of the plague be in the night-time, after tenne of the clock at the [119]soonest, and without concourse of people, and that the Corpse be laid at least foure foot deep under the ground.

"That all Dogs and Cats in the Towne be forthwith sent away out of the Towne, or such as are found in the Streets, or Courts of the Colledges, to be knockt on the head, and their carcasses carryed away and buried without the Works at a convenient distance."[119]

It is not to be wondered at if during the troubles which befell the nation in King Charles' reign, police suffered in common with all other institutions. Internal peace was not likely to thrive during those eleven years whilst no Parliament was summoned, whilst Wentworth was devoting his energies towards the creation of a standing army that was to make the Crown absolute, whilst soldiers were billeted broadcast on unwilling inhabitants, and as long as in many districts martial law continued to supersede the ancient judicial system.

The keynote of Charles' policy was, from the first, a determination to raise money by hook or by crook, wherever the cost might fall, and to this end, one field of trickery after another was exploited. One device (1626) was to make Sheriffs of those of his opponents whom the King feared, so as to secure their detention in their own counties; another was an attempt (1640) to reintroduce the forest laws, by determining afresh the boundaries of the royal forests,[120] and re-insisting on their old-time privileges for the sake of the revenues accruing therefrom. [120]Amercements were collected with an energy that was not content until the uttermost farthing had been gleaned: offences against the licensing laws were usually punished by fines, and the income arising from this source was not small, so it was enacted,[121] that if offenders did not pay up within six days, they were to be delivered to the constable to be whipped, and if the constable failed to execute his warrant, he was to be committed to prison by the Justice until he should induce someone else to do it for him.

Before approaching the subject of the Civil War and its after-consequences, it will, perhaps, not be out of place to pause for a moment, and looking back on the history of the past, to enquire, how much of the ancient police system of England survived at this period, how much of it was dormant, and what portions had altogether disappeared.

The Tything could no longer be said to exist: the increase of population, the growth of trade, and the improved facilities for moving from one part of the country to another, having rendered the retention of such a small sub-division impracticable. The parish took the place of the tything, and the parish-constable filled, to some extent, the position once held by the tythingman. We have seen how the office of constable, which theoretically ought to fall to all the inhabitants in rotation ("Religious Persons, Knights, Clerkes and Women" only excepted) came to be generally executed by paid, and practically permanent substitutes; but it must not be forgotten that [121]the liability of the principal was not at an end, nor the appointment of the substitute valid, unless the transfer was approved by the inhabitants, and until it was duly confirmed by the proper authority.

The decay of frank-pledge, as a practical system, had long been complete, but the general principle remained, and now and again we come across attempts at revival and other indications, which prove that the Saxon régime was not entirely forgotten. In his "Customs of the City of London," published in 1642, Sir Henry Colthrop quotes from Liber Albus: "A large Charter is granted for the liberties of Southwark, and for correction of offences there, with a view of Franck-pledge with arrests, and to bring the offenders to Newgate."[122]

Writing in the first half of the seventeenth century, Minsheu says that "Inlaugh signifieth him that is in some Franke-pledge," and goes on to remark that "Decennier is not now used for the Chiefe man of a Dozen, but for him that is sworn to the King's Peace ... and that no man ordinarily giveth other securities for the keeping of the King's Peace, but his owne oath, and that therefore none answereth for another's transgression, but every man for himself—and for the generall ground this may suffice."[123] The exceptions here implied, refer no doubt to the custom of binding over an offender to keep the peace. "Inlaugh" is obviously the antithesis of the more familiar "Outlaw," whilst "Dozen" is used in its original sense of [122]"Ten," and has nothing to do with the number "Twelve."

The liability of the Hundred to compensate the sufferers for the damages done therein still held good,[124] and constables had never been relieved, by Statute or otherwise, of their constitutional duty of presenting offences at the court of the Hundred or Leet. The High Constable was the chief executive officer of the Hundred, but as the scope of his office has been fully set forth in the form of oath already quoted, his exact position need not be further enlarged on, except to say that his disciplinary powers over the petty-constables seem to have been very limited. The Justices decided what the petty-constables were to do, and how they were to do it, despite the fact that the High Constable was the man who was responsible for the due conservation of the peace in his district: he had, in short, most of the responsibilities of a modern Chief Constable, with no power of appointing, dismissing, or controlling his assistants.

The obligation of all to bear arms had been re-enforced by Statute as recently as the year 1557,[125] and this liability remained the law of the land, at least nominally so, until the eighteenth century.

The Statute of Winchester defined the law as to Watch and Ward as heretofore, and although of course its precise regulations were no longer adhered to in detail, but modified continually with the changing circumstances of the times, no fresh authoritative declaration was issued on the subject.

[123]

Hue and Cry, also, had undergone little change and in 1626 is thus defined by Minsheu: "Hue and Cry—This signifieth a pursuit of one having committed felonie by the highway, for if the partie robbed, or any in the companie of one murdered or robbed, come to the Constable of the Next Towne, and will him to raise Hiew & Crie, or to make pursuit after the offendour, describing the partie, and shewing, as neere as he can, which way hee is gone: the Constable ought forthwith to call upon the Parish, for aid in seeking the felon: and if he be not found there, then to giue the next constable warning, and he the next, untill the offender be apprehended, or at the least untill he be thus pursued to the sea-side."

This brief survey of the police system of the early Stuart period not only shews how little progress had been made during the last five hundred years, but partly explains the rash haste with which all classes decided to appeal to the sword for the settlement of the differences that divided Crown and Commons. For some time back, in the absence of that restraining influence which an efficient police force might have afforded, people had readily run into factions; and, with arms in their hands, had supported their particular opinions by force, in defiance of all authority, and with a degree of violence that would never have been tolerated for a moment in any community where the value of peace-maintenance was duly appraised and properly insisted upon.

[124]

CHAPTER VII
MILITARY POLICE AND POLICE UNDER CHARLES II

If the feebleness of the police was in some degree responsible for the ready appeal to arms in 1642, the lawlessness that was so widespread at the close of the century, was largely the outcome of the disorganization of the national police system, which was the natural accompaniment of the Revolution. Civil War is invariably attended by an outbreak of crime that has no connection with the main quarrel, but which arises in the day of trouble because the powerlessness of the executive is the opportunity of the criminal. No longer is any one power supreme (crimes committed in one camp being generally condoned in the other), and a mania of insubordination drives ordinarily well-disposed persons to throw off the old restraints to which they instinctively submit in times of peace. When Civil War begins, the "King's Peace" is at an end, the Law is forgotten or despised, the whole body politic is in a state of fever, and the usual functions of orderly government are suspended.

If the Revolution in England produced less serious consequences than might have been expected, this result was due to the puritan zeal of the Parlia[125]mentary Army, which had no sympathy with any acts of violence that were not directed against those whom it held to be the enemies of liberty and religion, and which at least permitted no riotous licence amongst its adherents. Yet in spite of this desire of the popular party to maintain order, the whole civil machinery of the country was dislocated and out of gear as long as the war lasted; even the circuit of the Justice of Assize was discontinued; and marriages, no longer solemnised with the customary religious ceremony, were performed by Justices of the Peace, and in such a casual manner that few records were kept.

As soon as Cromwell's victory was complete he at once set to work to establish an orderly government, only to find that the old implements that had served his predecessors were now broken and well-nigh useless. In London, the Parliamentary stronghold, the re-establishment of order presented no insuperable difficulties, but in the rural districts the case was different. There the gentry, to which class both Justices of the Peace and grand jury-men belonged, were in the main royalists—whilst constables, tythingmen and petty jurymen were usually Roundheads. The resulting friction hampered the Protector's administration from the first; so that, much as he would have preferred to have made use of the constitutional machinery for peace-maintenance, he was often compelled to resort to novel expedients to police the new commonwealth. If it was denied to Oliver Cromwell to govern on constitutional lines, he held, nevertheless, the supreme command of a large and powerful army, such as no sovereign in England had previously had [126]the control of, and inevitably therefore, he fell back upon the military forces that had served him so well in the past, hoping by their aid to restore, if not to improve upon, the state of security that had been wrecked by the war.

An attempt to reform the county magistracy by the creation of a new commission of the peace in the year 1651 having ended in failure, the Protector had no choice but to hand over to the

Army those police functions which no alternative organization was competent to undertake, and so for the first time in English history, the civil power was subordinated to a military dictatorship, and for a while the sword supplanted the baton.

In the course of the year 1655 the whole of England and Wales was divided for administrative purposes into twelve police districts, viz.:—

i. Kent and Surrey.

ii. Sussex, Hants, and Berks.

iii. Gloucester, Wilts, Dorset, Somerset, Devon and Cornwall.

iv. Oxford, Bucks, Herts, Norfolk, Suffolk, Essex and Cambs.

v. London.

vi. Westminster and Middlesex.

vii. Lincoln, Notts, Derby, Warwick and Leicester.

viii. Northants, Beds, Rutland and Hunts.

ix. Herefordshire, Salop and N. Wales.

x. Cheshire, Lancashire and Staffordshire.

xi. Yorkshire, Durham, Cumberland, Westmoreland and Northumberland.

xii. Monmouth and S. Wales.

[127]

To each of these districts a military officer was assigned, and largely endowed with inquisitorial and penal powers. Though holding for the most part no higher army rank than that of colonel or major, these functionaries (who were appointed by Cromwell himself, and who remained under his personal supervision) were styled Major-Generals,[126] and under this title exercised an office which for the moment overawed the constitutional ministers of the peace. At first it was not intended that the ordinary magistrates should be superseded, for the Major-Generals were instructed to co-operate with "the other Justices of the Peace," and if in practice this co-operation degenerated into flat coercion, such a result must be attributed to the exigencies of the occasion, or to the misinterpretation of their orders by the Protector's agents, rather than to the deliberate design of Cromwell himself.

The programme in front of the military reformers was a sufficiently extensive one, comprising, as it did, measures "for the security of the peace of the nation, the suppressing of vice, and the encouragement of virtue."[127] To enable them to grapple with their herculean task, they were assisted by a special force of militia, 6420 strong, all but two hundred of whom were mounted, and the expense of the new administration was met by the imposition of a tax of ten per cent. on the estates of Royalists, on the old English principle that those responsible for disturbances [128]should pay for the re-establishment of order. As was only to be expected, political considerations suggested many of the police regulations now enforced—travellers from foreign parts were not free to remain on English soil till they had communicated to the Major-General of the district, their names, their destination, and their business, nor were they allowed to move from shire to shire without previously advising the Justices; whilst ex-cavaliers and other persons of known royalist sympathies were bound to notify every change of address to the soldier-magistrates, who were also empowered to disarm rebels and to distribute the confiscated weapons amongst supporters of the parliamentary cause. For the guidance of the Major-Generals a document was circulated, containing twenty-one headings, under which was set out a scheme for the better government of the people—horse-racing, cock-fighting, and bear-baiting were forbidden, drunkenness, blasphemy and sabbath-breaking were to be severely punished, and alehouses, not absolutely necessary for the refreshment of travellers, were to be suppressed.[128] The vigour with which this crusade against popular sports was pushed is well illustrated by the activity displayed by Colonel Barkstead, who with his own hand killed all the bears in Westminster, and ordered his men to wring the neck of every game-cock that they could find.

Under the military régime espionage was encouraged, and the new functionaries received special [129]instructions to watch carefully such persons as appeared to live beyond their means. At the same time better protection for the public highways was provided, sheriffs being ordered to apprehend vagrants, robbers and highwaymen throughout their respective districts, with the assistance, if necessary, of the military police; in this way the vagrant nuisance was considerably abated, if not for long, and in one neighbourhood at least complete success would seem to have been attained, for Whalley was able to boast, "This I may truly say, you may ride all over Nottinghamshire, and not see a beggar or a wandering rogue."

Although the meshes of what the Protector called his "little poor invention" were calculated to entangle petty sinners amongst his opponents whilst admitting of the escape of more dangerous offenders amongst his adherents, it would be unjust to suppose that Cromwell's police system was only a pretext for the exercise of political tyranny. Many of the pains suffered by royalists were directly attributable to their own faults, and, without deserting their cause, they might have with ordinary care have avoided many of the penalties they incurred. Generally speaking, the code was especially severe against moral as contrasted with criminal offences; gambling and profane swearing being punishable by heavy fines and imprisonment, whilst dissolute living rendered the offender liable "to be sent out of the Commonwealth," as transportation to Barbadoes was euphemistically termed. In addition to their already too numerous duties, the Major-Generals were expected to exercise a general supervision over the religious habits of the [130]people, the regulations of weights and measures and the control of certain trades also falling to their lot. In London and Westminster, where the Puritans had a preponderating majority, and where Major-General Skippon and Colonel Barkstead respectively held command, the police control grew particularly irksome and irritating, puritan zeal being carried to such a pitch that fiddlers found themselves in the stocks for no worse offence than playing a jig, and even the ordinary Christmas festivities were sternly repressed. Search was frequently made in the taverns and alehouses, and any servant or apprentice found there after 8 P.M. was seized and taken before a Justice of the Peace for punishment. The Commissioners of Customs also were instructed to cause their officers to make similar visits in order to prevent tippling amongst watermen,[129] whilst stage-plays and places of public amusement were vigorously proceeded against.[130]

The régime associated with the Major-Generals was short; these functionaries were practically extinct before the end of 1657, and all traces of their rule were quickly obliterated after the restoration of the Monarchy. But the episode is none the less interesting as being the only example in England of an almost unqualified military police ascendancy, such as has been common elsewhere.

In estimating the results produced by this system, [131]it must be borne in mind that the circumstances under which it was instituted were quite exceptional. The army which undertook the policing of the country was composed neither of foreigners nor of mercenaries; on the contrary, its members were the pick of the middle classes of England, and their object was the maintenance of liberty and religion, as they understood those terms, not conquest, nor oppression for oppression's sake.

Cromwell's lieutenants did their work with honesty and diligence, and, according to their lights, they held the balance of justice level between man and man. If their discretion had equalled their impartiality, posterity would be able to look upon their administration with unqualified approval, but the admonishing, meddling, and eavesdropping tactics that they saw fit to pursue only invited the reaction that so quickly followed on the heels of their employment.

As long as a strict military discipline remained in force, disorders were kept in check, but as soon as it was relaxed, the havoc caused by the war soon became apparent, and at no time in our history has there been such a need of a strong and capable police force as there was at the time of the Restoration. The country was overrun by vagrants and disbanded soldiery, numbers of people had suddenly been reduced to poverty, and numbers had as suddenly been raised to affluence; the revulsion of feeling that followed upon the downfall of the puritan party led to excesses of every kind, and licence and violence thrived in the general confusion; nor was it till Charles II. had been king for several years that any [132]attempt was made to grapple with the state of chaos to which the internal security of the kingdom had been reduced, and even then the matter was not faced with any resolution.

London was in a disgraceful condition. Few towns in Europe were at once so inadequately policed, so badly lighted, and in such an insanitary state as the capital city of England; proof of the lack of proper sanitation, and its unfailing result, was brought home to people in convincing form at the time when the nightly procession of dead-carts, filled with victims of the plague, was the only traffic to be seen in the streets; but although the great fire of 1666 improved out of existence some of the most pestilential quarters, London remained a city of squalor and darkness. Most of the thoroughfares were without pavements of any kind, and such as existed were so sunken and broken that they were a source of danger to those who stumbled along them; rubbish was shot out of upper windows into the street beneath, and the public squares were used as receptacles for all the filth of the neighbourhood. After nightfall the certainty of having to encounter drunken bullies and highway robbers confined to their houses those citizens whom urgent business did not compel to walk abroad; even in daylight there were districts where the peace officers dared not venture, and Macaulay tells us that within the sanctuary of Whitefriars "even the warrant of the Chief Justice of England could not be executed without the help of a company of musketeers."[131]

All this time the legislature was mute: throughout the reign of Charles II. hardly a single Act of Parliament was passed dealing with the policing of the twin cities that make up the metropolis. The municipal authorities did what they could, and by an Act of Common Council provided a force of about one thousand Bellmen, afterwards called Charlies, in memory of the monarch in whose reign they were first instituted. Unfortunately these watchmen were allowed to shirk their duties and were well known to be altogether inefficient, so much so, that when rowdy apprentices and other unruly assemblages gave trouble, as they too often did, no one thought of looking to such weak-kneed officials for the safety of the town. On such occasions companies of soldiers were requisitioned to protect the main thoroughfares, and, as a further precaution, chains were stretched from one side of the street to the other to prevent the free movement of the riotous bands.

Before the end of the reign, however, some advance was made towards rendering London a fit place to live in. Several squares were enclosed and planted; new and wider streets were built; but the greatest improvements of the time were due, not to the efforts of municipal authorities, but to the recently-formed Royal Society, which investigated the question of sanitary police, and offered suggestions that to some extent were acted upon, with the result that England has since been free from the plague, so fatal in former years. Commissioners of Sewers were appointed, and the duties of [134]scavengers and rakers, with regard to the cleansing of the metropolis, were formulated.

In other departments also, progress was manifest, especially in the lighting arrangements. By an act passed in 1672[132] it had been ordered that a certain number of candles should be displayed every night between Michaelmas and Lady Day; but in 1685 private enterprise was responsible for placing a light before every tenth door from dusk till midnight. The effect cannot have been dazzling, but even this moderate amount of illumination was more effectual in preventing crime than any number of the watchmen of the period were likely to be. About the same time regulations for the control of hackney carriages plying for hire were first published.[133]

In the rural districts peace-maintenance was, if possible, at a lower ebb than in London—the roads were almost impassable throughout the winter months, and highwaymen were as frequent as mile-stones. Peace officers were practically non-existent: Justices were careless and apathetic, and Lords of the Manor had neglected to hold Courts-Leet for the annual election of Constables. A statute of 1673[134] complains of the lack of constables, and authorises two Justices of the Peace in each district to fill up the vacancies immediately. This was the first occasion on which the power of appointing petty constables had been by Act of Parliament [135]conferred on the magistrates, and official sanction extended to what had for years been the almost invariable custom. For the better policing of highways, turnpikes were established,[135] and those who used the roads made to subscribe towards the necessary repairs, instead of the whole burden being thrown on the rural population, which, partly by forced labour exacted by law (the *Corvée* of Feudal times), and partly by a parochial rate, had been compelled to mend the roads that traversed their neighbourhood. It is to be feared that this long-delayed act of justice was attributable rather to the vile condition of the highways than to any tender consideration for the rural population.

The system of passports, which had been introduced some centuries before for the purpose of checking vagrancy, continued to find favour, and was believed in as a panacea for the prevention of all kinds of crime. It was thought, not without reason, that a thief could not long pursue his vocation undetected amongst neighbours, who were acquainted with his circumstances, and who saw how he occupied his time and how he spent his money, whilst a stranger who came to-day and was gone to-morrow, might rob from one end of England to the other with impunity. The police were therefore instructed to enforce the regulations against vagrants with increased vigour, and in the following manner. After a vagrant beggar had been whipped he was entitled to a testimonial signed by the minister of the parish and countersigned by the [136]constable or tythingman, setting forth the date and place of his punishment, something after this form. "W. W., a sturdy vagrant beggar (aged about forty years) tall of stature, red-haired, and long lean-visaged, and squint-eyed, was this 24th day of A in the 22nd year of the reign of Our Gracious Sovereign Lord King Charles the Second, etc., openly whipped at T in the County of G; according to the law, for a wandering rogue; and is assigned to pass forthwith from parish to parish by the officers thereof the next streight way to W in the county of B, where he confesseth he was born: and he is limited to be at W aforesaid within twelve days now next ensuing at his peril. Given under the hands and seals of C. W. minister of T. aforesaid, and of J. G. constable there, the day and year aforesaid."[136] Any vagrant found by a constable, and unable to produce such a testimonial, was straightway to be arrested, and became liable to more whipping, or if found incorrigible[137] to transportation "to any of the English plantations beyond the sea" by the order of a majority of Justices at Quarter Sessions. Although we no longer look upon vagrancy as "The Mother and Root of all Evil" as our forefathers did, and have relaxed the stringency of the laws against vagabondage, the tramp is still an object of legitimate suspicion, and a watchful eye is kept by the Convict Supervision Office over all convicts at large, who are bound to [137]produce their licenses when called upon by a police officer to do so, and are only allowed to travel from district to district under certain restrictions.

Among the many difficulties that those responsible for the preservation of the peace had to contend with, one of the most complicated was how best to deal with the lawless aggression of the Lowland Scots without involving the two nationalities in actual war. Henry VIII. endeavoured to solve the problem by the creation of a special local authority called "The Council of the North," but this was only a temporary measure, and not very successful, nor were the expedients adopted by Elizabeth any more effectual. Throughout the whole of the seventeenth century, the northern counties were continually overrun by predatory bands, called Moss-troopers, who taking advantage of the almost perennial hostility existing between the English and the Scots, harried the country-side, murdering, marauding, and lifting cattle: in case of pursuit, or after an unusually successful expedition, they had only to cross the border to avoid capture. According to Fuller,[138] their numbers amounted at one time to some thousands of men, who scoured the country in troops and exacted an annual tribute from the inhabitants of the valleys between the Solent and the North Sea. Although Fuller's was assuredly an exaggerated estimate, these enterprising freebooters were without question a most formidable fraternity. The Union of the Crowns of England and Scotland deprived them, it is true, of the international pretext they [138]had traded upon in the past, but their depredations continued just the same as before. With the hope of putting an end to these raids, a local police force was established in 1672,[139] and afterwards kept alive by successive Acts of Parliament. The Justices of the Peace for the northern counties were empowered by virtue of this Statute to make a charge of £500 against Northumberland, and of £200 against Cumberland, for the payment and support of a body of men, forty-two strong (viz., thirty Northumbrians and twelve Cumbrians), whose duty it was to "search out, discover, pursue, apprehend, and bring to trial by law,"—the raiders. In strict justice, the task of suppressing the Moss-troopers should not have been left to a local force, but the political relations between the two countries were already strained almost to breaking point, and the employment of troops on the borderland might, and probably would, have induced a rupture. Under the circumstances, therefore, the government of the day was probably justified in the course pursued, but on no account should the whole expense have been borne by the very counties which had already principally suffered through the inroads of the raiders.

Contemporary literature shews how lamentably insecure life and property had become in the days of the later Stuarts, and during the early Georgian period. Luttrell's diary is one long catalogue of crimes of violence, and he remarks, from his own experience, that "footpads are very troublesome in [139]the evening on all the roads leading to the city, which renders them very unsafe." In his history of England, Smollet declares that "thieves and robbers are now become more desperate and savage than they had ever appeared since mankind was civilized."

No thoroughfare was free from the tyranny of the fraternity of highwaymen, who were allowed to terrorize whole districts, and who enjoyed an almost unlimited freedom from interference. As their depredations grew more extensive, their insolence increased. Evelyn describes how a gang of robbers succeeded in appropriating the taxes that had been collected in the northern counties, as the bags containing the money were being escorted through Hertfordshire, on their way to London: the highwaymen first stopped and secured all travellers in the immediate neighbourhood, placed them under guard in a field, and after killing the horses of their captives to prevent pursuit, attacked the escort, put them to flight, and captured the treasure. The authors of this outrage were never caught.

Troops were sometimes made use of in a half-hearted sort of way to patrol the most infested localities, but the simple remedy of maintaining a properly paid and equipped police was never tried: the only expedient that the wisdom of the age could suggest was the offering of rewards to all and sundry to encourage the apprehending of highwaymen. This disastrous policy was inaugurated in 1692.[140] "Whereas the highways and roads," runs the preamble of the statute in question, "within the Kingdom of England [140]and Dominion of Wales have been of late times more infested with thieves and robbers than formerly, for want of due and sufficient encouragement given, and means used, for the discovery of such offenders," provision is accordingly made, that in the event of any person being killed in the act of taking a highwayman, his executors shall have the reward, and a free pardon is promised to accomplices and other criminals who shall cause such offenders to be brought to justice. The conditions under which this pardon was granted were as follows: "If any person or persons, being out of prison from and after the said five-and-twentieth day of March, commit any robbery and afterwards discover two or more persons, who already hath or hereafter shall commit any robbery, so as two or more of the persons discovered shall be convicted of such robbery—any such discoverer shall himself have, and be entitled to, the gracious pardon of their Majesties."

The provisions of this Act were afterwards extended to robberies in London,[141] and first and last were responsible for an appalling sum of wickedness. The bait of blood-money and the lack of a salaried or professional class of detectives were answerable for the appearance of amateur thief-takers; these men were mostly ex-thieves, who had given up their old vocation for the safer, more lucrative, but infinitely baser role of fattening on the conviction of the innocent, and on the execution of those whom they had themselves corrupted. The best known and most energetic member of this horde of vampires was the [141]notorious Jonathan Wild, who flourished at the beginning of the eighteenth century, and whose *modus operandi* is fully set forth for us by Henry Fielding in his satirical history of "Jonathan Wild the Great."

This arch-ruffian had a most complete knowledge of all the thieves in England, and at one time practically monopolised in his own person the trades of receiver of stolen property and trafficker in blood money. He established warehouses all over the country, and even bought himself a ship to export what he could not dispose of at home. To those thieves who submitted to his authority, and who brought him the proceeds of their robberies, he extended a protection that must have been dependent to a certain degree on the connivance of some person or persons in authority. Grandmaster of espionage, and holding in his talons the threads of all villainy, Wild could manufacture whatever evidence he chose, could ruthlessly destroy any who opposed him, and deliver up to justice those thieves who were bold enough to take their spoils elsewhere for disposal. When this supply of victims ran short, or when it suited his purpose to shield the real culprit, he was content to take the reward offered for the conviction of the innocent. It is comforting to know that his carcass, the foulest fruit the fatal tree ever bore, eventually swung at Tyburn, at the same spot where so many of his victims had preceded him.

The iniquitous system of paying blood-money for the conviction of certain classes of offenders continued for generations, but is now happily extinct. At the present day rewards are not offered by [142]Government except under very exceptional circumstances, and then only in cases where the identity of the criminal is clear, whilst rewards offered by private persons are placed under restrictions that prevent any revival of the abominable traffic that continued even into the nineteenth century. As late as 1816 George Vaughan, and others associated with him, were convicted at the Middlesex Sessions of conspiring to induce three brothers named Hurley, and a lad named Wood, only thirteen years of age, to commit a burglary at Hoxton, and by having them convicted of the fact, to procure for themselves the rewards given by Parliament for the conviction of housebreakers.

One of the chief embarrassments, after the inefficiency of the constabulary, which hampered the action of the authorities, and made the suppression of crime more difficult, was the popularity that the more notorious thieves enjoyed amongst a large section of the people; the sympathy, felt and expressed, for highwaymen of the Claude Duval type was widespread, and arose from a variety of sentiments. The mass of the people, who never suffered in their own pockets, were not altogether averse to seeing the rich plundered occasionally, especially as it was the policy of the robbers to be free and open-handed with a part of their booty. Another class of people who were well-disposed towards the highwaymen, gave their sympathy as a misdirected kind of protest against the severity of the law; and the "gentlemen of the road," as they were called, quick to perceive the advantage [143]that this popularity, from whatever source arising, gave them—sometimes, but not often—performed quite gentlemanly actions, in order to enhance and to advertise their reputation for good deeds.

The Abbé le Blanc, who spent some years in England early in the eighteenth century, declared that he frequently met Englishmen who were as proud of the exploits of their highwaymen as they were of the bravery of their soldiers, and in a letter to de Buffon he writes: "It is usual, in travelling, to put ten or a dozen guineas in a separate pocket, as a tribute to the first that comes to demand them," and adds that, "... about fifteen years ago, these robbers, with a view to maintaining their rights, fixed up papers at the doors of rich people about London, expressly forbidding all persons, of whatever quality or condition, from going out of town without ten guineas and a watch about them, under pain of death. In bad times, when there is little or nothing to be got on the roads, these fellows assemble in gangs, to raise contributions even in London itself; and the watchmen seldom trouble themselves to interfere with them in their vocation."[142] Without attaching too much importance to the statements of this foreign critic, it must be confessed that at no time in our history have the arrangements for maintaining the peace sunk to so low an ebb as when thief-takers like Jonathan Wild were officially recognised and allowed to co-operate with the constitutional police forces, and at no time has the flood of lawlessness reached such a [144]height as when highwaymen and footpads dictated their own terms to all who made bold to use the King's Highway. Yet the Government took no steps towards organizing an adequate defence, and utterly failed to provide any counterpoise to the criminal tendencies of the age; it was left to private enterprise to carry out the duties, or some of them, that Parliament neglected to perform. In 1696 a "Society for the reformation of manners in the cities of London and Westminster" was formed, and in 1702 was instrumental in securing the conviction of 858 "Leud and Scandalous persons." Two years later, the Governors of the London poor issued a proclamation, promising the sum of twelve pence to any person who should apprehend "any rogue, vagabond, or sturdy beggar," and, having brought him before a Justice of the Peace, cause him to be committed to the workhouse.

The particular kind of lawlessness, however, that chiefly exercised men's minds in the days of Queen Anne was the work of young men of the town, commonly known as "Mohocks," who established a reign of terror in London, and whose excesses the peace-officers were powerless to prevent. The worst outbreak occurred in 1712, and the doings of these young blackguards are minutely described in a pamphlet published in that year.[143] "The watch in most of the out-parts of the town stand in awe of them, because they always come in a body, and are too strong for them, and when any watchman [145]presumes to demand where they are going, they generally misuse them. Last night they had a general rendezvous and were bent on mischief; their way is to meet people in the streets and stop them, and begin to banter them, and if they make any answer, they lay on them with sticks, and toss them from one to another in a very rude manner. They attacked the watch in Devereux Court and Essex Street, made them scower: they also slit two persons' noses, and cut a woman in the arm with a penknife that she is lam'd. They likewise rowled a woman in a tub down Snow Hill, that was going to market, set other women on their heads, misusing them in a barbarous manner."

In spite of the public indignation that such brutalities aroused, the feeble and timid watchmen were not superseded, nor was any inquiry instituted to discover the reasons for their inability to cope with these scandalous proceedings. It was thought rather a good joke that watchmen should be knocked down, and constables overturned, whilst the fact that London was left in complete darkness during the greater part of the night seems to have occasioned but little concern. There is a saying to the effect that a good lamp is a good policeman; but the subjects of Queen Anne, as it seems, expected the peace to be maintained without the assistance of either the one or the other,—the lamps were only lighted at six o'clock in the evening, and those that had not gone out before were extinguished at midnight, and when the moon was full they were not lighted at all.

[146]

The outrages committed by the Mohocks were so serious and persistent that something had to be done towards putting a stop to them, and so recourse was had to the objectionable expedient of offering a government reward for the conviction of the members of the gang. On the 17th of March 1712, the Queen issued a Royal Proclamation in the following words—

"Anne R. The Queen's Most Excellent Majesty being watchful for the Public Good of her loving Subjects, and taking notice of the great and unusual Riots and Barbarities which have lately been committed in the Night Time, in the open Streets, in several parts of the Cities of London and Westminster, and Parts adjacent, by numbers of Evil dispos'd Persons, who have combined together to disturb the Public Peace, and in an inhuman manner, without any Provocation have Assaulted and Wounded many of her Majesty's good Subjects, and have had the Boldness to insult the Constables and Watchmen, in the Execution of their Office, to the great Terror of her Majesty's said Subjects, and in Contempt and Defiance of the Laws of this Realm, to the Dishonour of her Majesty's Government, and the Displeasure of Almighty God, &c., &c.... Her Majesty doth hereby promise and declare, That Whosoever shall before the First Day of May now next ensuing, discover to any of Her Majesty's Justices of the Peace, any Person who, since the First Day of February, last past, hath, without any Provocation, Wounded, Stabb'd, or Maim'd, or who shall before the said First Day of May, without any Provocation, [147]Wound, Stab, or Maim, any of her Majesty's Subjects, within the said Cities of London and Westminster, and Parts Adjacent, so as such Offenders be brought to Justice, shall have and receive the Reward of One Hundred Pounds, &c., &c."

The continuance of disorders, which Rewards and Royal Proclamations were unable to check, and the prospect that the Jacobites would not tamely accept the rule of the House of Hanover, combined to make the question of peace-maintenance a very difficult problem for Queen Anne's successor. It is not surprising, therefore, that one of the first legislative enactments of George the First had for its object the suppressing of public tumults. The Act referred to is commonly called "The Riot Act,"[144] and became law in 1715. This Statute introduced no new principle—similar enactments, or at any rate measures which had the same object in view, had been frequently brought forward by Tudor sovereigns and by their predecessors, but in 1715 the offence of rioting (together with the penalties attaching thereto) was more clearly defined than had formerly been the case, and extended powers were conferred on a single Justice of the Peace or other authorized officer, acting alone, for "preventing tumults and riotous assemblies, and for the more speedy and effectual punishing the rioters."

After reciting that "the punishments provided by the laws now in being are not adequate to such heinous offences" the Statute enacts, that if any persons to the number of twelve or more, being [148]unlawfully, riotously, and tumultuously assembled together, to the disturbance of the public peace, at any time after the last day of July 1715, and after being commanded by any one or more Justice or Justices of the Peace, or by the sheriff, etc., by proclamation in the Kings name, to disperse themselves, shall unlawfully continue together for the space of one hour after such command, then such continuing together to the number of twelve or more, shall be adjudged felony without benefit of clergy, "and the offenders therein shall suffer death as in the case of felony without benefit of clergy."

The method of making the proclamation is as follows:—The Justice of the Peace or other authorised person "being among the said rioters, or as near to them as he can safely come" shall command silence, and after that shall openly and with loud voice make proclamation in these words:—"Our Sovereign Lord the King chargeth and commandeth all persons, being assembled, immediately to disperse themselves, and peaceably to depart to their habitations, or to their lawful business, upon the pains contained in the act made in the first year of King George, for preventing tumults and riotous assemblies. God save the King." To constitute a riot it is essential that alarm should be caused amongst the King's subjects, and if the four last words of the proclamation are omitted the reading of the Riot Act has no virtue. If after proclamation has been made the rioters do not disperse within an hour, any or all of them may be apprehended by force, and if they make resistance, the persons killing or injuring [149]them are indemnified and discharged of all liability with respect to any death or lesser injury they may happen to inflict.

The general tone of public opinion was constantly being lowered by the degrading spectacles that were everywhere displayed. Government itself set the example of brutality and violence by countenancing the procession to Tyburn, the use of the pillory, and the setting up of whipping-posts in the public streets; with the result that imitators sprung up in abundance to practice the lessons so sedulously taught by the authorities. The punishment of the pillory was in itself sufficiently severe, but the method of its infliction practically amounted to the official legalising of Lynch Law, because the populace were permitted to torture the sufferer almost to any extent; stone-throwing was nominally forbidden, but the prohibition was not enforced, and, if a victim died of the ill-usage to which he was subjected, no one was punished.

The police, who were feeble and timid when danger threatened, and who could never be trusted to quell the most insignificant riot, grew bold on occasions, when, without risk to themselves, they could pounce upon some weak or unpopular individual. Although whipping could be legally inflicted only by order of the magistrate, it was no unusual occurrence for a constable to take a man to the nearest whipping post, and there have him thrashed without reference to any superior authority whatever.

For the safeguarding of prisons, banks, and other [150]important places, military guards were often used to reinforce the ordinary watchmen, and, when so employed, the soldiers were accompanied by constables, whose duty it was to question passers-by, to hand suspicious characters over to the guard, and to bring them before a Justice of the Peace on the following morning. These duties, simple as they were, seem to have been negligently performed by the peace-officers, for complaints of neglect of duty were frequent; when Brigadier Mackintosh and his companions escaped from Newgate, they were lucky enough to pass the guard without examination, because the constable was absent from his post, and, in his absence, the military sergeant in charge had no authority to detain fugitives.

Further evidence, were any required, of the unsatisfactory condition of the parochial constabulary in London is abundant—not only was delinquency on the increase, but internal squabbles were everywhere rife amongst the local bodies intrusted with the preservation of the peace. In 1727 the Vestry of St George's, Hanover Square, for example, established a force of thirty-two watchmen and four bedels for that parish; several of the inhabitants, however, refused to pay the Watch-rate, and set up an opposition establishment which they called "The Inhabitant Watch" consisting of some sixteen persons, who repudiated the authority of the existing constables, and, on one occasion, flatly refused to arrest certain offenders even when required to do so by the High Constable.

An ineffectual attempt to reform the police of [151]London was made in 1736, in which year an Act of Parliament[145] was passed, giving powers to the Common Council of the City to raise a sum of money sufficient for all police purposes, to appoint as many peace officers as they thought proper, and to issue new and improved orders for the guidance of the nightly watch. By the same statute, Aldermen were made responsible for their respective wards, constables were empowered to arrest night-walkers, malefactors, and other suspected persons, and watchmen, in the absence of the Constable, might perform the duties of that functionary. Liability to watch and ward extended to all the inhabitants of London who were not "rated and assessed," by virtue of the Statute of Winchester.

At about the same time, the police administration of the rural districts was the subject of legislation, it being enacted[146] that any constable neglecting to make Hue and Cry shall be fined five pounds, and the liability of the hundred, in which a felony has been committed, for the escape of the felon is again insisted upon. By another Statute,[147] passed four years later, High Constables were ordered to levy a County Rate in the provinces and to pay the proceeds over to a treasurer appointed by Quarter Sessions, to be applied by him to the general police purposes of the County.

It is obvious that the Civil Power ought to be prepared for any possible emergency, but before 1829 this was far from being the case, and we find that when any exceptional conditions arose, tem[152]porary expedients had to be hurriedly devised to meet the crisis, affairs being allowed to slip back into their normal state of unpreparedness immediately the pressure was relieved. Such was the nature of the arrangements improvised during the rebellion in favour of the Young Pretender in 1745, when London prepared to defend itself against the enemy that marched southwards from Perth as far as Derby, almost without a check. The trained bands, who a hundred years before had barred the advance of Charles I. at Turnham Green, were called out, and, for a period of five months, the City Militia superseded the normal police establishments.

At this time the trained bands consisted of six regiments, viz., The Yellow, The White, The Orange, The Blue, The Red, and The Green. Their numbers amounted to close on ten thousand men, who at the crisis undertook to protect London, not only against a possible attack of an enemy from without, but also against the depredations of thieves and rioters within. The different regiments were told off to come on duty in rotation, for twenty-four hours at a time, and were disposed for police purposes in the following manner. Near the Mansion House was placed the main guard, and here the Commanding Officer was to be found during his tour of duty; other guards, under subordinate officers, being stationed at various points in the city.

During the day, only "home-sentinels," as they were called, were posted, but after sunset both "out-sentinels" and patrols were added; these patrols, called "petty-rounds," periodically visited [153]the neighbouring sentries; in the event of any rioting or other disturbance taking place, they had to return immediately, and inform the officer in charge. He was then instructed to march out his party to suppress it, at the same time notifying his commanding officer of the extent of the disorder, in order that the latter might send the necessary reinforcements, not only from the Main Guard, but from the other guards also, in sufficient numbers until peace was restored. Moreover, a general supervision was maintained by means of "grand rounds," which starting from the Main Guard patrolled the whole circuit to see that sentries were alert, that patrols were acquainted with their duties, that the countersign was correctly given, and to conduct prisoners to head-quarters for subsequent disposal by the magistrates. At daybreak reveille was sounded, and all out-sentinels relieved; but the home-sentinels were continued at their posts throughout the day.

The retreat of the invaders, and their final rout at Culloden, rendered the further embodiment of the citizen soldiers unnecessary, but during the period of their employment they performed their police duties with so much success, that robberies in the streets of London were for the time almost entirely suppressed, and the King's Peace was maintained in unexampled tranquillity. It does not appear that the Militia abused the power placed in their hands in any way, whilst the superiority of their rule over that of the watchmen was so pronounced, that there was some talk in after years of permanently handing over the policing of London to the trained bands; but the national distrust of a too powerful gendarmerie prevailed, and the old régime was allowed to continue. If the suggestion had come to anything, it would of course have been necessary to modify their organization which was of a strictly military character; but when the proposal was rejected an excellent opportunity was lost of obtaining the services of a really efficient body of men, at an expense to the ratepayers far below that of the existing watch, which then cost about £23 per night for the City proper, besides what was paid by banks and private individuals for special services.

CHAPTER VIII
BOW STREET POLICE AND MAGISTERIAL REFORM

It was not until the middle of the century that any intelligence was brought to bear on the problem of police, or that any promise appeared of a better state of things in that department of government. For an awakened interest and the resulting improvement we are mainly indebted to the famous novelist, Henry Fielding, who spent the closing years of his short life in a vigorous campaign against the growing domination of society by the criminal classes. Appointed to the Westminster bench at the age of forty-three, he exhibited in his new capacity an acquaintance with law and a knowledge of human nature, that were but rarely found in the ranks of the magistracy of the day: his charge to the Grand Jury, delivered in 1749, reads more like the deliberate composition of a justice of assize of large experience than the work of a junior magistrate just appointed to the office.

In the hope of rousing the civil power from its somnolent state, Fielding published a treatise called "An Enquiry into the Cause of the late Increase of Robbers," in which he gave an interesting account of the habits and customs of the people, with observations on the poor law, and on the apprehension, trial, and execution of felons. He attributed the prevalence of crime principally to the luxurious habits indulged in by the populace, especially gambling and drunkenness. With gin at a penny the quartern, and high play the absorbing passion of all classes, it was small wonder that crime was on the increase. In his attempts to improve the police, Fielding was ably seconded by his half-brother Sir John Fielding, who succeeded him as magistrate at Bow Street, and there inaugurated some valuable and far-reaching reforms.

By the employment of regularly-paid detectives he did more to render the streets of London safe than the whole body of watchmen, beadles and constables, to the number of about two thousand, had previously been able to effect, and soon afterwards obtained permission to establish, by way of experiment, a small police force organised on novel lines. This force, called the Bow Street Foot Patrol, was divided into eighteen parties, thirteen of which (called Country parties) patrolled the principal highways outside the metropolis, whilst the remaining five (known as Town parties) watched the streets of the central district. The remuneration of the patrols was high in comparison with the wages then customary, no patrolman receiving less than two shillings and sixpence a night. The system proved a great success, and a few years later its sphere of usefulness was enlarged by the formation of a horse patrol, which was posted for the protection of travellers on one or other of the main roads [157]leading into the country. Though consisting only of eight men, who, however, were well mounted and well armed, it afforded a better state of security to the suburbs than they had previously enjoyed.[148]

The success that attended Sir John Fielding's innovations was prompt and abiding. Bow Street quickly became pre-eminent as the only court where justice was dispensed in a business-like manner, and its officers, under the name of Bow Street Runners, became famous for their skill and sagacity. Sir John Fielding was blind, but his infirmity did not prevent him from constantly attending to his magisterial work. When seated in court he used to wear a white silk bandage over his eyes, and the striking figure of the tall blindfolded knight was a dramatic picture long remembered at Bow Street. His knowledge of everything that concerned the criminal classes was remarkable. It was said of him that he never failed to recognise an old offender, though the only indication he had to go by was the sound of the prisoner's voice. He was the author of several pamphlets on police questions, the most important being that published in 1755 under the title of "A plan for preventing robberies within twenty miles of London"; the details of which may be briefly stated as follows:

He suggested that the landowners and occupiers of high-class residential property near London should combine to form societies for the apprehension of burglars and other depredators. Each society was to select a treasurer to collect an annual subscription [158]of two guineas a-piece from the members. When a robbery was committed, the injured party was to immediately despatch a mounted messenger to the magistrate at Bow Street, warning on his way all the turnpike keepers, advising them as to the property stolen, and of any other particulars of importance. The magistrate was then to be empowered to draw on the funds of the society in the hands of the treasurer, for any expenses that might be incurred in the course of the pursuit and subsequent prosecution of the criminal.

This pamphlet was followed by a second called "An account of the origin and effects of a Police, set on foot in 1753 by the Duke of Newcastle, on a plan suggested by the late Henry Fielding."[149]

The publications of the brothers Fielding were to some extent instrumental in directing the public conscience towards a consideration of the state of the criminal law, which, year by year, had tended to increase in severity, without thereby effecting any diminution in the tale of offenders. "Extreme justice is an extreme injury," wrote Sir Thomas More, but abstract ideas of justice were little entertained in the days of the Georges; Tyburn and transportation were the only recognised remedies for the more serious breaches of the law, and men were slow to realise that it is better to make the commission of crime difficult than to punish it with indiscriminate severity. But from this time onwards arose a genuine wish for some change, a desire to [159]repress crime as humanely as possible; a half-formed idea found partial expression that perhaps, after all, the pain suffered by the culprit ought not to exceed the benefit conferred on the community by the punishment exacted; henceforward the Statute Book was not disgraced by fresh barbarities, and in course of years the old ones were gradually eliminated. In 1783 the procession to Tyburn was discontinued, and the use of the drop to accelerate death by hanging, introduced; the pillory was abolished in 1816 for all offences except perjury; whipping in public was done away with the following year, and transportation finally ceased in 1867.

Instead of legislating on the lines suggested by Fielding, whose scheme of police was proving practical and successful, the government preferred to revert to the methods of Queen Elizabeth,[150] and in 1755 was responsible for an Act[151] that was nothing but an attempt to revivify the Westminster Statute of 1584, the only new feature being the appointment of a committee called "The Jury of Annoyances," a body designed to see that the pavements were kept [160]in repair, and to prevent obstructions and encroachments thereon; this addition, it was supposed, brought the Act up to modern requirements. The number of constables to be yearly appointed for the City and Liberty of Westminster was fixed at eighty, furnished proportionally by the different parishes; any man who had already served, personally or by deputy, was not to be again chosen until seven years had elapsed since he last held office.

Two years later another Act,[152] to explain and amend the foregoing, followed, by which a regular chain of responsibility was created; the petty constable had to obey the High Constable; and he, again, had to observe the lawful commands of the Dean or High Steward, who still remained the paramount police authority in the district.

In 1772, the House of Commons appointed a Committee to inquire into the burglaries that had recently become so frequent in London and Westminster, one hundred and four houses having been broken into between Michaelmas 1769 and March 1770. This committee was the first of a long series authorised by Parliament with the idea of improving the police; every few years a new committee was appointed, and each in turn recorded a wearisome tale of resolutions without finding a remedy or indeed arriving at any satisfactory solution. One and all reported that the existing watch was deficient, a fact long patent to everybody without the assistance of select committee-men; they deplored the want of uniformity and co-operation in wards and parishes, [161]and recorded the shortcomings of beadles, constables, and watchmen; but whilst suggesting various minor reforms, they failed to see that no real progress was possible until a clean sweep had been made of the old system and its abuses.

The principal witnesses examined before this first committee were Sir John Fielding of Bow Street and Mr F. Rainsforth, the High Constable of Westminster; the former spoke as to the position of the magistracy and the state of the liquor traffic; the latter confined his remarks to the inefficiency of the peace-officers. The following extracts from Mr Rainsforth's diary for the 23rd of March 1770, which he read to the committee, shew us the kind of thing that used to go on.

"Saint Margaret's—Three quarters past eleven: constable came after I was there: Houseman and Beadle on duty: 41 watchmen, with St John's United, at 8½d. per night, with one guinea at Christmas, and one guinea at Lady Day, and great coats as a present: their beats large: was obliged to take a soldier into custody for being out of his quarters, and very insolent, with several more soldiers in the street at 12 o'clock: called out 'Watch,' but could get no assistance from them.

"St Clements' Danes—Past 3: no constable on duty: found a watchman there at a great distance from his beat: from thence went to the night-cellar facing Arundel Street in the Strand, which is in the Duchy, and there found 4 of St Clements' watchmen drinking. St Mary-le-Strand no attendance, having only two constables, which only attend every [162]other night, 3 watchmen, Duchy included, at one shilling each. A very disorderly cellar near the new church for selling saloop, etc., to very loose and suspected persons: St Clements' watchmen 32 at one shilling."

After hearing much evidence of this description, the committee passed thirteen resolutions, none of which, however, were of a very vigorous character. They recommended an increase in the number of watchmen, higher pay and a better method of appointing them; they suggested that the name "beadle" should no longer be used, that ballad-singers should be suppressed, and that steps should be taken to put a stop to the custom of granting wine and spirit licences indiscriminately to all who applied for them, adding by way of a conclusion to the whole matter, that the Roundhouses, as the constables' lockups were called, should not be used for the sale of intoxicants, and should be large enough to accommodate the prisoners arrested by the watch; it having frequently been found necessary to release disturbers of the peace and other minor offenders to make room for more serious cases!

In consequence of the report of the Parliamentary Committee, a bill was introduced into the House of Commons to provide an improved watch system for the "City of Westminster and parts adjacent ... uniformly ordered and regulated throughout the whole district." This Act,[153] passed in 1773, directs that trustees shall meet annually to appoint "what [163]number of watchmen they shall judge necessary to be kept and employed" for the ensuing year, specifying how many are to be apportioned to "beats" and "stands" respectively, and how many are to be told off for patrols. The local authorities are not, however, given a free hand in the administration of the interior economy of their trust: the minimum establishment that must be kept up by each parish is fixed by law, and varies from sixty watchmen on the beats and stands, and eight on patrol for St George's Hanover Square, down to the single watchman required for the "purlieus of the Savoy." Watch-houses must be substantially built, and watchmen are to be armed with staff and rattle, provided at parish expense, as well as with lanterns paid for out of their own pockets; the minimum wage must not fall below one shilling and threepence per night unless a man is employed by the year, in which case his nightly remuneration need not exceed one shilling: the hours are from 10 P.M. until 5, 6, or 7 A.M. according to the season of the year.

The duties of the watch comprise the apprehending of disorderly and suspected persons and handing them over to the constable; testing the fastenings of houses, shops and warehouses, and warning the occupier when necessary; twice every hour the watchmen must patrol his beat, and "as loudly and audibly as he can, proclaim the time of the night or morning." On coming off duty, the watchman has to submit his staff, rattle and lantern for the inspection of the constable; neglect of duty entails a [164]fine of ten shillings, and any person who assaults a watchman in the execution of his office renders himself liable to a £5 penalty; watchmen are forbidden to frequent alehouses during their tour of duty, and provision is made for the punishment of those publicans who harbour them.

There is much that is good in this Act, but it applied only to Westminster, and half of its provisions were never carried out. Instead of the uniform order that was to be established, the old confusion continued, the fine of five pounds was insufficient to protect the watchmen from assault, and the peace officers still tippled in alehouses, whilst thieves were comfortably carrying home the booty they had so easily secured.

The utter inadequacy of the whole system of defence against civil tumults, and the complete helplessness of London to protect itself against mob violence, was brought home to its inhabitants in a startlingly convincing manner in the course of those six terrible days during which their city was within an ace of being destroyed at the hands of the rabble let loose upon her streets by the crackbrained fanatic, Lord George Gordon.

The events that took place in the first week of June 1780, and which are to some extent familiar to us through the pages of "Barnaby Rudge," would never have happened if, in the earlier stages of the outbreak, the rioters had had opposed to them even a couple of hundred resolute constables, accustomed to deal with mobs, and working under the direction of officers experienced in the tactics of street-fighting. [165]At no time is an efficient civil force of such inestimable value as it is at the first appearance of great popular ferment; for in accordance with the strength or weakness of the police at that moment, is the course of after events decided. A crowd is like a great volume of water, harmless as long as its embankments are kept in repair and, if necessary, strengthened, but capable of an infinite amount of mischief if once allowed to break its barriers.

Anything like a full description of the Gordon riots lies outside the scope of this book; but a brief account of the principal features of the outbreak will very properly find a place here, in order to illustrate the degree of violence that an English mob is capable of, when allowed to get out of hand, and for the purpose of comparing these riots with others that took place on subsequent occasions after our modern police had been established. London is the mother-city of the English-speaking races, all of which have modelled their police forces on the metropolitan pattern; and the Gordon riots, which were the most violent ever experienced in this country, have therefore served as a lesson to cities as distant from us and from each other as Sydney and New York, forewarning those responsible for the maintenance of the peace in those places of the extent of the danger that threatens when proper precautions are neglected.

The disturbances in question arose out of an agitation directed against the Roman Catholics, whose position had been much improved by a recent Act of Parliament, the agitation culminating in a demand for the repeal of the unpopular con[166]cessions. A monster petition was prepared, and it was decided to present it to Parliament, with such a display of force that a refusal would be unlikely. Accordingly, at 10 o'clock on the morning of the 2nd of June, as many as 60,000 people assembled in St George's Fields to accompany Lord George Gordon in his attempt to intimidate the legislature. Marching to Westminster by different routes, the crowd closed all the avenues to both Houses, stopped peers and commoners on their way thither, and treated those who fell into their hands with insult and personal violence, smashing their carriages, tearing their clothes and in some cases removing their wigs; many members of Parliament were forced to put blue cockades in their hats and shout "No Popery" before they were released, others only regained their freedom on promising to vote for the repeal of the obnoxious act.

Whilst these proceedings were taking place, a squadron of horse arrived; but on being hooted and threatened, the troopers declared that their sympathies were altogether with the people, and then trotted off amidst the cheers of the crowd, who soon afterwards began to disperse, to riot in other parts of the town. That evening the Roman Catholic chapels attached to the Sardinian and Bavarian embassies were looted and burned.

Rioting continued during the three days that followed, the paralysed executive submitting in helpless impotence, and it was not until the fifth day that the climax was reached. The mob now suddenly broke out into an almost inconceivable state of fury, and overran the whole of London, [167]pillaging and burning as they went, and spreading terror in every direction: all business was suspended and most of the houses were barricaded; many persons, hoping to pacify the destroying furies, hung blue flags out of their windows and chalked the words "No Popery" on their shutters. An organized attack was made on Newgate, and when the old prison walls successfully withstood all the efforts of the mob to injure them, the furniture from the governor's house was thrown out of the windows and piled up for a bonfire, with the idea of consuming the great wooden gates; when these at length gave way, the rabble poured into the gaol through the smoking gateway, shortly to return bringing with them three hundred liberated prisoners, many of whom were under sentence of death already, and over-ripe for any atrocity. Matters now grew worse than ever, distilleries were broken open, and the raw spirits poured down the gutters to be lapped up by a crowd that was already mad. An attempt to break into the Bank of England was prevented by the guard stationed there, but many houses, including Lord Mansfield's and Sir John Fielding's, were burnt to the ground, and all books and documents destroyed.

When thirty-six incendiary fires were raging simultaneously, and when the King's Bench and Fleet prisons had shared the fate of Newgate, the troops and militia, who were employed with vigour only at the eleventh hour, began to get the upper hand of the rioters, and then only by dint of firing volleys into the mass. Gradually through the next two [168]days some semblance of order was restored, and by the third morning the riots were at an end. The official return handed in to the Secretary of State showed that 210 people had been killed by the troops and 248 wounded, several of whom subsequently died; but the bill was not complete: the public hangman claimed 21 more victims, and a much larger number were transported for life. The Lord Mayor of London was tried for his faulty arrangements and for his alleged supineness, but was let off with a fine of a thousand pounds. Lord George Gordon's insanity saved him from the consequences of his misdeeds.

These fatal riots should have taught the lesson that soldiers are ill-suited to the task of putting down civil tumult, and that their use entails an unnecessary amount of bloodshed, especially when their action is so long delayed that an increased severity becomes necessary. Unfortunately the lesson, if learnt, was not taken to heart: at any rate no adequate remedy was proposed at the time. On one point only was any light immediately thrown. Hitherto some doubt had existed as to the legality of employing the military to put down riots, but on this occasion the King sought the advice of the Attorney-General,[154] who gave it as his opinion, that, as soldiers were also citizens, they could constitutionally be used to prevent felony, even without the Riot Act being read. It was well that this point was cleared up, because circumstances will occasionally arise when troops must be sent for as a last [169]resource; but it is remarkable that, after the failure of the soldier to keep the peace had just been demonstrated in so signal a manner, no one should have supplied the obvious rider, and suggested the substitution of a more satisfactory agent. Half a century slipped by before the necessary change began in England; but on the principle of applying the remedy to any limb except the diseased one, Dublin was quickly provided with what London lacked, and in 1786 was passed the "Dublin Police[155] Act,"[156] under which three Commissioners were appointed, and given the command of a paid and well-organised constabulary. In the course of the following year the whole of Ireland came under the protection of the new guardians of the peace, who, developing as time went on, eventually reached that state of efficiency that is now invariably associated with the name of the Royal Irish Constabulary.

The magistrates of the period set the worst possible example to their subordinate officers, and there were but few of them who did not deserve the name of "Trading Justices," that was so commonly applied. Those who did not actually accept bribes were usually ready to make a little extra money by the improper and wholesale bailing, not only of offenders who ought to have been kept in confinement, but of innocent persons also, who ought to have been immediately and unconditionally set at liberty. The system was to issue warrants against [170]helpless people for imaginary crimes, and then to let them out on bail, the magistrate netting the sum of two shillings and fourpence every time he repeated the trick. James Townsend, a Bow Street runner, who gave evidence on this subject before a parliamentary commission in 1816, explained how lucrative this practice used to be, "and taking up a hundred girls, that would make at two shillings and fourpence, £11, 13s. 4d. They sent none to gaol, for the bailing them was so much better."

There is much to be said for the plan of employing country gentlemen to administer justice, without stipend, in the neighbourhood of their own estates; but in London, where all the criminal talent of the three kingdoms was collected, and where the duties of magistrates became both difficult and onerous in consequence, only inferior men could be induced to undertake the office, and then only for the sake of the patronage they could control, and for the perquisites they were able to pick up. They were distinguished neither for social position, nor for legal knowledge, and readily succumbed to every temptation that offered. As long as the magistracy was corrupt, Acts of Parliament were powerless to purify the police: the duty of the Government was plain if not easy; the Commission of the Peace for Middlesex had to be immediately purged of the Trading Justices, and a scheme had to be introduced under which capable and upright men would be secured to take their place: the hands of the new magistrates, when appointed, had to be strengthened and sufficiently enlarged to enable them to grapple with the [171]problem of keeping order in London, a city which besides being the most populous in Europe, had the reputation of being the most difficult to manage, its inhabitants quickly resenting any action of the executive that threatened to interfere, in the smallest particular, with their liberties or their customs. At the same time it was necessary to devise a check upon the magistrates, powerful enough to prevent a recurrence of the old abuses.

The Middlesex Justices Bill, which was laid before the House of Commons in March 1792, was an attempt to satisfy the above-mentioned conditions, and was framed on the model of the stipendiary establishment already existing at Bow Street, where satisfactory results had been obtained. It was proposed to create five new police offices (shortly afterwards increased to seven), and to appoint three Justices to each, at a remuneration of £300 a year apiece. This salary was only to be paid on the explicit understanding that they were neither directly nor indirectly to apply to their own benefit any of the fees received by them, from whatever source arising, all such fees to be devoted in future to reducing the expenses of the office. The courts were to be open daily for the transaction of business, one magistrate always to be in attendance, empowered to dispose summarily of the cases brought before him without the assistance of a jury. Provision was also made for the appointment of six constables to each office, at a wage not exceeding twelve shillings a week, invested with authority to apprehend any person suspected of malpractices who [172]was unable to give a satisfactory account of himself. Finally, the constables were to be under the control of the magistrates, and the magistrates were to be answerable to the Secretary of State, in whom was to be vested the power of dismissal, as well as that of appointment.

When introduced, the Bill was severely criticised, Fox and Sheridan, who were two of its strongest opponents, both declaring that the principle of a magistrate punishing without the intervention of a jury was barbarous and unconstitutional, and that the proposal to set up constables with increased powers was an unwarrantable attempt to oppress the poor, already ground down under the heels of the rich. It was advanced that the influence exerted by the Ministry of the day over the magistracy was already excessive, and that the real object of the bill was to still further increase this influence, by adding the power of conferring salaries to that of making appointments.

The framers of the Bill, whilst denying the truth of these statements, and confident of the ultimate triumph of the principles they advocated, were willing that the measure should at first become law for a limited period only, and were content that Parliament should have the opportunity of amending, or even annulling its provisions, if on trial they should prove unsatisfactory.

The Middlesex Justices Act first came into operation, therefore, as an experiment. The seven public offices were established in different parts of the Metropolis at convenient distances from each [173]other, the twenty-one Justices were appointed, and the forty-two constables were sworn in, an insignificant force indeed with which to contend against the whole criminal array of London, but of great historical interest as a development of the Bow Street system, the two together forming the first regularly organized and paid force ever established in England. The acknowledgement of the desirability of employing stipendiary magistrates in crowded centres was no less important, and gradually led up to the system that is found so valuable to-day, not only at the metropolitan police courts, but also in those great towns where the principle has, in recent years, been adopted.

The reform of the magistracy that was taken in hand in 1792 was not so thorough as it might have been, and the opportunity that then offered of removing once and for all every unworthy taint from the administration of justice in the metropolis was only partly taken advantage of.

The Middlesex Justices Bill was conceived in too parsimonious a spirit, and the right sort of men did not come forward to fill the important posts of police justices, many of the new magistrates, in fact, being recruited from the ranks of the old discredited class, which it was one of the principal objects of the Bill to displace. Neither the justices nor the constables received a salary large enough to make them independent of improper sources of income, the latter being openly permitted to engage in various lucrative transactions that had nothing to do with their office. It is said that constables attached to [174]the public offices would not infrequently fill the role of counsel for the prisoner, as well as holding a brief for the prosecution.

The small force called into being by the Act of 1792, and which, including the Bow Street officers, amounted to about fifty men, was designed only against individual criminals; the idea of preventing or repressing riots by means of a civil police force was hardly considered to fall within the range of practical politics. At the moment when the success of the revolutionary leaders had achieved the overthrow of the French Monarchy, and had culminated in the execution of Louis the Sixteenth, established authority all the world over was in danger of subversion. The violent utterances of certain Radical Societies shewed that there were many in England who violently sympathised with the Revolution, and the riots that took place in many of our towns proved that the excesses which had turned the streets of Paris into shambles, were finding an echo amongst the discontented and disorderly on this side of the Channel.

Considering the urgency of the matter, the attitude assumed by the Government then in office seems altogether incomprehensible. The political horizon was assuredly dark enough to warn the most heedless; and the signal manner in which the military had failed to keep order during the Gordon Riots conclusively demonstrated how unreliable was that arm for the purposes of peace maintenance. Yet the only steps taken by the responsible authorities were to embody the Militia, and to pass an [175]ill-considered measure called "The Alien Act,"[157] which required that all foreigners resident in England (unless duly naturalized), should provide themselves with passports, or forthwith leave the country.

That we survived the crisis without having to face a similar conflagration was hardly due to the foresight of our rulers, who, though well aware that our preventive appliances were rusty and out-of-date, neglected to replace them by others, or even to modernize them.

[176]

CHAPTER IX
PAROCHIAL POLICE OF THE EIGHTEENTH CENTURY

Before proceeding to a narration of the successive steps that culminated in the radical reorganization authorized in 1829, it is necessary to describe the nature and extent of the various police establishments as they existed at the close of the eighteenth century.

Exclusive of Special Constables, who, though legally available, were but rarely if ever employed, there were, at this time, five distinct classes of Peace Officers:

(i.) Parochial Constables, elected annually in Parish or Township and serving gratuitously.

(ii.) Their Substitutes or Deputies serving for a wage voluntarily paid by the Principals.

(iii.) Salaried Bow Street Officers, and Patrols expressly charged with the suppression of highwaymen and footpads.

(iv.) Stipendiary Police Constables attached to the Public Offices established under "The Middlesex Justices Act."

(v.) Stipendiary Water-Police attached to the Thames Office, as established by Act of Parliament in 1798.

[177]

It will be noticed that of these five classes, numbers i. and ii. were common to the whole of England, whilst numbers iii. iv. and v. were peculiar to London and its immediate neighbourhood, but, for our present purpose, it will be more convenient to consider the provincial constabulary as altogether distinct from the various Metropolitan Police bodies. Theoretically and constitutionally, there should have been little or no difference between the policing of London and that of any rural district, but the stage of development reached in the Metropolis already foreshadowed the impending changes, whilst in the country the standard of police had as yet deviated hardly at all from the mediæval pattern.

Leaving the London police establishments, therefore, for future consideration, we find that in rural districts, and in provincial towns, High Constables and Parish Constables, acting under the direction of the Justices of the Peace, continued to exercise the time-honoured powers which had been handed down to them from forgotten generations. To get a clear idea of how the old-time system adapted itself, more or less, to the changed conditions that prevailed in the nineteenth century, the best way is to turn to what we may call the police text-books of the period such as the "Treatise on the Functions and Duties of the Constable," by Colquhoun (1803), or "The Churchwardens' and Overseers' Guide," by Ashdowne, published at about the same time. "The High Constable," says Colquhoun, "has the superintendence and direction of the petty constables, head[178]boroughs, and other peace officers in his hundred or division. It is his duty to take cognisance of, and to present, all offences within his hundred or division which lead to the corruption of morals, breaches of the Lord's Day, Drunkenness, Cursing and Swearing. To bring forward sufficient number of constables to maintain decency and good order during the execution of malefactors or the punishment of offenders, and to attend in person to see that the peace officers do their duty. To summon petty constables to keep order in the Courts of Justice &c...." With regard to tumults and riots, "to do all in his power to arrest offenders, and so to dispose of his constables as to suppress the disorders in question, also to give assistance to neighbouring divisions ... to present all persons exposing for sale unwholesome meat ... and to take cognisance of false or deficient weights and measures." In another place he declares that petty constables should regularly perambulate their districts once at least in every twenty-four hours, and visit all alehouses once a week "to see that no unlawful games are permitted, and that labouring people are not suffered to lounge and tipple until they are intoxicated." The duty of petty constables when riots are threatened is thus described. "The instant a constable hears of any unlawful assembly, mob, or concourse of people likely to produce danger or mischief within or near his constablewick or district (he must) give notice to the nearest Justice, and repair instantly to the spot with his long or short stave, and there put himself under the [179]direction of such magistrate or magistrates as may be in attendance."

"The Churchwardens' and Overseers' Guide and Director" is arranged in the form of a vocabulary, and in alphabetical order gives explanations of the principal matters with which Parish Officers are chiefly concerned. "Constables," we learn, "are to make a Hue and Cry after the offenders where a robbery or felony is committed, to call upon the parishioners to assist in the pursuit: and if the criminal be not found in the liberty of the first constable, he is to give notice to the next, and thus continue the pursuit from town to town, and from county to county; and where offenders are not taken, constables are to levy the Tax to satisfy an execution on recovery against a Hundred, and pay the same to the Sheriff &c...."

"Hundreds or Wapentakes," according to Ashdowne, "are generally governed by a High Constable, under whom a Tythingman or Borsholder is generally appointed for each Borough or District within the Hundred. Hundreds are liable to penalties on exportation of wool, liable also for damages sustained by violently pulling down buildings; by killing cattle; cutting down trees, ... by destroying turnpikes, or works on navigable rivers; by cutting hopbines; by destroying corn to prevent exportation; by wounding officers of the Customs; by destroying woods &c.... Hundreds are also bound to raise Hue and Cry when any robbery is committed within the Hundred; and if the offender is not taken, an action may be maintained against [180]the Hundred to recover damages."[158] Under the heading of "Swearing" is arranged the following information:—"Persons guilty of profane swearing, and convicted thereof, to forfeit to the Poor of the Parish. Day-Labourers, common soldiers, or common seamen, 1/-. Persons under the degree of gentlemen, 2/-. Gentlemen or persons above the degree of gentlemen, 5/-. The above penalties to be doubled for a second offence, and trebled after a second conviction."

Of Tythingmen the same author writes:—"There is frequently a Tythingman in the same town with a constable, who is, as it were, a deputy to exercise the office in the constable's absence; but there are some things which the constable has power to do that tythingmen cannot intermeddle with. When there happens to be no constable of a parish, the office and authority of a Tythingman seems to be the same under another name."

[181]

If anyone should be inclined to doubt the remarkable stability of the Constable's office, and all that pertains to it, he may find it instructive to look back a few hundred years, and refer to what Lambard and others have to say about Tythingmen and Constables, part of which is quoted in the third chapter of this book.

To the scope and intention of the functions exercised by parish officers as stated by Colquhoun and Ashdowne, if somewhat old-fashioned, no exception need be taken. The trouble was, however, that the office-holders did not live up to the standard inculcated by their teachers. The commonsense and reasonableness of the whole system fell to the ground whenever ignorant and unworthy agents were entrusted with its administration, and such, unfortunately, was the character of the large majority of the police personnel. The parish constable was incompetent, and the duties imposed on him were either evaded, or performed in a purely perfunctory manner. Under the circumstances such a tendency was perhaps inevitable, for it is not to be expected that unpaid services will be well performed by the poorer classes without constant supervision. Struggling men, who have to work hard to provide for themselves, and for their families, are not likely to overtax their energies in the service of the State without reward, and those substitutes who received a few shillings a year from their principals were only careful not to exceed the minimum amount of labour which could be exacted from them compulsorily.

[182]

Further consideration of the Rural Constabulary must be postponed until we come to deal with the reorganization which was set on foot in 1839. For the present we must return to the Metropolis, where the doomed parochial system was now tottering to its fall, and where the need for reform was more pressing than elsewhere. At the time we are considering, London boasted a variety of police establishments, all more or less disconnected. The City had one organization, Westminster another, the public offices distributed justice after a fashion in their respective districts, and Bow Street prided itself upon holding a position of complete isolation and independence. Nor was this all—the whole of the metropolis was split up into parishes, and each parish made its own arrangements for keeping the peace, or dispensed with police altogether, as it saw fit. Twelve London parishes were thus entirely unprotected: St James' and Marylebone employed Chelsea pensioners, the City supported 765 watchmen, Edgeware had no policeman and no patrol, Camberwell armed its night watchmen with blunderbusses, whilst St Pancras had no less than eighteen distinct Watch Trusts, a source of weakness rather than of strength, because they never co-operated with each other. In Kensington the police force consisted only of three headboroughs, excellent men perhaps; but as Peel remarked, "if they had been angels, it would have been utterly impossible for them to fulfil the duties required from their situation." Deptford, being without a single professional watchman, was at one time patrolled by the inhabi[183]tants, who enrolled themselves into companies twenty strong for that purpose, quickly disbanding, however, as soon as the robbers moved into another district. In some parishes, again, there were patrols and no beats, and in others there were beats and stands but no patrols, despite the recommendations of Special Commissions and the provisions of Acts of Parliament.

The degree of security extended to the ratepayers by the local authorities was thus a very variable quantity; but it is not too much to say that without exception the constitution of all the parochial police bodies was antiquated and radically unsound, and that Watch and Ward was at this time more indifferently kept than had previously been the case throughout the whole history of the Metropolis.

In the year 1800 Parish Constables were generally permanent deputies and of inferior origin; nor was any trouble taken to secure officers of the right stamp. The wages paid to Parish Watchmen were miserable, and the men usually engaged were those whose antecedents and qualifications precluded them from obtaining more lucrative or reputable employment. These "Charlies" (as they were popularly called, after their predecessors the Bell-men, instituted in the reign of Charles the Second) were for the most part infirm from age and starvation, drunken, the creatures of street-walkers and publicans rather than servants of the public, and altogether contemptible. Dressed in heavy capes, muffled up to the ears, provided with long staves and dim lanterns, they issued from their watchboxes twice an hour for a minute or two to [184]call the time and the state of the weather. As clocks and barometers they may have been of some service; or, as somebody once put it, to wake a man up after his house has been robbed to tell him the bad news; but for the prevention of crime, they were worse than useless. Striking their staves on the pavement, and shewing their lanterns, they gave timely warning of their approach; and if the thieves thought it worth while to take any notice at all of such a trivial interruption, they had only to remove themselves temporarily into the next parish to be secure from pursuit.

As an object for practical joking, and as a theme for ridicule, the Charlies provided some amusement to the Jerry Hawthorns and Corinthian Toms of the period, but this was the extent of their usefulness. Quite a considerable literature hinged on their grotesque incompetency, but in their praise not a syllable was uttered; everyone made fun of them. They were humorously described as "persons hired by the parish to sleep in the open air," and another topical saying was to the effect that "Shiver and Shake" ought to be substituted for "Watch and Ward," because they spent half the night shivering with cold and the other half shaking with fright. It was a popular amusement amongst young men of the town to imprison watchmen by upsetting their watchboxes on top of them as they dozed within; and the young blood who could exhibit to his friends a collection of trophies such as lanterns, staves, and rattles, was much accounted of in smart society. The newspapers were never tired of skits [185]at the expense of the parochial watch: the following extract from *The Morning Herald* of October 30th, 1802, will serve as an example:—

"It is said that a man who presented himself for the office of watchman to a parish at the West End of the Town very much infected by depredators, was lately turned away from the Vestry with this reprimand—I am astonished at the impudence of such a great sturdy strong fellow as you are, being so idle as to apply for a watchman's situation, when you are capable of labour." Another publication calling itself "The Microcosm of London" gives its readers a satirical account of the nightly watch in these words. "The Watch is a Parochial establishment supported by the Parochial rate, and subject to the jurisdiction of the magistrates: it is necessary to the peace and security of the metropolis, and is of considerable utility: but that it might be rendered much more useful cannot be denied. That the Watch should consist of able-bodied men, is, we presume, essential to the complete design of its institution, as it forms a part of its legal description: but that the watchmen are persons of this character, experience will not vouch: and why they are chosen from among the aged and incapable must be answered by those who make the choice. In the early part of the last century, an halbert was their weapon: it was then changed to a long staff: but the great coat and lantern are now accompanied with more advantageous implements of duty—a bludgeon and a rattle. It is almost superfluous to add, that the watchhouse is a place where the appointed watch[186]men assemble to be accoutred for their nocturnal rounds, under the direction of a constable, whose duty being taken by rotation, enjoys the title of Constable of the Night. It is also the receptacle for such unfortunate persons as are apprehended by the watch, and where they remain in custody till they can be conducted to the tribunal of the police office, for the examination of a magistrate."

The watchhouses here referred to were dirty and insecure hovels, with an underground cellar secured by a grating, behind which prisoners were confined, sometimes for forty-eight hours, but in the case of minor offences a tip of half-a-crown to the constable was generally sufficient to secure release.

In 1804 there were 2044 parochial constables and watchmen in the Metropolis, including the 765 employed by the City, that is to say, about one watchman to every seventy or eighty houses.

The City of London was much better policed than the rest of the Metropolis. It was said that so superior were the arrangements eastward of Temple Bar to those of the more westerly districts, that a pickpocket was easily recognised when he came to the City boundary, because he always walked so fast, and so often looked over his shoulder, as if he suspected that someone was after him. The watchmen appointed by the Lord Mayor and Aldermen were selected from a better class of men than were those who held office in Westminster and other parishes; they were also better paid and more carefully superintended. In 1815 the Lord Mayor himself, on more than one occasion, visited the [187]watch by night and had the men mustered, discharging on the spot those whom he considered unfit. Briefly the organisation was as follows—the City was divided into four divisions with three day patrols to each division, in all twelve patrolmen at one and a half guineas a week each. By night, whilst the constables and watchmen were on duty, the patrols were reduced to eight, two to a division; their duties were, to visit the watchhouses at least twice a night, to see that the constable of the night was not absent from his post, signing their names at every visit in a book kept for the purpose at the several watchhouses. The Constables of the Night were paid no salary, but were generally in receipt of fees from the elected householders whose deputies they were. They were bound to be present with the watch all night long, and were held responsible that the watchmen did their duty. In time of riot, or when disturbances were apprehended, the Lord Mayor had power to summon them, together with the watch, at any hour—by day as well as by night, for the maintenance of the peace. The task of supervising the City police was entrusted, not to a High Constable, but to the two City Marshals, whose duty it was to pay surprise visits to the watchhouses at uncertain hours, to certify that the patrolmen's books were duly signed up, and to report every morning to the Lord Mayor concerning the "internal quiet of the City of London." They also bound themselves on oath to proceed against no man through malice, and to screen no man through favour or affection.

Both in the city and in other parts of London, [188]the management of the traffic was in the hands of special officials called Street-keepers; but beyond the regulation of vehicular traffic within the limits of the parishes where they were employed, they had no general police duties to perform, and were not under the control of the magistrates, nor subject to the police authorities.

The Burgesses of Westminster still suffered their police administration to be bound by the ecclesiastical traditions of bygone centuries; and if we make an exception in favour of the "Jury of Annoyances," established in 1755, we may say that little evidence of progress was discoverable within the Liberties of the Western City. The Act creating the Annoyance Jury was passed in the twenty-ninth year of George II., and two years later was amended and enlarged. The Court of Burgesses was now empowered to maintain forty-eight inhabitants of Westminster for the suppression of public nuisances: members of this jury had authority to enter any shop or house, and if they found any unlawful or defective weight or measure therein, to destroy the same, and to amerce the offender a sum not exceeding forty shillings for each offence. In 1764 the Jury was divided into three divisions, called St Margaret's Division, the St James' Division, and the St Martin's Division, each containing sixteen members; at the same time it was ordained, that all presentments had to be in writing under the hands and seals of at least twelve jurymen. In 1800 the Annoyance Jury was still nominally responsible for the cleanliness, sightliness, and sanitary condition of [189]Westminster, but, as a matter of experience, the removal and prevention of nuisances was left almost entirely to the discretion and taste of the more fastidious householders.

As has already been said, the Middlesex Justices Act was at first an experimental measure; in 1801 it was repealed, but most of its provisions were at once re-enacted by a statute[159] which placed the public offices on a more permanent basis, and raised the salary of the magistrates and the wages of the police officers. There were now ten of these offices, viz., Mansion House, Guildhall, Hatton Garden, Worship Street, Whitechapel, Shadwell, Southwark, Queen Street Westminster; Great Marlborough Street, and Wapping. Mansion House and Guildhall belonged to the City proper, and Wapping was the headquarters of the River Police. To each office were apportioned three magistrates, eight constables, and a clerk or two. The magistrates sat in rotation, and, within the limited areas of their respective jurisdictions, acted independently of their colleagues. There was little uniformity or co-operation. Each office had a general duty of apprehending and punishing any criminals found within its boundaries, but had no connection with the Nightly Watch. The different parishes concerned had transferred to the public offices the duties connected with Hue and Cry, whilst retaining in their own hands the responsibilities of Watch and Ward. The relations existing between the parochial and stipendiary authorities were not cordial, in fact there was frequently a pro[190]nounced enmity between the parish constable and the police constable, whilst the amateur peace officer not infrequently set at defiance the professional magistrate. The impossibility of controlling the local watchmen conduced to a very unsatisfactory state of affairs, as is seen by the following evidence given before the 1816 Committee by Mr Robert Raynsford, the magistrate of Hatton Garden. "At present, as the law now stands," he said, "we have no power at all over the parish watchmen: but when this question was agitated on a former occasion, the parishes had so rooted an aversion to the interference of the magistracy, that I believe there were petitions from most of the parishes: at the same time there are offences committed in the streets, close by a watch-box, and we are told that the watchman was fast asleep, or would give no assistance: we have no power of sending for the watchman, or if we did, we have no power of punishing him. I think it would be an improvement if they were put under the direction of the Police."

It will be remembered that the Middlesex Justices Act had placed the police offices under the control of the Home Office, which had the power of appointing and dismissing the magistrates: this was right and proper, but it would have been far better if any further supervision exercised by the Secretary of State had been confined to the larger and more general issues connected with the police establishments, and had stopped short of the injudicious meddling that went on. The magistrates might surely have been trusted with the selection of their [191]own constables, but, for some occult reason, successive ministers seem to have thought it their duty to diminish the authority of the magistrates by actively interfering with the nomination and election of the rank and file. Under these circumstances it is strange that the magistrates were as well served by their subordinate officers as they seem to have been, yet, everything considered, the stipendiary policeman proved so superior to the amateur constable that Maurice Swabey, the magistrate at Union Street, declared, that he would rather have six additional officers than fifty parish constables.

From the list of the Public Offices above enumerated, the most interesting has intentionally been omitted, because its unique position calls for separate and more detailed notice. Besides being of earlier date than the other offices, Bow Street exceeded them also in importance, and was distinguished as the centre of the police activities of the time. From Henry Fielding, who presided in 1753, to Sir Franklin Lushington, who recently succeeded Sir John Bridge, the Chief Magistrate at Bow Street has nearly always been a man of mark amongst his brother stipendiaries, and in their day the Bow Street Runners (as the officers attached to this Court used to be called) were of quite a different type from their comrades employed in the junior offices.

Though only eight in number (afterwards increased to twelve) these runners exerted a preponderating influence, which largely altered the aspect of the contest between the professional thieves and the helpless public on whom they preyed. The Bow [192]Street policemen were the first peace officers to make a serious study of the art of detecting and running down criminals: they were experts whereas all their predecessors had been amateurs; no longer dull officials performing routine duties in perfunctory fashion when "not otherwise engaged"; but keen hunters with all their faculties stimulated by the prospect of the blood money and other rewards they hoped to earn. When they appeared on the scene the professional depredator no longer had things all his own way; instead of the parish constable who could be outwitted and bamboozled at every turn, the cracksman or forger found himself confronted by a wary adversary, well armed, and up to every move on the board. That the Bow Street Runners achieved much good in breaking up predatory gangs, and in bringing notorious offenders to trial, is not to be denied, but it is no less certain that they were the source of much evil. Actuated by the hope of gain rather than by any sense of duty, their motives were as ignoble as their methods were shady. They played only for their own hand, and all their best endeavours were bent towards the arrest of the particular criminal whose conviction would bring the greatest profit to themselves, and not to the pursuit of the fugitive from justice whose capture was chiefly desirable on public grounds. Prevention did not enter at all into their conception of police duty, and their services were of course only at the disposal of those who were rich enough to pay handsomely for the privilege. The extent to which this system of feeing was carried may be guessed [193]from the fact that Townsend left £20,000 behind him, and that Sayer's heirs divided no less than £30,000 at the death of their benefactor.

In order to obtain information, the runners made it a rule to frequent low "flash-houses," as the resorts of thieves were called, and to associate with the vicious and desperate characters to be found there. When examined before a Parliamentary Commission, several of these officers freely admitted that it was by the employment of such tactics that they expected to obtain the most valuable information, and gave it as their opinion that flash-houses ought to be encouraged rather than suppressed, on account of the facilities they afforded the runner in his search for a man who was "wanted."

There were, no doubt, many honest men amongst the Bow Street Officers doing their duty to the best of their ability after their lights, and although their methods would not be tolerated for a moment at the present day, they were much in advance of their predecessors. Certain of them attained a wide celebrity. Such men as Lavender, Nelson and others—unique characters in their way—made it their business to go everywhere and know everybody: they carried a small baton surmounted by a gilt crown, and this badge of office admitted them not only to such unsavoury dens as "The Dog and Duck" and "The Temple of Flora," but even into the Royal Palaces, where two officers, we learn, were constantly stationed "on account of the King being frequently teased of lunatics." Runners were often specialists, occupying themselves in one line of business to the neglect of [194]others: thus, whilst that well-known gossip Townsend chiefly confined himself to safeguarding the property of his wealthy clients, and to capturing noble duellists, Keys devoted himself to circumventing coiners and forgers of bank notes, and a third was principally engaged in the detection and apprehension of "Resurrectionists."

There is no doubt that more than one of the Bow Street policemen were actually in league with the depredators they were paid to catch, though they were generally too alert to be found out; but the confidence of the public in their thief-takers received a rude shock when Vaughan, of the Horse Patrol, was proved to have arranged a burglary for the sake of the reward that would have come to him on the conviction of the felons. "Set a thief to catch a thief" may sometimes be good policy, but it is nearly always bad police.

The Patrols, Horse and Foot, which were attached to the Bow Street Office, had been in existence some fifty years or so, but had only consisted of a handful of men quite insufficient for the amount of work that was expected of them. In 1805 Sir Richard Ford, the Chief Magistrate, obtained permission to extend the system of mounted police so as to provide patrols for all the main roads to a distance of about twenty miles from Bow Street. The strength of this new force was fifty-two patrols, two inspectors, and a clerk: they were recruited almost exclusively from retired cavalrymen, and were familiarly known as Robin Redbreasts on account of the red waistcoat that was a conspicuous part of their uniform. They [195]were better paid than their predecessors, the wages of a "patrol" being twenty-eight shillings a week, with allowance for horse keep, and the salary of a "conductor" standing at £100 a-year and a guinea a-week for forage and shoeing. Their energies were principally directed against highwaymen, and they quickly cleared Hounslow Heath and other infested localities from this class of plunderer. The Horse Patrol cost the Government £8000 a year, not a high price to pay for the suppression of those impudent robbers "the gentlemen of the road." The foot patrol policed the inner circle within a radius of about four miles.

The legal powers of Bow Street were never very strictly defined, but it was generally understood that the jurisdiction of the Office was confined to the County of Middlesex (the City of London excepted), and to the main roads in the neighbourhood of the metropolis which were patrolled by Bow Street Officers. Under the direction of the Home Secretary, the Chief Magistrate had, in fact, the control of a small and independent force applicable to the general police requirements of the capital and its environment.

CHAPTER X
POLICE AT THE DAWN OF THE NINETEENTH CENTURY

In the year 1801, the population of London and Middlesex hardly exceeded a million, but how many of the individual units that went to make up this total were engaged in criminal pursuits, it is of course impossible to estimate with any degree of accuracy, because the bulk of the crime was undetected and consequently unrecorded. From such data as we possess, however, it is certain that the proportion of thieves and other delinquents to honest men must have been alarmingly high. Between 1801 and 1811 the population increased some sixteen per cent., and during the same period the number of commitments rose nearly fifty per cent.[160] This increase in the number of rogues whose careers were cut short by capture, speaks well for the Bow Street Runners from one point of view; but it also indicates no less surely that these officers were making no progress at all in the art of preventing crime, which instead of diminishing as time went on, continued to grow in volume year by year. Indeed the state of the metropolis was such, that social reformers might well have despaired of ever seeing an improvement; [197]every corrupting influence, and every criminal tendency seemed to flourish unchecked and unrebuked in the congenial atmosphere of the London slums: children, neglected by their parents and uncared for by the State, got their only schooling in the gutter, where they educated themselves, and each other, in all the tricks of vice and dishonesty. Night after night, undisturbed by watchmen or other peace-officers, hundreds of urchins of both sexes huddled together for shelter and company under the fruit-stalls and barrows of Covent Garden Market. Day after day, these homeless and unhealthy vagabonds quartered the town, street by street, and alley by alley, in search of any prey that they might be able to lay their hands on. Their pickings and stealings were turned into money with fatal ease at the shop of any one of the eight thousand receivers of stolen property, who were supposed to ply their trade in London; and however meagre might be the income realised by the juvenile criminal, drink in plenty, with gin at tenpence a pint, was within the reach of all. Such licensing laws as existed, were seldom enforced, and even after the scandalous public lotteries had been suppressed, public-houses continued to hold minor lotteries, called "little-goes," for all comers, men, women and children.

Mondays and Fridays were the great days for bullock-hunting, an inhuman and brutal sport that throve in the neighbourhoods of Hackney and Bethnal Green, with the sanction, if not with the connivance, of the peace officers of those parishes. The procedure of the bullock-hunters was as follows. [198]A fee having been paid to a cattle drover, an animal was selected from his herd, peas were put into its ears, sticks pointed with iron were driven into its body, and the poor beast, when mad with rage and pain, was hunted through the streets with a yelling mob of men, women, and dogs behind it; the weavers left their looms to join in the pursuit, and passers-by continually augmented the crowd, until the exhausted victim could no longer be goaded into any shew of resistance or movement, when it was left to die where it fell, or when sufficiently recovered, to be removed to some butcher's slaughter-house.

On Sundays the favourite resort was a field adjoining Bethnal Green Church, and here some hundreds of men and boys assembled during the hours of divine service, to indulge in less exciting games, such as dog-fighting and duck-hunting. On holidays and fair-days these

Saturnalian proceedings grew more outrageous than ever. In a letter descriptive of the occurrences that used to take place at an annual fair held in the West-end of London, which the Receiver of the Metropolitan Police wrote to Lord Rosslyn in 1831, occurs the following passage: "It will hardly be credited that within five or seven years ... people were robbed in open day ... and women, stripped of their clothes, were tied to gates by the roadside; the existing police being set at defiance."

John Sayer, the Bow Street officer, stated before a Parliamentary Committee, that there were streets in Westminster, especially Duck Lane, Gravel Lane, and Cock Lane, infested by a gang of desperate [199]men, and so dangerous that no policeman dared venture there, unless accompanied by five or six of his comrades, for fear of being cut to pieces. These are not highly coloured fairy-tales, but actual facts as recounted in the Blue-books of the period, recounted moreover without exciting any particular notice at the time. In 1812, the crime of murder was so common, and so much on the increase, that a Parliamentary Committee was appointed to hold an inquiry as to the best means of combating the savage tendencies of the people. Offences against property were even more prevalent than crimes of violence. Spurious coin and counterfeit banknotes deluged the country.[161] In the parish of Kensington alone there were sixteen successful, and three unsuccessful, attempts at burglary in six weeks, and John Vickery, an experienced Bow Street officer, calculated that in one month property to the value of £15,000 was stolen in the City of London, without one of the guilty parties being either known or apprehended.

Thieves and receivers, drivers of hackney coaches, and sometimes toll-gate keepers, conspired together to rob the travelling public. Their favourite *modus operandi* was as follows—the thief climbed on the back of the conveyance, unfastened the ropes that secured the luggage, and with the assistance of an accomplice, removed the trunk or other booty when close to the house of the confederate receiver. As soon as the loss was discovered, the coachman repudiated all knowledge of the affair, and having at [200]the first opportunity put away the false and resumed his registered number, became to all appearance an honest cabman, against whom the police could prove nothing. The transformation was not difficult, because numbers were not then painted on the coach as on hackney carriages they now have to be, but were displayed on a removable iron label.

Still more serious were the conspiracies in which solicitors and police officers were concerned, which had for their object the levying of blackmail from bankers and others. In this organized system of fraud the following method was usually adopted—a man of education, with money behind him, would plan a bank robbery, purchase the necessary information, and hire expert thieves to do the actual work. The robbery having been duly effected, some time would be allowed to elapse, and then the prime mover in the affair, through his agent the police officer, would notify to the manager of the bank that the stolen notes or securities had been traced, and might be recovered, if a large enough reward was forthcoming. This offer was invariably coupled with the *proviso* that, in the event of the proposed restitution being carried out, no further questions should be asked, nor further proceedings taken.

The trick seldom failed, because the parties who had been robbed knew, that in the absence of any detective police agency worthy of the name, acceptance of the terms offered them was the only chance they had of recovering their property. Under the circumstances, they could hardly be expected to be [201]public-spirited enough to incur the heavier loss, and at the same time, through advertising the affair, suffer some diminution of credit, for the sake of the principles involved.

The Committee which sat in 1828, and which investigated the whole question, considered it advisable not to publish the evidence brought before them, but stated that they had abundant proof that frauds of this description had for years been carried through with almost uniform success, and to an extent altogether unsuspected by the public. They were satisfied "that more than sixteen banks had been forced to pay blackmail, and that more than £200,000 worth of property had, in a short space of time, been the subject of negotiation or compromise," and stated that about £1200 had been paid to blackmailers by bankers alone, "accompanied by a clearance from every risk, and perfect impunity for their crimes."

Between 1805 and 1818 there were more than two hundred executions for forgery alone, that is to say at the rate of one execution in every three weeks. When one considers that only a few of the forgers were caught, that of these not all were convicted, and that of the convicted but a moderate percentage were hanged, we get some idea of the prevalence of this particular offence. The alarming frequency with which mobs began to appeal to violence to compel attention to their grievances, real or supposed, by force of arms, was one of the most dangerous symptoms of the age. The Food Riots of 1800, the Luddite disturbances of 1811-1816, [202]Spafield (1816), Manchester (1817), Peterloo (1819),[162] and the riots throughout the manufacturing districts in 1828-9, were all cases in point which convinced the thoughtful that, unless something better than the shoddy defence, which was all that the civil power could then muster, was quickly forthcoming, the mob would soon obtain a complete mastery, to the destruction of all law and order, just as had recently happened in France.

The mania for duelling, again, which was now at its height, was an indication that the prevailing spirit of lawlessness was not confined to the masses. When hereditary lawgivers, and even Cabinet ministers, could find no better way of settling their differences than by calling each other out, little wonder that the rank and file followed suit, and took the law into their own hands. It is no valid argument to say that duelling was merely a passing fashion; by the Law of England any duel is a gross breach of the peace; and that such deliberate infractions should have become fashionable only proves that the law was held in contempt, and that the police system which failed to compel people to keep the peace was totally inadequate to the requirements of the times. There was a period when the vendetta was the natural defence adopted by semi-[203]civilised communities to diminish the frequency of murder, and to protect the honour of their women: in time blood feuds gradually died out, not because any great change had overtaken human nature, but because there was no longer any need for the individual or the family to perform duties which could be executed with greater discrimination, impartiality, and thoroughness by judges and policemen. After the disappearance of the vendetta the custom of duelling remained. It was felt that personal honour was too delicate a matter to be delegated to any outsiders, and that questions in which honour was concerned must continue to be settled by the principals themselves. Eventually however, the same influences that rendered blood feuds unnecessary removed the excuse for the practice of duelling; under modern conditions, a man can usually vindicate his honour by an appeal to public opinion, or, in the last resort, by an action for slander, without having to submit his cause to the uncertain arbitrament of the rapier or the pistol.

On the whole, there is no exaggeration in saying that, at the dawn of the nineteenth century, England was passing through an epoch of criminality darker than any other in her annals; the resurrectionist atrocities of Burke and Hare, the more inhuman villanies of Williams and

Bishop the cold-blooded depravity of Vaughan and his accomplices, and the other lurid crimes which belong to this age, surpass in enormity anything before or since.

Such then was the desperate state of society at [204]the dawn of the century. What arrangements did the country make to protect itself against the consequences of this accumulation of crime? What organization was provided for the enforcement of order, and for the protection of life and property? For its first line of defence England trusted to the supposed deterrent effect of a rigorous penal code; the more humane and effectual method, prevention, being lost sight of in the mistaken belief that it was possible to extirpate crime by the severity with which it was punished, a belief that survived in face of the fact, that as punishment increased in bitterness, so did offences grow in frequency and in violence.

The penal laws were written in blood. Colquhoun estimated that there were 160 different offences which were punishable by death, without benefit of clergy: a man could be hanged for larceny from the person if the value of the article stolen was more than one shilling: Townsend stated before the parliamentary commission of 1816, that he had known as many as forty people hanged in one day: on another occasion seven persons, four men and three women, were convicted at Kingston of being concerned in robbing a pedlar, "they were all hanged in Kent Street, opposite the door." Such indiscriminate infliction of the extreme penalty of the law could serve no useful purpose,[163] on the [205]contrary it undoubtedly aggravated the very offences it was intended to check. The punishment for a trivial theft being identical with that meted out for the most heinous crime, all sense of proportion in the different degrees of moral guilt was lost. "As well be hanged for a sheep as for a lamb" represented a point of view not unnatural under the circumstances, and expressed the actual mental attitude of the average criminal.

It can easily be demonstrated that an inverse ratio exists between the efficiency of police and the severity of sentences.[164] The more difficult the commission of crime is made, the less necessity will there be for deterrent measures that savour of vindictiveness. The intimate knowledge that an effective police have of the habitual criminal class is not only a safeguard against the conviction of the innocent, but renders it possible to deal leniently with the juvenile, and with the casual, offender. Within reasonable limits, the fear of almost certain detection is a far stronger deterrent than the distant prospect of severe punishment. Sir Samuel Romilly speaking in the House of Commons in 1810 said, "if it were possible that punishment, as a consequence of guilt, could be reduced to an absolute certainty, a very slight penalty would be sufficient to prevent almost every species of crime, except those which arise from sudden gusts of ungovernable passion. If the restoration of the property stolen, and only [206]a few weeks, or even but a few days imprisonment, were the unavoidable consequence of theft, no theft would ever be committed. No man would steal what he was sure he could not keep."

Romilly made strenuous efforts to persuade the government to reduce the number of offences punishable by death, but without immediate success. Sir James Mackintosh followed in his footsteps, and in 1822 proposed to the House that measures should be adopted "for increasing the efficiency of the Criminal Law by mitigating its vigour." It is worthy of remark that, at this time, Peel opposed the principles advocated by Mackintosh and Romilly, though seven years afterwards he was the author of the Act that gave effect to a part of Romilly's ideal, "a vigilant and enlightened police, and punishments proportioned to the offender's guilt."

The savage rigour of the penal code defeated its own ends in many ways. People would not give evidence that might condemn a man to such barbarous treatment; juries would not always convict, even when the evidence was perfectly clear.

Consequently the law often became a dead letter, and the prospective criminal had many inducements to tempt him to break it; for, in the first place, he probably would never be caught; and in the second place, the chances were, that the jury would evade the responsibility of giving a verdict, that might lead to a sentence, that would be an outrage to their humanity.

With crime so increasingly prevalent, there might have been some justification for great severity of [207]punishment, if it had been found by experience that strong repressive measures had invariably been followed by a permanent reduction in the number of criminals; but this is not the lesson that history has taught. It is true that exceptional cases have arisen from time to time in which signal severity meted out to a prominent offender has proved the safest and best course. Prompt and exemplary punishment, even in excess of his deserts, inflicted on a ringleader, has often been the only way to enforce discipline or to prevent the spread of dangerous mutiny; but such cases are rare, and owe their success as deterrents to their rarity, and to the attention that they excite at the time; whereas a consistent course of excessive severity has never been a lasting success, unless combined with powerful preventive measures,[165] and then such a course is no longer necessary. Highway robbery and sheep-stealing were common when they were capital offences, now they are seldom heard of, and the thieving that invariably went on at the foot of the gallows was sufficient proof that the popular belief in the deterrent value of public executions was a popular fallacy.[166]

The futile cruelty of the frequency with which capital punishment was inflicted was equalled if [208]not exceeded by the manner in which the secondary punishments were administered. Transportation was introduced[167] in the reign of Charles II., but at first was not, strictly speaking, a legal punishment, but rather an exercise of the royal clemency towards those in "the King's Mercy"; and it may be said to have taken the place in the social scheme of the old system of outlawry which, in former times, enabled a capital felon to save his life by abjuring the realm.

Labourers were required to develop the resources of America and the West Indies, and to this end criminals under sentence of death were often pardoned on the understanding that they transported themselves to those colonies. Several convicts, however, were clever enough to secure the pardon and yet avoid fulfilment of the condition on which it was granted. By 1717 so many of these persons were at large, that arrangements were made[168] by which felons were to be kept in prison until they could be handed over to agents, who were required to give security that the undesirables in question were really deported. Fifty years later the practice of transportation was common, and had come to be esteemed as an easy and profitable means of getting rid, once [209]and for all, of offenders caught transgressing the laws made by society for its protection. Though called transportation the system really amounted to perpetual slavery; it could nominally be inflicted for fourteen years, but was almost invariably for life. The convicts were handed over to contractors at so much a head, and shipped off to America to work on the plantations: many died on the voyage, thus reducing the profits of the traffic; in fact a Bristol contractor complained that if another plague broke out on his ship he would have to give up the business. To prevent this waste, an Act was passed in 1767[169] which provided that, for the future, contractors should take the convicts immediately they were sentenced, for fear that they should deteriorate during their sojourn in prison, and consequently fetch less money.

After the American Revolution we lost this source of revenue, and penal establishments at Bermuda, Gibraltar, and in New South Wales took the place of the plantation in the social scheme. At the same time a change took place in the method of conveying convicts to their destination; they were no longer bought for the sake of the work that could be got out of them, but contractors were paid for carrying them to the penal establishments. The frightful mortality on board the ships continued, however, until the terms of the contract were altered; as soon as the practice of paying a fixed price for every man embarked was discontinued, and the payment of a larger sum for every man landed alive substituted, [210]the convicts were treated more like human beings, and the death-rate on these voyages was no longer excessive.

Transportation signally failed as a deterrent, partly because the punishment was carried out so far from home, and partly on account of the unequal manner in which the penal system was administered. In the Crown Colonies, such as Bermuda, the servitude was of the hardest description, but in Australia the custom arose of assigning convicts as servants to colonists. This gave facilities for all kinds of abuses. A glaring and often-quoted instance of the kind of thing that went on may be cited. A certain bank clerk who had robbed his employers was convicted and sentenced to be transported to Australia, but the stolen property was not recovered. The convict was duly conveyed to New South Wales; soon afterwards his wife arrived in the same colony, and having selected her husband as a servant, the two lived together in security and wealth on the proceeds of the robbery.

Deterrents must be advertised in order to be effectual; the county gaol by the roadside is an ocular reminder of the reality of punishment, but a vague knowledge that felons were serving their time in the Antipodes was a far less potent preventive: indeed transportation came to be regarded as desirable by many, who gladly submitted to expatriation for the sake of getting a fresh start in life in a new land at the public expense. Escott remarks that whilst Australia was at once a penal settlement and a thriving colony, "the strange spectacle was seen [211]of honest artisans emigrating of their own accord to spots where felons also were relegated for their offences."[170]

The second line of defence upon which the country relied for the diminution of crime was an unpaid parochial police, sometimes assisted, and sometimes thwarted, by the various stipendiary establishments already described, and this combination, as we have seen, was almost as untrustworthy as the penal system had proved itself to be.

The constables or headboroughs, and the thief-takers, or as we should now call them, detectives, were more vigorous than the watchmen, but in some respects they were also more dangerous to society; the former lived largely by blackmail and the latter on blood-money. The salary of the headborough for Shoreditch was only ninety shillings a year, the post was not one of honour, and the stipend surely too insignificant to be an attraction; yet there was no lack of applicants, who by the diligent gleaning of perquisites and by the industrious collection of blackmail, saw their way to make a good living out of the office. As much as thirty-six shillings a day could be earned by a headborough by appearing in a prosecution at the Old Baily, and bribes from those employed in the liquor traffic were a still more profitable source of income.

In 1815 alone, eighty thousand pounds was given in blood-money, an expenditure that might almost be considered as a Government subsidy for the [212]encouragement of felony. Forty pounds was the reward offered for the conviction of certain offenders, and it was obviously to the advantage of the thief-taker not to interfere with a promising young criminal until he should commit a forty pounds crime; premature detection was tantamount to killing the goose that should lay the golden egg, and the common cant phrase of the day, when referring to a juvenile offender, was, "he doesn't weigh forty pounds yet." The mischievous tendency of this system of rewards cannot be exaggerated, it vitiated the whole police constitution; nor was there any chance of recovering property until a sufficient reward was advertised to stimulate those who alone were familiar with the haunts and methods of thieves and receivers.

"Officers are dangerous creatures," said Townsend, after more than thirty years' experience as a Bow Street Runner; "they have it frequently in their power (no question about it) to turn the scale, when the beam is level, on the other side: I mean against the poor wretched man at the bar; Why? this thing called nature, says profit is in the scale: and melancholy to relate, but I cannot help being perfectly satisfied that frequently that has been the means of convicting many and many a man.... I am convinced that whenever A is giving evidence against B he should stand perfectly uninterested.... Nothing can be so dangerous as a public officer, where he is liable to be tempted."

The following is a list of the rewards, that could be earned by police and others:—

[213]

1. Highway robbery—

    From the Sheriff   £40 0 0}   £50 0 0

    From the Hundred   10 0 0}

2. Burglary—

    From the Sheriff   40 0 0}   50 0 0

    A Tyburn Ticket worth   10 0 0}

3. Housebreaking in the daytime   do.   50 0 0

4. Counterfeiting gold or silver coin   40 0 0

5. Do. copper coin   10 0 0

6. Stealing from any shop, warehouse or stable, to the value of more than five shillings   10 0 0

7. Horse stealing	20 0 0
8. Stealing cattle or sheep	10 0 0
9. Compounding a felony	40 0 0
10. Wounding and killing a Revenue Officer	50 0 0
11. Certain Offences under the Black Act	50 0 0
12. Persons returning from transportation	20 0 0
13. Embezzling the King's Stores	20 0 0
14. Apprehending deserters from the Army	1 0 0
15. Apprehending rogues and vagabonds	0 10 0
16. Apprehending idle and disorderly persons	0 5 0

A Tyburn Ticket was a certificate granted by a judge or Justice to the person who captured and prosecuted a felon to conviction; it freed the holder [214]from all liability to serve as a Constable, and exempted him also from many other Ward and Parish obligations. The Ticket was transferable, and so had a pecuniary value which varied in different parishes, generally ten pounds or more. A Tyburn Ticket had been known to fetch as much as forty pounds.

The law being powerless to prevent crime, and the police being unable to give protection, people exerted themselves to safeguard their own interests in their own way; shopkeepers combined to provide patrols to watch the fronts of their shops, householders armed themselves for the defence of their houses, whilst steel man-traps and spring-guns were set up in gardens and coverts. In consequence of the number of innocent persons maimed and killed by these not very discriminating agencies, Lord Suffield, in 1825, introduced a Bill with the object of making their use illegal, but it was not until May 1827 that an Act was passed, prohibiting the setting of spring-guns, man-traps, and other engines calculated to destroy human life, or inflict grievous bodily harm.[171]

It is not too much to say, that a survey of all the institutions of England, as they existed at the beginning of the nineteenth century, would reveal the fact, that whereas many departments of government were feeble and many corrupt, in no department were ignorance, corruption, and inefficiency so pronounced as in that of police. If, however, any should wish to find a rival institution to share this [215]unenviable position of discredit, he would not have far to look, but could discover the object of his search in the disgraceful mismanagement that pervaded every corner of our gaols, from prison-gate to condemned cell. If the criminal, whilst at large, could count on a minimum of interference with his career of depredation, he had at the same time to reckon with a maximum of ill-treatment if ever he was deprived of his liberty. It almost seemed as if the authorities, piqued at their ill-success in the departments of prevention and detection, were determined to wreak their vengeance on the unfortunate few who fell into their hands. Neglect was the keynote in every part of the penal administration, the public suffered through the neglect that failed to provide a modicum of protection, and the prisoners suffered through the neglect of the governors and warders to provide them with the necessaries and decencies of life.

A description of the extortions, inhumanities, and crimes against the most elementary laws of sanitation, that were rife in prison-houses and convict establishments, would here be out of place. A full account is to be found in the interesting volumes in the pages of which, Major Arthur Griffiths has exhaustively dealt with the subject; but to shew with what reckless disregard for consequences prisoners were treated, and how little attention was paid to the reclamation of juvenile offenders, it is sufficient to mention the fact that in Newgate, a felon, who had been sentenced to transportation, was retained in England, to act as a schoolmaster to the boy [216]prisoners. Under the unreformed prison system, gaols were little better than universities of crime, that conferred the diploma of "habitual" on the criminals who graduated there, and it was said that half the burglaries that were committed in London were planned in Newgate.

---

[217]

CHAPTER XI
PIONEER REFORMERS

Just when the immediate outlook was the most gloomy, and at an hour when the future seemed most barren of any hopeful sign, unseen and unsuspected influences were already at work; influences which were destined first to arrest, and eventually to repel, the increasing flood of criminality, as well as to alleviate the hard lot of the unhappy convict. Up to this point the annual total of crime had ever been mounting higher and higher whilst the tale of abuses had continued to increase. But the malady had now come to a head, and intelligent public attention was at length focussed on a difficult and unpopular subject, which hitherto had been deliberately avoided by all but the very few who had been familiarized with its magnitude by routine, and who had mostly grown callous to its evils by use. When John Howard began to minister to prisoners, and when Jeremy Bentham began to propound his doctrine of utilitarianism, no one foresaw that the devotion of the one would achieve a transformation of the whole prison system, nor that the profound common-sense of the other would triumph over the irrationality which for centuries had vitiated the penal administration of England.

[218]

Foremost amongst the many objects for which Bentham worked were the amendment of the criminal code, the improvement of the Poor Laws, the abolition of transportation, sanitary and prison reform, systematic registration, and the instituting of public prosecutors, in short better police all round and in the widest sense of the term. Though most of Bentham's best work was done in the eighteenth, his doctrines received but little attention in this country before the nineteenth century, and the practical reforms which he advocated, though for the most part inaugurated in his own lifetime, were the immediate achievements of his disciples and friends. His own special hobbies were not altogether successful, the panopticon idea did not repay him for the labour and the money which he lavished upon it, and his philosophy did not prove the complete panacea for human ills that he anticipated; but through the medium of his friend Romilly he slew the Draconian monster, and he pointed out the path which Colquhoun followed and which ultimately led to the genesis of modern police.

The pamphlets of the two Fieldings, and the exertions of other minor reformers who succeeded them, had no doubt done something to stir up public opinion and to pave the way for a better system, but their combined influence was only effectual up to a certain point, and the virtue of the remedies they proposed was not sufficiently potent to get to the root of the all-pervading mischief. The credit of being the first to perceive the true functions of a rational police force, as it should be, belongs to [219]Bentham,[172] and the credit of formulating the details and presenting them in a tangible and practical shape to his contemporaries is due to Dr Colquhoun, who, in 1796, published his famous treatise "On the Police of the Metropolis."

If we think of Colquhoun as the architect who designed our modern police, and of Peel as the builder who constructed its framework, we must remember that there were others who had a hand in the good work, and that a long time elapsed between the drawing of the plans and the erection of the edifice. If it is allowable to carry the simile a stage further, we may say that the Government pigeon-holed the draughtsman's plans for many years before the order was given for the foundation stone to be laid. This delay must not be attributed to indifference, but rather to necessity. It is, perhaps, a truism to say so, but in order to carry any valuable reform to a successful issue, thought must precede action. Law is the public opinion of yesterday put in force to-day, and as Professor Dicey has somewhere pointed out, legislation has almost always been the outcome of the opinion of thirty years before. No better example of the truth of this general formula could be instanced than the case of the police reforms of the nineteenth century: Bentham, Colquhoun, Romilly and others did the [220]necessary thinking and sowed the seed in the public conscience; a period of thirty years elapsed whilst the seed was coming to maturity; meanwhile Peel and the Duke of Wellington watched the gradual ripening of public opinion and provided the necessary legislation as soon as the people were ready for it.

Colquhoun, who, like Fielding, was a Middlesex magistrate, saw that the essential need was method. He recognized that before any material improvement could be looked for, or any real security obtained, the miserable jumble of wards, parishes, hundreds and boroughs, each with its private establishment of watchmen and constables, who were debarred from acting one yard outside their own boundaries, would have to be swept away, and a centralized agency substituted under the superintendence of "able, indefatigable and intelligent men."

The criminal classes, at this time, had an organization far superior to any that Society could oppose to it; in fact, if a committee of pickpockets and burglars had been entrusted with the task of creating and arranging a system of police, they could hardly have devised any scheme under which they would have secured to themselves greater freedom from molestation. Colquhoun pointed out how all this might be changed: he would have a register prepared of all the known offenders, containing a complete history of their connexions and haunts, together with a list of all property stolen; he would establish such a correspondence between the town and country magistrates that the movements of suspected persons might be effectually watched, and [221]finally would "interpose those embarrassments which a vigilant and active police may place in the way of every class of offenders, so as to diminish crimes by increasing the risk of detection." He also collected a mass of evidence bearing on the causes that were responsible for the prevalence of crime, and proposed that a scientific campaign against the enemies of Society should be inaugurated, under the direction of experts, who should be free to devote the whole of their time and energies to the task. His proposition, in fact, amounted to the creation, if possible, of a centralized police, related to the general government through the Home Office, and officered both in the superior and subordinate grades, by men specially trained for the purpose. It was on these lines, of course, that Peel set to work twenty years later, but there is little doubt that he would have failed to carry his measure, in the face of the opposition which it aroused, if men's minds had not been to some extent prepared beforehand by the convincing arguments brought forward in "The Police of the Metropolis."

It must not be imagined that the period immediately preceding the formation of the new police was a time of expectant idleness, or that nothing was being done beyond the publication of treatises. Experiment and legislation were both at work; Parliamentary Committees, which sat in the years 1812, 1826, 1818, 1822 and 1828, to investigate the subject of police, collected a mass of evidence, much of which was useful; and the Select Committee on Vagrancy, appointed in 1821, performed a necessary [222]and valuable task. Distinct progress was also made towards the correction of prison abuses and in the direction of the reform of the penal code, whilst several statutes which were out of sympathy with the new standard of humanity were very properly repealed. The pillory was virtually abolished in 1816, public flogging of women was made illegal in 1817,[173] that anomalous institution "benefit of clergy" disappeared in 1826, and the death penalty could not be inflicted on persons convicted of forgery after 1830. Of new enactments belonging to this period, the most important was the "Alehouse Act" of 1828,[174] which reduced to one statute all the licensing laws passed in former years, and which to this day remains the foundation of our present system. Broadly speaking the object of the Act was decentralization, and its effect to place the whole licensing jurisdiction in the hands of the Justices of the Peace in their several districts.[175] The laws relating to remedies against the Hundred were amended and consolidated in 1826,[176] and shortly afterwards regulations affecting the jurisdiction of Courts of Quarter Sessions came into force.[177]

[223]

Colquhoun's activity did not stop short at the production of his first book, a work which roused the Government from its lethargy, and which even awakened the interest of the King, he issued a police gazette containing a full description of all known offenders, which circulated in all parts of the kingdom, and was the means of bringing many miscreants to justice; he strongly endorsed Bentham's suggestion that a public prosecutor should be appointed, in order that private persons should be relieved of the odium and expense of coming forward to prosecute offenders, who might enjoy a measure of popularity, or whose conviction might be desirable on public grounds, even if no individual had suffered specific injury; and in the year 1798 he was induced to turn his attention to the question of river-police. The rich cargoes of West India merchantmen lying in the Thames had long offered temptations, and the absence of police gave frequent opportunities which London thieves could not resist. Robberies were of daily occurrence, and the value of the property annually stolen from ships and wharves has been computed at half a million sterling.[178] Under these circumstances, the principal ship-owners, despairing of ever obtaining protection from Government in return for the heavy taxes they paid, applied to Colquhoun to help them to defend their goods. He assented, and produced a work called "A Treatise on the Commerce and Police of the River Thames," which was soon followed by the establishment by

Government[179] of an efficient water-police, with headquarters at Wapping, and composed, [224]for the most part, of sailors who had served their time in his Majesty's Navy.

In 1821 the Home Secretary, Lord Sidmouth, who had given much attention to police questions, determined if possible to put an end to the discreditable state of the London streets, where of recent years robberies had increased to an alarming extent. With this object in view, he decided to confine the services of the Bow Street patrols to the Metropolis, and gave orders that, in future, the wide circuit they had previously guarded was to be reduced, and their energies concentrated within the circumference of the central region. Dividing this limited area into sixteen districts, he attached to each a party of four men under a Conductor, and retained at Bow Street a reserve of one Conductor and fourteen men at the disposal of the Inspector there, for use in any sudden emergency. The suburbs and outlying districts were momentarily left unprotected by this withdrawal of the Bow Street Officers; so to repair this defect, the Horse Patrol, which in 1805 had been reorganized by Sir Richard Ford, was further improved and its numbers increased. The force was now divided into two branches, the mounted and dismounted, each of which was again split up into four divisions: the strength of the establishment was fixed at 161 of all ranks, apportioned as follows—

- Mounted—2 Inspectors, 4 deputy inspectors, 54 patrols.
- Dismounted—4 Inspectors, 8 sub-inspectors, 89 patrols.

[225]

As was formerly the case, the horse patrol consisted of ex-cavalry men, and they were dressed and accoutred in the following manner—

Blue double-breasted coat with gilt buttons, scarlet waistcoat, leather stock, white leather gloves, black leather hat, Wellington boots and steel spurs, whilst each man, when on duty, was furnished with a pistol, sabre, truncheon and pair of handcuffs.

Only married men were employed, and cottages were provided for them at convenient spots close to the roads they had to patrol, their wives were forbidden to keep pigs or poultry, a wise prohibition designed to secure to the government-horses their full allowance of forage.

The mounted and dismounted patrols worked in connection with each other; the latter were responsible for the immediate neighbourhood of London to a distance of five miles from its centre, and the former looked after the remoter districts included in a circle with an average radius of twenty miles; their principal routes were—to Enfield by Hampstead and Highgate in the North, to Epsom by Croydon and Richmond in the South, to Windsor by Uxbridge in the West, and Eastwards to Romford on the left bank of the Thames, and towards Maidstone on the right bank. Their orders were to proceed along the specified road at such a pace as would bring them to the end of their beat at the appointed time—halt ten minutes and then return meeting the other patrolmen half-way; when passing travellers they were ordered to make themselves known by calling out in an audible tone "Bow Street Patrol"; and on arriving at the home-end of [226]their beat they were timed to meet the dismounted patrol, and had to communicate to them any news of importance. Every patrol, when on duty, was expected to be fully equipped, with his pistol loaded, and his sword-belt outside his coat; if his horse should go lame he had to dismount, and on foot patrol half his usual distance; in the event of a robbery or other breach of the peace coming to his notice, his duty was to join his companion, if possible, and that of the two together to pursue and endeavour to apprehend the offender or offenders, summoning outside assistance if necessary. If they effected a capture their prisoner was to be safely secured till morning, when they had to bring him to Bow Street.

The orders issued to the dismounted patrol, *mutatis mutandis*, were practically identical with those already detailed: the men were warned never to go out on their rounds without truncheon, cutlass and warrant; and they had to meet the mounted patrol at the extremity of their beat, or report the circumstances under which they failed to carry out their instructions.

The Bow Street patrols were efficacious to a certain extent. Their presence gave confidence to travellers, and highway robberies on the main roads were put a stop to; but they were of little use against burglars, and altogether failed to suppress the footpads who took to the lanes and by-ways when the high-roads were protected, nor could the removal of stolen property be prevented as long as the patrolmen were only kept on duty for half the night. The small [227]force at the disposal of the Chief Magistrate at Bow Street, for the purpose of safe-guarding the outlying districts, had to patrol such a large area, and their movements were in consequence so regular, that it was easy for thieves to calculate the hour at which the peace officer was due at any given point, and equally easy to avoid him by concealment in a cross-road or behind a hedge until he had passed: a thief named Wilson long avoided capture in this manner, and when he eventually fell into the hands of the police, it was discovered that he had in his possession a regular time-table on which was marked at what o'clock the patrols might be expected at various points on all the main roads.

Twelve months after Lord Sidmouth's improvements had been initiated, a further advance was made, this time at the instance of Robert Peel, by the establishment of a Day-Patrol to supplement the Bow Street force. The new police body was very small, and only of an experimental nature; but it served the purpose of its institution, and the success achieved by the three Inspectors and twenty-four men who composed this little force was a strong argument for a subsequent extension on similar lines.

These reforms, following close upon each other, showed that at last Government was disposed to make a sustained effort to put the police on a better footing, and to give effect to the recommendations of the Parliamentary Committees, which it had summoned year after year, but whose advice it had hitherto as regularly neglected.

---

[228]

CHAPTER XII
"THE NEW POLICE"

The depth of lawlessness under which London lay submerged, and the deplorable condition of the feeble bulwarks that the richest city in the world had so long been content to rely on, have been considered at some length, because it is only by contrasting the security of recent years with the lawless confusion previously existing, that an intelligent appreciation of the debt we owe to Sir Robert Peel is made clear.

The evidence given before the various Parliamentary Committees reveals to us an impartial contemporary view of things as they then were, and it requires but little acumen to see for ourselves how well we are served by our police to-day. The improvement that has taken place has been something more than a well-defined instance of the general amelioration in our institutions, which was the feature of the nineteenth century: the year 1830 saw an almost instantaneous change in the police of London, a transformation from an inconceivably rotten and antiquated system into one which immediately became an example to the world, and one which still remains a credit to our civilization. [229]Simultaneously with the police revival there suddenly dawned an unwonted era of security out of the dark and dangerous shadows of the past: that this was due to Peel's Act, and to no other cause, is conclusively proved by the fact that the rural parts of England, to which the Act did not apply, had no share in the improvement which was at once manifest in the metropolis. The sharp contrast between the state of London under the old *régime* and its condition under the new administration is well illustrated by a comparison of two critical articles taken from the leading reviews of the day. A year before the introduction of Peel's bill the *Quarterly Review* said—"There can be no doubt that the whole of the existing watch system of London and its vicinity ought to be mercilessly struck to the ground. No human being has the smallest confidence in it.... Their existence is a nuisance and a curse"; and some years afterwards, when people had begun to realise how indispensable their police had become, the *Edinburgh Review* refers to the Metropolitan force in these words: "The arrangements are so good, the security so general, and the complex machinery works so quietly, that the real danger which must always exist where the wealth and luxury of a nation are brought into juxtaposition with its poverty and crime, is too much forgotten: and the people begin to think it quite a matter of course, or one of the operations of providence, that they sleep and wake in safety in the midst of hordes of starving plunderers."

The change was the more sudden because it had [230]been so long deferred. When the transition stage was over there could be no sustained conflict between the new champions of order and the old allies of disorder, because the latter had been allowed to hold the boards until their charlatanism and worthlessness were thoroughly exposed. People might, and actually did, say that the new system was bad and would lead to all kinds of disaster, but no one was bold enough to assert that the old system was good. Population had increased enormously, people were richer, more civilized and more humane than they had ever been before, and yet they put up with the same old apology for police that their grandfathers had been dissatisfied with and ashamed of. In some respects it is fortunate for us that this was so; for when the inevitable change was brought about, we got a better article than we should have done if an earlier model had been adopted, or if the abuses had not been allowed to flourish until they had become sufficiently glaring to demand radical measures for their removal.

Of the many Parliamentary Commissions, which since the year 1770 had investigated the police problem, the only one which did its work in a satisfactory manner was that convened on Peel's initiative in 1828. This Commission went into the question very thoroughly, and came to the conclusion that "it was absolutely necessary to devise some means to give greater security to persons and property." As soon as the Commissioners' report was issued, Peel decided to act upon it immediately, and on the 15th April 1829, introduced his bill in the House [231]of Commons. After briefly reviewing the prevailing state of insecurity, and commenting upon the notoriously defective police arrangements in vogue, he declared that no longer must petty parochial jealousies be allowed to outweigh higher and more extended principles. He then unfolded to the House his general plan. Recognizing the impossibility of simultaneously providing the entire metropolis with trained policemen, he proposed, in the first instance, to start on a modest scale, hoping that by the gradual absorption of parishes, the central agency would become exercised in the management and control of the police, until in course of time it should be competent to take charge of the whole constabulary of London:[180] the first experiment would begin with Westminster; Kensington and Hammersmith would come next; and eventually every parish, any part of which was within fifteen miles of Charing Cross, would be taken over.

Most recent attempts to reform the police had been entered into under the influence of panic, and when some patched-up defence could be extemporised against the danger that threatened, those responsible for the public quiet had been content. Peel's aims were more comprehensive: he set himself to design a framework sufficiently rigid to withstand the stress of the moment, and elastic enough to admit of expansion along the lines of future development.

[232]

A nice judgment was required to determine how far the old materials could be made available for the reconstruction, to decide how much to retain and how much to discard. Certain sound and well-proved principles, admirably suited to the national temper, underlay the structure which he was bent on modernizing, and these, he saw, could not be dispensed with. No mania for novelty blinded him to the value of much of the groundwork of the old system; and his reforms, therefore, were in the best sense conservative, for whilst there was no break in the continuity of whatever was good, neither was there any deliberate retention of anything that was bad. It is largely due to Peel's moderation that, the more one studies the anatomy of modern English police, the more one discovers birthmarks of its Anglo-Saxon parentage.

Two months after its introduction, Peel's measure became law. The famous Act of Parliament[181] creating the Metropolitan Police Force was entitled "An Act for improving the Police in and near the Metropolis." The preamble declared that, it having been found expedient to substitute a more efficient system of police for the local establishments of nightly watch and nightly police which had proved inadequate for the prevention and detection of crime, a new office of police was to be constituted, under the immediate authority of the Home Secretary. The Act is a long one, but its main provisions are simple and concise. His Majesty appoints two Justices of the Peace to conduct the [233]business of the Police Office, and to frame regulations for the management of the force, subject to the approval of the Secretary of State. The financial department is placed under an official called the Receiver, and the Police Rate (which must not exceed eightpence in the pound) is to be collected by Overseers like the Poor Rate. The existing watch shall continue to discharge its duties in the various parishes until notification is made that the new police is appointed, and then all watch-boxes, arms, etc., shall be handed over, and the present watch rates shall cease. The limits of the "metropolitan police district" are defined to comprise Westminster, and such parishes in Middlesex, Surrey, and Kent, as are enumerated in the Schedule of the Act. The Metropolitan police district is partitioned off into various "divisions" according to counties, those of Middlesex being as follows, Westminster, Holborn, Finsbury, Tower, Kensington, Brentford, and a division comprising certain extra-parochial places such as Grays Inn, Furnivals Inn and Ely Place. A short supplementary Act[182] relieves the chief magistrate at Bow Street of the direction of the Horse and Foot Patrols, and places them under the new police office.

This Office, as created by the Act of Parliament, the chief provisions of which are above detailed, was situated in Westminster and was called Scotland Yard. It differed from the older Offices in many respects, for whilst it was given no judicial functions to perform, it was charged with the duty of supervising the police machinery of the metropolis. It thus became [234]a centre from which to amalgamate the heterogeneous elements that went to make up London's police, and from which to administer the reclaimed territory in an ever-widening circle, until the whole metropolitan area, amounting to nearly seven hundred square miles, was freed from the trammels of Bumbledom, and brought under the control of a bureau directed by "able, indefatigable, and intelligent men."

The intimate connection that had always existed between Justice of the Peace and constable was not severed at the birth of the metropolitan force, and the first officers of the new establishment, appointed under the provisions of the Act, were two Justices. Colonel Rowan, a soldier of distinction who had already gained some experience with the Royal Irish Constabulary, and Richard Mayne, an eminent lawyer, were the men selected. The task could not have fallen into better hands, and to the energy and tact displayed by the first Commissioners[183] must be attributed, in great measure, the success achieved by the new force from its inception. In the course of an appreciative report, dealing with the results obtained by the New Police, a Parliamentary Committee, which sat in 1833 and 1834, paid a high compliment to these gentlemen. "Much, in the opinion of your committee, is due to the judgment and discrimination which was exercised [235]in the selection of the individuals, Colonel Rowan and Mr Mayne, who were originally appointed, and still continue to fill the arduous office of Commissioners of police. On many critical occasions and in very difficult circumstances, the sound discretion they have exercised, the straightforward, open and honourable course they have pursued—whenever their conduct has been questioned by the public—calls for the strongest expression of approbation on the part of your committee."

The task in front of the Commissioners was far from being an easy one: they had to raise a new force, but more important still was the business of restoring to the discredited office of Constable some of its native dignity and prestige. To this end it was necessary to get rid, as quickly as they dared, of all the unworthy ministers whose shortcomings had emboldened the lawbreakers and whose backslidings had disheartened the law-abiding; in so doing they had to incur the odium of causing the wholesale dismissal of public servants, who, worthless as they were, had no other trade to fall back upon. Nor was this the end of their difficulties. They had to organize and train a very considerable army of recruits, they had to drill this force and educate it to discharge duties requiring tact and forbearance, they were assisted by no expert opinion, and had little previous experience to guide them. The novelty of the problem increased the difficulty of its solution. They had to encounter a popular prejudice that was almost unanimously opposed to them, and although a false step might have produced the most [236]disastrous consequences, no delay was allowed them for consideration or experiment.

Having undertaken the task, however, they were not the men to turn back, and in an incredibly short space of time they had the whole machine in working order; the metropolitan area was mapped out into police divisions, the divisions divided into sections, and sections subdivided into beats: the various grades of Superintendent, Inspector, Sergeant, and Constable were created, and to each grade was assigned its proper duties. By June 1830, the Metropolitan Police consisted of 17 Superintendents, 68 Inspectors, 323 Sergeants, and 2,906 Constables, or 3,314 of all ranks, distributed in the following manner:

Return of Metropolitan Police, 1st June 1830.

Key:
Col A: Superintendents.
Col B: Inspectors.
Col C: Sergeants.
Col D: Constables.

Letter.	Name of Division.	A	B	C	D	Total.	Estimated Population.
A	Whitehall	1	2	14	96	113	5,893
B	Westminster	1	4	18	145	168	51,618
C	St James	1	4	16	167	188	94,418
D	Marylebone	1	4	18	147	170	85,040
E	Holborn	1	4	16	147	168	73,208
F	Covent Garden	1	4	16	145	166	61,618
G	Finsbury	1	4	20	210	235	102,561
H	Whitechapel	1	4	18	168	191	111,382
K	Stepney	1	6	28	262	297	113,516
L	Lambeth	1	4	18	168	191	45,646
M	Southwark	1	4	16	168	189	78,169
N	Islington	1	4	24	222	251	74,455
P	Camberwell	1	4	19	195	219	64,967
R	Greenwich	1	4	20	182	207	72,540
S	Hampstead	1	4	22	190	217	70,260
T	Kensington	1	4	20	148	173	49,668

V	Wandsworth	1	4	20	146	171	57,532
	Totals	17	68	323	2906	3314	1,212,491

[237]

This table shows at a glance how rapidly the parochial police was giving ground before the advancing battalions from Scotland Yard. In less than twelve months, in place of the five districts originally taken over, we find practically the whole of London and its suburbs policed by the new constabulary. The skeleton of this force's organization is also indicated in the above table, the details only require to be filled in. The Metropolitan Police District, it will be seen, was divided into seventeen Police Divisions, each designated by an appropriate local name, and by a letter of the alphabet. These Divisions were then divided into Sub-divisions, Sections, and Beats. There were eight Sections in a Division, and eight Beats in a Section. In every Division a Police-Station was provided, in as central and convenient position as possible, where the business of the Division was conducted on a plan approved by Scotland Yard, and common to all alike. The Constabulary force was organized in police companies, one company to a Division, under the command and direct supervision of its officer, the Superintendent. Furthermore, each company was split up into sixteen parties, each party consisting of one Sergeant and nine men, four Sergeants' parties being equal to one Inspectors' party. To put it in tabular form—

Constables	in charge of	Beats,	wages	19s. a week.
Sergeants	"	Sections,	"	22s. 6d. a week.
Inspectors	"	Sub-divisions,		£100 per ann.
Superintendents	"	Divisions,		£200 per ann.

[238]

Nine men, it will be observed, were apportioned to only eight beats; the sixteen odd men, *i.e.*, one from each party, constituted a Divisional Reserve. Every Constable and Sergeant was distinguished by an embroidered number and the letter of his Division, in order that he might readily be identified; the earlier numbers (from 1 to 16) denoted Sergeants, the higher numbers Constables. Each Constable was provided with a Beat-Card, giving the names of the Streets, etc., in his Beat.

At first the twenty-four hours were divided into two day reliefs and two night reliefs, half of the entire force being on duty by day and half by night. This arrangement was not a success, and was subsequently altered, when the day duty was performed in two reliefs and the night duty in one relief: under this system two-thirds of the force were employed by night, one-third by day, individual men doing eight months' night work and four months' day work during the year. By this means a greater degree of security was attained when it was chiefly required, and the health of the men suffered less than under the former plan.

Such in outline was the organization of the Metropolitan Police; absolute and arbitrary uniformity, however, was not insisted upon, but when necessary the system was modified to suit local requirements; thus, there were not exactly 144 Constables in each Company, but the number varied from 262 in the Stepney (K) Division down to 96 in the Whitehall (A) Division. The first mentioned of these two Divisions was densely populated, whilst [239]the other contained but few people, and the Whitehall Company, therefore, which was mainly composed of picked men, was generally available should any sudden emergency arise in other quarters of the town.

Prominent amongst the earlier constitutional functions conferred upon the English constabulary for the prevention of crime were those of Presentment and Inquiry. We have seen how, with the decay of the police system which once effectually maintained the peace, these primary duties had fallen into disuse, and how in consequence, the principle of "quick and fresh pursuit" had been neglected—partly by reason of the defective information possessed by the executive, and partly on account of the inefficiency of the inferior officers. Under the new *régime*, however, these most essential constituents of successful police action were reintroduced, a conspicuous feature of the new police being the excellence of the arrangements arrived at for the supply of information as to the persons and habits of delinquents. To this end, a report or "presentment," containing the results of all inquiries made during the last twenty-four hours was daily rendered to the Commissioners, who were thus enabled to take steps for the prevention of any threatened breach of the peace. When a serious crime had been committed, not only were the known facts of the case immediately circulated amongst all the members of the London force, but necessary particulars were periodically notified to a wider circle through the columns of the "Police Gazette," [240]a new official organ which superseded the old Bow Street publication known as "The Hue and Cry."

The police constable who made his appearance in 1829 was a very different kind of man from any of his predecessors in the same office. The new force was recruited from the best procurable material, and those who sought admission to its ranks were expected to possess good physique, intelligence above the average, and an irreproachable character. Hitherto a variety of officers had been employed in their separate capacities of constable, watchman, street-keeper, and thief-taker: now, all these duties had to be performed by the same individual. The new policeman, also, was required to have sufficient acquaintance with ordinary legal procedure to enable him to collect and arrange the available evidence in such a manner that, when his case came into court, the magistrate could dispose of the matter without vexatious delays induced, either by blunders committed, or by necessary formalities omitted. The difficulty of securing a sufficient number of men with the necessary qualifications at the rate of remuneration offered was immense; and although great care was exercised in the choice of candidates, but a small proportion of those selected were retained for any length of time. The extent to which this weeding-out process was carried may be estimated from the fact that between 1830 and 1838 there were nearly five thousand dismissals, and more than six thousand resignations, most of the latter not being altogether voluntary. This was in marked contrast to the [241]happy-go-lucky method of the old parochial bodies, who readily accepted infirm old men, ex-thieves, and sometimes thieves without the "ex," provided only that they were cheap.

For the guidance of all ranks, a set of rules and regulations were drawn up embodying principles and maxims upon which our modern police codes rest. "At the commencement of the new establishment," say the Commissioners, "it is the more necessary to take particular care that the constables of the police do not form false notions of their duties and powers. The powers of a constable, as will appear hereafter, are, when properly understood and duly executed, amply sufficient for their purpose. He is regarded as the legitimate peace officer of his district; and both by the Common Law and by many acts of parliament, he is invested with considerable powers, and has imposed upon him the execution of many important duties.... It should be understood at the outset that the principal object to be attained is the prevention of crime. To this great end every effort of the police is to be directed. The security of person and property, the preservation of the public tranquillity, and all other objects of a police establishment will thus be better effected than by the detection and punishment of the offender after he has succeeded in committing the crime. This should constantly be kept in mind by every member of the police force, as a guide for his own conduct. Officers and police-constables should endeavour to distinguish themselves by such vigilance and activity as may render it extremely difficult for anyone to [242]commit a crime within that portion of the town under their charge.

When in any division, offences are frequently committed, there must be reason to expect that the police in that division is not properly conducted.

The absence of crime will be considered the best proof of the complete efficiency of the police. In divisions where this security and good order have been effected, the officers and men belonging to it may feel assured that such good conduct will be noticed by rewards and promotions."

Touching the duties of the individual constables, Mr Mayne, who drew up the regulations, went on to say "He (*i.e.* the constable) must remember that there is no qualification more indispensable to a police officer than a perfect command of temper, never suffering himself to be moved in the slightest degree by any language or threats that may be used: if he do his duty in a quiet and determined manner, such conduct will probably induce well-disposed bystanders to assist him should he require it."

These regulations require no comment, they speak for themselves: but in view of the intense and unreasoning hostility direct against the police both by press and public, not only in 1830, but also on more recent occasions, it is fortunate that this evidence of the conciliatory spirit in which the reforms were introduced, should be on record. It is hardly necessary to add that the high standard set up by the first Justices of the Metropolitan Force has never been departed from by the successive Commissioners of Police, from that day until now.

[243]

The immediate result of the institution of an effective police force, whose main object was prevention, was precisely that which was to be expected: convictions for crimes of violence decreased, because evil-disposed persons knew that they could no longer commit them with impunity, and convictions for minor offences increased, because the vigilance of the new policemen brought to their proper punishment many a petty depredator who had easily hoodwinked his familiar friend, the old parish officer.

Under the date of November 3rd, 1829, or little more than four months after the passing of the Act, the Duke of Wellington was able to write to Peel—"I congratulate you on the entire success of the Police in London, it is impossible to see anything more respectable than they are"—and Peel to answer "I am very glad indeed to hear that you think well of the Police. It has given me from first to last more trouble than anything I ever undertook. But the men are gaining a knowledge of their duties so rapidly, that I am very sanguine of the ultimate result. I want to teach people that liberty does not consist in having your house robbed by organised gangs of thieves, and in leaving the principal streets of London in the nightly possession of drunken women and vagabonds."[184]

Nothing has yet been said about the expense of the new establishment. At what cost to the ratepayers was this increased security obtained?

Such a question is not easy to answer with any degree of certainty. Before 1829 many [244]parishes were practically without police of any kind, and if they spent little in Watch-rates they paid dearly in the heavy tolls exacted by "the organised gangs of thieves" referred to by Peel. Other parishes kept their accounts so carelessly that their records are useless for purposes of comparison, and it is therefore impossible to tell how much money they wasted. The 1834 Committee, which investigated this question of comparative expense, had all the available material before them, and they gave it as their opinion that strict economy pervaded the new system. In support of this opinion, they quoted the case of the parish of Hackney, which was moderately well policed as things went then. Prior to the introduction of the reformed police, the ratepayers of Hackney contributed £3,380 per annum, whereas at the maximum police rate that could be levied under the new system (viz. eightpence in the pound) the bill was only £3,164.

[245]

CHAPTER XIII
PUBLIC OPPOSITION TO THE "NEW POLICE"

The formation of the new police force in the metropolis aroused the fiercest opposition and remonstrance. Invective and ridicule were heaped upon the measure from all sides. The hopeless incompetence and the discredited character of the blackguardly Charlies were at once forgotten, nor were the prevalence of crime and the insecurity of life and property at all considered by those who made it their business to foment the popular antagonism.

Week by week certain newspapers continued to publish the most preposterous attacks: no story was too improbable to gain credence. A *coup d'etat* was contemplated—it was Sir Robert Peel's intention to place the Duke of Wellington on the throne—English liberty was to give place to military tyranny—under the pretence of providing protection for the people the government aimed at the creation of a secret political inquisition,—in fact anything that was at once inconsistent and absurd was listened to with avidity and partly believed.

[246]

At first sight it seems almost incredible that any part of the nation, except the criminal class, should have felt and exhibited such bitter hostility to legislation that we now see had been too long delayed; but the reluctance of the people to welcome the innovation was not so unreasonable as it now appears. It is easy for us to be wise after seventy years' experience of the admirable results that have followed upon the Act of 1829; but in that year the only example of modern militarily organized police before the eyes of the people, was that under which Paris had groaned since the time of La Reynie. Chateaubriand's philippics directed against the French system were eagerly read and quoted, and it was felt that London could not avoid the condition of interference with individual liberty that obtained across the Channel. People could not associate in their minds a proper police organization and the maintenance of justice, and remembered that "injustice is always most formidable when armed."

The events of the French Revolution were still in the public mind; and many Englishmen, who had looked on with horror at the spectacle of a neighbouring country writhing in the grip of anarchy, narrowly watched the course of events at home, in fearful anticipation lest any of the causes which had brought about the debâcle in France should be reproduced in this island. Nothing under the ancient régime had pressed the French people so hard nor bitten so deep as the police tyranny of the eighteenth century; and when the day of reckoning [247]came, the one rallying cry which never failed to stir the Parisians to an extremity of fury, was that for the abolition of the "lettre de cachet"[185] and for the overthrow of the lieutenant of police and his gang. And no wonder! Liberty was impossible under a system which arrogated to itself the right "de tout voir, de tout connaître, et de tout juger;" when no man could call his conscience his own, and when no fireside was secure against the paid informer. "If three men meet together, I can rely on it that at least two of them are on my side" boasted Sartines, a famous Chief of police. What plan could be more demoralizing than the one which sets the servant to spy on the master, the son to watch his father? What system so base as that under which the same hand that presses yours in friendship is the first to arrest you, what instrument so fatal to liberty or justice as the "lettre de cachet" which proclaims the innocence of the man who was legally convicted yesterday, and sends to the Bastille to-morrow the man who was honourably acquitted to-day?

People in England who knew these things, not unnaturally asked themselves the question, Why, with our eyes open, should we forge against ourselves a weapon similar to that, whose sharp point has goaded our neighbours till they were driven to set alight the torch of revolution and to destroy the whole fabric of government?

[248]

The fear that the continental system[186] of police might be introduced into England was not the only ground upon which this strenuous opposition rested. Another factor was the deeply rooted antipathy that the English have always displayed to any armed force that they feared might deprive them of their liberty. The inherent national suspicion of standing armies is well known: James II. tried to govern by the aid of one, but his attempt ended in failure owing to the opposition of the people; William III. wished to maintain a large permanent force, but so hateful was the mere name of a standing army in English ears, that Lord Somers, the king's minister, was constrained to talk of it as a temporary measure, to allay the popular irritation. Even to the present day, our comparatively small army, half of which is permanently on foreign service, only exists at the will of Parliament, and from year to year; whilst the fact that only two regiments, the lineal descendants of the trained-bands, are allowed to march through the streets of London with fixed bayonets, is an interesting survival, as shewing the distaste that the display of armed force in their midst has always produced amongst our countrymen. If this was the feeling with regard to the army, which was to a certain extent indispensable and which was only maintained, ostensibly at all events, for use against foreign enemies, it was not to be wondered at, if the [249]hostility to a strange body of men uniformed and drilled like soldiers, who were admittedly employed to keep their fellow-countrymen in order, was more pronounced.

The mildest form of police supervision was believed by many to necessitate the use of domiciliary visits, universal espionage, and official interference with the concerns of daily life. Men could not foresee the possibility of an armed constabulary keeping their hands off law-abiding citizens, and directing their energies solely against law-breakers. It has been said, that had the original police constables been first seen in their present head-dress, the result would have been dubious, but the glazed hat was just homely enough to save the situation.

In their fears, the opponents of the police bill underrated the efficacy of the two safeguards that have proved amply sufficient to defend society against the employment of any objectionable or tyrannical methods by the members of the force. The first safeguard was, that the new police was placed under the immediate control of the Home Secretary, who was directly responsible to the Cabinet, and through the Cabinet to the country, for the actions of the metropolitan force. The second safeguard lay in the power of the public press. The routine duties of a constable were, and are necessarily, performed in the eye of the public, and every bystander is free, through the columns of the newspapers, to tell the rest of London what he has seen. This facility he is [250]seldom slow to avail himself of, and so any act of oppression, any dereliction of duty, on the part of the police is discussed by thousands of people by the following morning.

The Turks have a proverb "The dog barks, but the caravan passes on"; and in this case the necessity for ending the existing state of affairs was so overwhelming, that the appeals, threats, and forebodings of the opponents of reform were powerless to prevent, or even retard, its progress. From its first commencement the new force learnt how to combine authority with moderation, and the storms of clamour that attended its birth were disguised blessings that conduced to its subsequent efficiency.

The opposition of the less reputable part of the press, and the very lukewarm support that was all it received from the remainder, were not without their effect on the force, though the result produced was far from being that hoped for by the agitators. The Commissioners, instead of being discouraged, were stimulated. With rare wisdom, assuming that the complaints which were continually being published against the constables were made in good faith, they carefully investigated each fresh indictment, with the result that, not only was the constabulary purged of its unworthy members, but the better sense of the country, appreciating the devotion to its interests practised by the Commissioners, was the sooner convinced of the advantages that follow from the establishment of a permanent and properly organized "standing army against crime." Some of the malcontents, however, who, from the first, had been so [251]bitter in their opposition to Sir Robert Peel's design, by no means relaxed their hostility after a reformed police was an accomplished fact, but on the occasion of a projected Royal Procession through London in 1830 again attempted to inflame the ignorant, and to provoke them to violence against the new guardians of the peace, by the distribution of anonymous placards. One of these placards read as follows:—"Liberty or Death! Englishmen! Britons!! and Honest Men!!! The time has at length arrived. All London meets on Tuesday. Come Armed. We assure you from ocular demonstration that 6000 cutlasses have been removed from the Tower, for the use of Peel's Bloody Gang. Remember the cursed Speech from the Throne!! These damned Police are now to be armed. Englishmen, will you put up with this?"[187] The authors of this precious appeal must have had a pathetic belief in the efficacy of strong language, if they thought that the prospect of a collision with six thousand policemen armed with cutlasses would be a sufficient inducement to bring together an armed mob to oppose them; but popular feeling ran so high that it was decided to abandon the Royal Procession, and elaborate precautions were taken to prevent a riot. The day passed, however, without serious consequences.

At the time of the accession of William IV., the whole country was restless and ripe for mischief. The irritation caused by the rejection of the Reform Bill by the House of Lords stirred up a feeling of violent opposition amongst the masses of the people, [252]directed, not only against the Upper House, but against the whole executive machinery of the Constitution. The worst outbreak occurred at Bristol, where the gaols, public buildings, and many private houses were burnt, and the whole town sacked as ruthlessly as if it had been an enemy's stronghold. Birmingham was the headquarters of an association said to consist of 200,000 members, enrolled with the avowed intention of coercing the government by the use of armed force, if they were unable to achieve their objects by legitimate means. In London, an organization, calling itself "The National Political Union" had been established with affiliated branches all over the metropolis: these branches, or "classes," as they were called, each consisting of from 80 to 130 members, held secret meetings at which the most violent language was often indulged in: the Union leaders were wont to insist on the necessity of the associates arming themselves, in order that the police might be successfully resisted, and a certain Mr Hetherington went so far as to publicly advertise that he would give a reward of £5 to the best marksman in the ranks of the Union. The most formidable "class" was the 73rd, popularly known as the "fighting class," recruited chiefly from the Camberwell district, which, for some reason or other, seemed to be peculiarly hostile to the police: other centres were less openly violent, and, for the most part, contented themselves with the publication of political manifestoes and proclamations. The wording of these latter were, as a rule, more curious than edifying. Members of Parliament were called "mock [253]representatives" and "borough-mongers' creatures," the House of Lords was referred to as "the hereditary hospital of incurable national nuisances," whilst the King was described in these words: "Alas, poor William Guelph! he is merely the puppet of a base scoundrelocracy."

Fortunately for the peace of London, the National Political Union lacked influential leadership; and this want, coupled with the fact that, by the institution of the Metropolitan Police, a powerful weapon had just been placed in the hands of the government, prevented the occurrence of disasters, similar to those which had devastated Bristol. But amongst the many difficulties that surrounded Colonel Rowan and Mr Mayne, the most exasperating originated in the hostile attitude of these Unions.

It was, therefore, much to be regretted that any just cause for complaint should have been given to that discontented section of the populace, which was anxiously looking out for an opportunity to discredit the new establishment. Unfortunately the hoped-for opportunity was soon afforded by the improper and unauthorised conduct of a policeman, Popay by name, who took it upon himself to act as a spy, and by pretending to be an advanced radical, to gain the friendship and confidence of the members of one of the classes of the union, in order to betray them to his superiors.

It appears that when it came to the knowledge of the police authorities, that speeches of a threatening nature were delivered at the meetings of the various centres, the district superintendents were instructed [254]to send a man in plain clothes to make reports, not with any intention of entrapping the speakers, but in order that any projected breach of the peace might be prevented. Popay was accordingly sent to the Camberwell neighbourhood, and either misunderstanding his instructions, or, as is more likely, purposely exceeding them in the hope of earning the approbation of his officers, entered upon an elaborate career of deceit and double-dealing. Disguised under an assumed name, and pretending to be a struggling artist, he professed revolutionary principles of an advanced character; and having enrolled himself in the local class, quickly became one of its ruling spirits, inciting the other members to proceed to extreme lengths, railing against the government, abusing the police, and even subscribing to the funds of the society. This sort of thing continued for some months, until it happened one day that a Camberwell reformer, whilst passing a police office, saw Popay sitting at the window with a ledger before him. When questioned as to the business that took him there, Popay said that he had only casually been called in, because the police had got their accounts into a muddle, and had asked him to set them right. Suspicion having been aroused, however, further enquiries were made, and it soon came to light that the *soi-disant* ardent politician was actually one of Peel's hated myrmidons, with the result that the outcry about police tyranny began all over again.

The new agitation did not materially differ from the old one: the same exaggerations and the identical [255]falsehoods, threadbare already, were again made use of. One new feature, however, was introduced in the shape of a petition, which was presented to the House of Commons, signed by one Frederick Young and nine other inhabitants of Camberwell and Walworth, setting forth their grievances with a great parade of humility. "Some of your petitioners," they wrote, "have frequently seen those whom they know to be policemen disguised in clothing of various descriptions, sometimes in the garb of gentlemen, sometimes in that of tradesmen and artizans, sometimes in sailor jackets, and sometimes in ploughmen's frocks: that thus feeling themselves living among spies, seeking their lives, and sorely feeling the taxes heaped upon them for the maintenance of those spies, they make this appeal to your honourable house," etc., etc.

Although the mis-statements and exaggerations contained in this petition were patent to all, the House of Commons very properly considered the matter to be a serious accusation against the entire police force, and at once appointed a Committee to enquire into the truth or falsity of the system of espionage, which was alleged to be universal. After the most careful investigation the Committee gave it as their opinion, that the authorities should be exonerated from the charge of connivance, but that Popay's conduct had been highly reprehensible, adding by way of comment that "with respect to the occasional employment of policemen in plain clothes, the system as laid down by the heads of the police department affords no just matter of complaint, [256]whilst strictly confined to detecting breaches of the law and to preventing breaches of the peace, should these ends appear otherwise unobtainable: at the same time, the Committee would strongly urge the most cautious maintenance of those limits, and solemnly deprecate any approach to the employment of spies, in the ordinary acceptation of the term, as a practice most abhorrent to the feelings of the people, and most alien to the spirit of the Constitution."

The Popay incident would not in itself have been of more than passing interest, had it occurred at some later period when results had justified the creation of the metropolitan police, but happening as it did, whilst everything was still in the experimental stage, and at a time when the new constables were, so to speak, on probation, the certainty that even a single policeman had been guilty of such conduct was a severe blow to the well-wishers of the force.

The culminating point of the tide of unpopularity which threatened to overwhelm Sir Robert Peel's police was reached soon afterwards. In the month of May 1833, it was advertised that a public meeting, under the auspices of the National Political Union, would be held in Coldbath Fields. Lord Melbourne, the Home Secretary, fearing disorder would result, informed the organizers that the gathering would not be permitted to take place, and instructed the Police Commissioners to have the ring-leaders arrested if they should attempt to disregard his veto.

[257]

The steps taken by Colonel Rowan to carry out these orders were as follows: 70 men of the "A" division were selected for the duty and despatched under a superintendent to Coldbath Fields, with instructions to seize the leaders the moment they began to address the crowd, and, if the attempt was persevered in, to disperse the meeting. It was not considered advisable to occupy the ground in force before the agitators assembled, because, strictly speaking, the police had no authority to prevent peaceable citizens from walking across this particular piece of ground if they were minded to, and because it was foreseen that, should the mob find their rendezvous already strongly held, they would attempt to carry out their programme at some other spot, where there was no police force strong enough to interfere with them. Colonel Rowan attended in person to direct the operations of the police, and to read the Riot Act, if either of these steps should appear necessary; as a further precaution, a considerable body of constables were kept in reserve close by, in order that there should be no danger of the police being worsted in any encounter that might take place. This reserve, which consisted of about 400 men, was kept out of sight, it being thought that, in the excited state of public feeling then prevailing, the display of an overpowering force would be calculated to irritate the mob, and to attract in consequence a still larger crowd than might otherwise be expected to assemble.

At the time appointed numbers of people began to congregate on the waste ground at Coldbath Fields, and soon afterwards the speeches commenced. [258]As soon as it became clear that the meeting was identical with that proscribed by the Home Secretary, the men of "A" division, after having been warned by Colonel Rowan to be cool and temperate in their demeanour, were ordered to carry out the instructions previously given them. At the same time a portion of the reserve was moved from the stables (where the men had been waiting) to support the first party, and it was during this advance that a collision took place at a street corner with a mob of people, who immediately began to throw stones, by which several constables were injured. Thereupon the superintendent gave the word to charge, and in the melée which followed truncheons were made use of, and three policemen were stabbed, one of them being killed on the spot. Meanwhile the crowd was incited to further resistance by the action of a man called Stallwood, who falsely representing himself to be a magistrate, harangued the police from the balcony of his house, and told them that they were acting illegally in making use of force before the Riot Act had been read. The struggle was of short duration. The people began to disperse in all directions, and numerous arrests were made by the police, who committed the error of following up their victory with too much vigour, carrying pursuit in some instances to a considerable distance from the scene of the original conflict.

This first collision between the Metropolitan force and the people gave rise to a series of charges against the police, which, if they could have been substantiated, might have ended in the undoing of all the good achieved after so many years, and [259]brought about with so much labour and difficulty. It was said that the police were intoxicated and, in that condition, had made an unprovoked assault on inoffending citizens, knocking down women and children with brutal impartiality, and then stunning them with their truncheons as they lay on the ground. Fortunately an exhaustive enquiry was held, with the result that the action of the police was satisfactorily vindicated. An unanswerable argument against the accusers was that, whereas several constables were badly knocked about, and one killed, not a single case of serious injury was to be found on the other side.

Public animosity, however, did not pause to reason; and at the inquest which was held on the body of the murdered policeman Culley, the jury, sympathizing with, or intimidated by, the popular feeling, brought in a verdict of "justifiable homicide." A verdict so flagrantly in the teeth of the evidence could not be allowed to stand: the Crown applied to the Court of King's Bench, and the inquisition was very properly quashed.

A Committee of the House of Commons was then appointed to enquire into the conduct of the police, who came out of the ordeal with more credit than the Government did, for it was proved that the Police Commissioners only carried out the instructions of the Home Secretary, who, when trouble arose, sought to escape all responsibility, and to throw the blame on Colonel Rowan. Whatever may be thought of Lord Melbourne's action, it is [260]certain that he did not err on the side of over-generosity, and the slender support which he somewhat grudgingly gave to the police authorities was hardly of a nature to encourage them in their uphill task. It may be that this cold-shouldering of its youngest child by a government department was not altogether a misfortune, for a popular reaction in favour of the police quickly followed, and friendship was expressed in quarters where nothing but hostility had been looked for: vestries which had recently petitioned against the formation of the force now passed resolutions in its praise, and nearly all those parishes situated just outside the boundary applied to be admitted into the Metropolitan police area. Before long provincial towns and outlying districts began to solicit the loan of police officers trained in the London school; and in eight years some two hundred places, including Birmingham, Bristol, Hull, Liverpool and Manchester were supplied with experts, who carried with them to their new sphere of action the methods they had learnt in the metropolis, and whose excellent work in the provinces did much to disprove the ridiculous fables, which had once gained credence, as to the overbearing incompetence of the new constabulary.

Public opinion is notoriously unstable; and in recent years the police have probably suffered to a greater extent than any other institution from the alternating favour and disfavour of the populace.[188] The comparative popularity enjoyed by the Metropolitan police force in 1834 was only a precarious possession, gratifying enough at the moment, but of [261]little permanent value. No such disadvantage, however, attaches to a testimonial deliberately given by a representative tribunal, especially when such testimony is in direct contradiction to anticipations recently expressed by an equally competent and similarly constituted body. The 1822 Committee were of opinion that it would be difficult "to reconcile an effective system of police with that perfect freedom of action and exemption from interference which are the great privileges and blessings of society in this country." The 1834 Committee, on the other hand, having satisfied themselves that these gloomy forebodings were groundless, reported to the House of Commons as follows: "Looking at the establishment as a whole, it appears to your Committee that the Metropolitan police has imposed no restraint, either upon public bodies or individuals, which is not entirely consistent with the fullest practical exercise of every civil privilege, and with the most unrestrained intercourse of private society."

CHAPTER XIV
POLICE REFORM IN BOROUGHS

It is sometimes assumed that the Metropolitan Police Act solved, once and for all, the question as to the manner in which London was to be policed for the future. Such, however, was far from being the case. The old prejudice was not lived down in a day; and the jealousy of those who saw what they were pleased to consider their vested rights slipping out of their grasp into the hands of the newcomers, caused the remnant of the old office-holders to make frantic efforts to recover what they had lost, and to hold fast what they were in danger of losing. There were still many irreconcilables, who looked upon the new force as a gang of usurpers and treated it with distrust and suspicion accordingly, hoping that some false move on the part of the police authorities, or some unlooked-for happy chance, might change the fortunes of the day. Luckily no such set-back occurred, and by slow degrees the ultimate success of the principles enunciated by Peel became more and more assured, and Scotland Yard triumphed to the discomfiture of all possible rivals.

From the very commencement Sir Robert Peel had declared that unity of design was essential to success; but when the reorganization took place, Parliament shrank from the bold course marked out for it, and instead of making a clean sweep of all that was useless, whilst transferring to the new police anything in the old system that was of value, preferred to retain some of the existing unsatisfactory agencies, and to allow them to continue to manage or mismanage their own affairs as before.

The establishments within the boundaries of the Metropolitan Police area that survived the reorganization of 1829 were[189]—

i. The Bow Street Horse-Patrol, under the control of the Chief Magistrate at Bow Street.

ii. The police constables under the separate control of the Magistrates of the Police Offices, to which they respectively belonged, being the following offices—Bow Street, Hatton Garden, Union Hall, Worship Street, Lambeth Street, Queen Square, Marlborough Street, High Street Marylebone, and the Town Hall Southwark.

iii. The River Police, under the control of the Magistrates of the Thames Police Office.

iv. The City of London Police, under the control of the Municipal authorities.

Each of these independent establishments carried out its police functions according to its own peculiar ideas and local traditions. One and all were jealous of their powerful neighbour at Scotland Yard; and when they dared to do so, were not ashamed to countenance the petty and spiteful tactics that their subordinate officers lost no opportunity of indulging in.

It will be remembered that a short supplementary Act[190] had contemplated the transference of the powers possessed by the Chief Magistrate at Bow Street over the Horse Patrol, to the Metropolitan Police Commissioners. This intention was not given effect to at the time, the

Patrol being left under the command of its old chief, Mr Day; and the Act was repealed in 1833.[191] It was not until October 1836, or more than seven years after the passing of Peel's measure, that the Horse Patrol became an integral part of the Metropolitan Consolidated Police, an amalgamation which, besides increasing the actual efficiency of both forces, effected an annual saving of more than a thousand pounds.[192] The horse-patrolmen became mounted constables, being attached as such to the exterior divisions, where the beats were long; and this arrangement has been continued to the present day.

It took longer to arrive at a satisfactory settlement with regard to the small detached bodies of police belonging to the nine stipendiary offices enumerated above. No one wished to interfere with the judicial functions of these police-courts; but it was highly desirable to effect a separation between the judicial and executive branches, and to bring under proper supervision and control the undisciplined plain-clothes policemen who thought more of picking up a good living for themselves, [265]and of "scoring off" their uniformed rivals, than they did of the preservation of the peace. The manner in which the general business of these police offices was conducted left much to be desired, whilst the arrangements for the conveyance of prisoners, and for their detention when awaiting disposal and under remand, were about as bad as they could be. As many as thirty prisoners of all conditions, of various ages, and of both sexes, were often crowded together in a prison van, in which there was only accommodation for twenty, and left there for hours in the dark whilst the van was making the tour of the police offices. When no conveyance was available, prisoners were sometimes conducted from the place of detention to the police-court handcuffed and fastened together by a long chain. It was alleged, probably with truth, that the officer in charge would allow his prisoners to be supplied with drink by sympathetic onlookers as, in Indian file, the procession passed through the public streets.

Such abuses were put an end to when the inevitable consolidation took place and the separate jurisdiction of the stipendiary offices ceased. The necessary duties about the courts were for the future ably performed by sergeants and constables of the new police, and the old staff, including the Bow Street Runners, were pensioned off or absorbed into the Metropolitan force. This centralization not only materially conduced to increased efficiency and diminished expense, but by severing the too intimate connection that had previously existed between [266]magistrates and policemen, was calculated to reassure the public, in so far that a magistracy untrammelled by police responsibility would be less prone to be over-indulgent towards any excesses of which the Constabulary might at any time be guilty.

The case of the third independent body was altogether different. The duties that fell to the River Police were special duties, and specially trained men were required to perform them adequately. The Thames police establishment, which was recruited chiefly from ex-sailors and watermen, consisted of sixty constables under the direction of twenty "surveyors"—each surveyor being in charge of a boat manned by three men; their powers comprised the right to board vessels in search of contraband or stolen articles, and generally to discharge the duties of excisemen and policemen combined. Since the year 1798, when the River Police was remodelled on the lines suggested by Colquhoun, it had proved an efficient body, and there were no obvious abuses or shortcomings that necessitated a radical change; the arguments for and against amalgamation were therefore more evenly balanced than was the case with the stipendiary offices, but it was felt that as both banks of the Thames were patrolled by the Metropolitan Police, it was rather absurd that the river between should be under a separate organization and control. It was accordingly decided to continue the work of consolidation, and many of the powers previously exercised by the magistrates of the Thames Office were transferred to the Commissioners at Scotland Yard, [267]the personnel of the river force being left as before.

The police arrangements in the City of London have already been described; certain modifications and improvements had been recently introduced, but the general scheme remained virtually the same as it had been any time during the last quarter of a century. It is true that a better class of man was employed than was formerly the case; but the system was not good, marred as it was by a lack of uniformity within, and a failure to co-operate with the kindred agencies without, the city boundaries. The expense too was excessive, and there was a period between the relief of the day patrols and the mounting of the night watch when no police at all were on duty. There can be little doubt that if the civic authorities had permitted this unsatisfactory state of affairs to continue much longer, government would have insisted upon consolidation, thus putting an end to the separate and exclusive jurisdiction in matters of police which, for five hundred years, had been the privilege of the City of London. Such a step, however, was rendered unnecessary by the timely precautions adopted by the Lord Mayor and Aldermen, who, taking the Metropolitan police as a pattern, entirely reorganized the city force, bringing it up to date both in respect to numbers and efficiency, and so ordering it that there should be no cause for friction between the city constables and metropolitan policemen, and no cause for jealousy other than that which proceeds from a healthy sentiment of *esprit de corps*. The legislature was [268]all the more ready to acquiesce in this compromise, because the City, asking for no assistance from the Treasury, bore the whole expense connected with the improved constabulary out of its private revenues.[193]

By the end of 1839 the consolidation was complete, and within a circumference distant fifteen miles from Charing Cross there remained but two police forces, both organized on similar lines and each designed on intelligent principles, in the place of the heterogeneous medley of samples formerly existing. In this same year, the efficiency of the Metropolitan Police was increased, and its sphere of usefulness enlarged, by an Act[194] which enables additions to be made to the police district by an Order in Council, and which empowers its officers to act as constables in and for certain specified districts outside the Metropolitan Police Area, such as, for example, the City of London, all navigable parts of the River Thames, and any place within ten miles of a Royal Palace. Authority was also given to police-constables to suppress gaming houses, disorderly houses, and illegal games (such as cock-fighting, prize-fighting, bull-baiting, and the like), to supervise licensed premises and pawnbrokers, and to regulate fairs and street-musicians.[195]

The success that had attended the reorganization [269]of the police of the metropolis, and the gratifying results that, on the whole, had followed the experiment, encouraged the hope that the benefits conferred by an efficient constabulary would soon be shared by the boroughs throughout the country. It would be an endless task to attempt a description of all the various police systems which found favour in the provincial towns, especially as in no two places was exactly the same pattern adopted; and it will be quite sufficient for our purpose if we briefly notice the arrangements come to for the prevention of crime and the maintenance of order in the case of a few selected boroughs.

In 1833 Bath had a population of about 20,000, or if we include the suburbs, 55,000; there was no permanent body of professional peace officers, only tythingmen or constables to the number of 110. This small force was split up into three parts, each part independent of, and antagonistic to, the others: on the occasion of a parliamentary election, when party feeling ran high and serious disturbances took place all over the town, the Walcot and Bathwick divisions gave their assistance, but the city police refused to act, even when they were appealed to by the Mayor in person. If a felony was committed in the city, the guilty party could only be apprehended on the warrant of a city magistrate, and, if the felon should succeed in reaching the suburbs, the city constables could not execute the warrant until it was backed by a justice of the county of Somersetshire.

In Gloucester no watchmen were employed before 1822, and the whole available constabulary force [270]consisted of the Sergeant-at-Mace, and the other officers of the Corporation, assisted by twelve constables appointed by the magistrates. The ancient Court of Pie-poudre flourished until 1770 or thereabouts, after which it gradually fell into disuse. In 1831 two day policemen were appointed in imitation of the London system.

Coventry, with a population of 28,000, supported 60 peace-officers under the command of a chief-constable, and from 8 to 10 watchmen under the orders of an official called "the Inspector of the Watch." In case of emergency the town looked for protection to the services of special constables who had been enrolled in times of tumult to the number of four or five hundred. Generally speaking the police were unpaid, but when employed in quelling a riot, the constables were sometimes given a shilling or eighteenpence for refreshments.

Dover had two distinct forces, one under the control of the magistrates, and the other (established under the "Pavement Act"), wholly independent. The total number of constables was from 25 to 30, but they had nothing to do with watching the town.

At this time Hull contained 36,000 inhabitants, and was policed on a very economical plan. The chief constable supervised thirty-nine officers who were only paid for work done; that is to say, the constables were allowed so much an hour for time actually spent in apprehending felons or vagrants, on the principle: no prisoner, no pay.

The dock companies employed a percentage of [271]their day-labourers to act as night watchmen, and, under a local act, 72 watchmen were appointed for the town and outlying districts. In Portsmouth 22 peace officers pretended to protect nearly 50,000 people, and in Liverpool, where the prevalence of crime was so pronounced that the town was often spoken of as the "black spot on the Mersey," the only police force existing in 1834 was a body of 50 watchmen (of the usual type), to keep order amongst 240,000 inhabitants.

These brief but representative examples will give some idea of the diversity of police systems and police expedients to be found in the larger towns. If each borough had been left to work out its own salvation according to its own predilections, constabulary forces more or less efficient would eventually, no doubt, have sprung up here and there; but the absence of uniformity and co-operation, which necessarily must accompany such a spasmodic process, would have seriously retarded the ultimate triumph of good government throughout England.

There were three principal reasons why the immediate provision of a general scheme of police reform in the Boroughs was urgently required at this particular moment. Criminals of all kinds are ever on the alert to find an Alsatia where they can ply their trades without the unwelcome interference of their hereditary enemy, the policeman, and the formation of the Metropolitan force was the signal for a wholesale exodus of depredators from London towards other and more secluded centres of activity. The smaller country towns and rural districts offered [272]few attractions to enterprising thieves, and so boroughs like Liverpool,

Manchester and Bristol, where considerable plunder was to be had at little risk, were the chosen retreats of many who no longer dared to brave it out in London.

If any reliance may be placed on contemporary statistics, this migration entirely altered the distribution of the criminal classes: it was estimated, incredible as it may seem, that in 1797 nearly ten per cent. of the population of London supported themselves "by pursuits either criminally illegal or immoral":[196] in 1837, the proportion of known bad characters to the population was calculated at only 1 to 89 in the Metropolitan Police District, but at 1 to 45 in the Borough of Liverpool, 1 to 31 in the City of Bristol, and 1 to 27 in the Town of Newcastle-on-Tyne.[197] One cannot believe that these calculations were based on perfectly accurate information, but on the other hand it is unlikely that the results are so wide of the mark as to be altogether without value, and after allowing a large margin for error, proof enough remains that the enhanced security of London had, to some extent, been purchased at the expense of the inhabitants of other towns.

The desire to acquire wealth without working for [273]it—to "live idly yet to fare well"—is the main incentive that makes men criminal, and experience proves that if those who live by their wits are sufficiently harassed, they soon show their wit by returning to the humdrum path of honesty till such time as the vigilance of their enemies is relaxed. "Allow the thief no rest" is a sound maxim of preventive police; and if in 1829 it had been possible simultaneously to provide efficient police for all the towns of England, many and many a thief would have been driven to exchange his old occupation for some less precarious trade.

The second reason why delay was dangerous was because of the enormous increase of population in the manufacturing towns. Trade was brisk, money plentiful, and the rapid development of the railway system caused an increasing stream of workers to flow from the country into the industrial centres. The population of Birmingham, for instance, increased in this way from 90,000 in 1815 to 150,000 in 1832.

The last of the three reasons which contributed to make this particular moment especially opportune for insisting that the provincial towns should provide themselves with an improved and adequate police, was because Municipal reform was the question of the hour, and it was therefore extremely important that the new-fashioned Boroughs should neither perpetuate faulty tradition nor originate impracticable experiment.

The history of English Boroughs cannot here be discussed; it will be sufficient to remark that, early [274]in English history, charters, giving powers of self-government, had been granted to many towns and by many successive sovereigns. The creation of Corporate Towns was esteemed one of the highest prerogatives of the Crown, but the powers so conferred were seldom employed to the best advantage; and the fact that failure was especially pronounced in the matter of peace-maintenance is sufficiently illustrated by the examples already given of borough police forces, as at this time constituted.

Legislative reform was set on foot in 1833 by the "Lighting and Watching Act" of William IV.,[198] which provided that inspectors should be appointed and given a large measure of control over the local police establishments of all English towns with the exceptions of London, Oxford, and Cambridge; this Act was, however, of little permanent value,[199] and is only worthy of notice as the first attempt to provide a day police outside the metropolis. In the following year the whole question of charters, etc., was investigated by Special Commissioners, who issued a report embodying recommendations, which, for the most part, were given effect to by the "Municipal Corporations Act" of 1835.[200] After repealing all Acts, charters, and customs inconsistent with itself, this statute proceeds to create municipal corporations for [275]the larger towns; such corporations to be styled "The Mayor, Aldermen, and Burgesses." The Mayor is declared to be a Justice of the Peace for the borough, and no property qualification is now required of him. The Common Law method of appointing constables is placed on a new basis, for the Act entrusts the making of Head and other constables to a body composed of the mayor and councilmen, called "The Watch Committee," the members of which are empowered, at their discretion, to make regulations for the management of the police, and to discharge or otherwise punish any constable found remiss in his duties, provided that three members at least are present when the award is made.

Borough constables are given powers to act in the county as well as in the town, and are authorized, not only to apprehend disorderly persons at any time, but during the night may take bail by recognizance from persons brought before them for petty misdemeanours, such recognizance to be conditioned for the appearance of the parties before the magistrate.

Watch Committees are required to provide station-houses, and every quarter must transmit to the Home Secretary a return shewing the number of men employed, the nature of their arms and accoutrements, together with an account of all salaries, clothing, and standing regulations for the forces; provision is made for the appointment, under certain conditions, of stipendiary magistrates at the request of the Council; the office of Borough Coroner is [276]instituted; and finally, the Act requires two or more Justices to nominate and appoint by precept in writing, in October of each year, as many as they see fit of the inhabitants of the Borough to act as Special Constables there, whenever they shall be required by the warrant of a J.P.

The institution of special constables was a natural accompaniment to the general drift of circumstances which, for a long time, had been modifying English police. Originally, as we have seen, every free Englishman was compelled to take an active part in maintaining the peace: subsequently, by common consent and merely for the sake of convenience, the performance of police functions passed into the hands of individuals, either chosen or hired for the purpose, it mattered not which. As long as the principle of an inherent liability to universal service was generally well understood and acted upon, or, in other words, as long as the Sheriff's *posse* was available in emergencies, no legislation was required on the subject, because at Common Law a sufficient force of special constables already existed; but when this common responsibility for action was in danger of being forgotten, or, what amounts to much the same thing, when the existing machinery was incapable of giving effect to it, some new expedient had to be devised to take its place.

The first Act of Parliament authorizing the appointment of special constables was passed in 1673,[201] and was a tardy attempt to repair the havoc caused by the Civil War, but like many laws that [277]found their way into the Statute Book during the seventeenth century, it might just as well have remained unprinted, for all the use that was made of it. It was not employed to restrain the Mohocks, nor to suppress the Gordon rioters, nor to save Bristol from the incendiaries. In 1831, however, began a sustained effort to systematize the overwhelming reserve of force at the disposal of the government of the country; this was the combined work of "The Special Constables' Act"[202] of 1831, of the "Municipal Corporations Act"[203] of 1835, and lastly of an Act[204] which became law shortly after the accession of Queen Victoria. These three Statutes dealt with the subject in detail, by defining what constitutes a special constable, by specifying his powers, and by stating when and by whom he is to be appointed. Between them they authorize "two or more justices, upon information on oath of any credible witness, that tumult, riot, or felony has taken place, or may be reasonably apprehended, such justices being of opinion that the ordinary officers are not sufficient for the preservation of the peace and protection of the inhabitants and property," to "nominate and appoint by precept under their hand so many as they shall think fit of the householders or other persons (not legally exempt from serving the office of Constable) residing in the parish or place or in the neighbourhood, for such time and in such manner as to the same justices shall seem fit," and ordain that they "shall send notice of such appointment to the Secretary of State and the Lieutenant of the county. Specials may act, not only in the parish or place for which appointed, but throughout the jurisdiction of the Justices appointing, and on the order of Justices of their own county, may act in an adjoining county."[205] Generally speaking, special constables have all the powers, and are subject to all the responsibilities, that ordinarily attach to police constables within their constablewicks.

The years 1829 and 1839 mark the limits of the most important decade in our police history. During this period of time the English boroughs acquired the means of securing themselves against the rising tide of crime which had threatened to overwhelm them; and an adequate defence against mob violence was made available by the legislation which restored, and reduced to a system, the power of the executive to enlist as many special constables as might be necessary for the maintenance of law and order. Whilst the former year will always be considered, and rightly so, as the most prominent landmark of the great revival from which dates an almost constant growth of police efficiency, the latter is hardly less noteworthy. 1839 not only saw the metropolitan forces for the first time firmly established on a permanent and satisfactory basis, it witnessed also the earlier stages of that movement in the rural districts which eventually provided the whole of England with a trustworthy constabulary.

CHAPTER XV
POLICE REFORM IN COUNTIES

Before describing the successive steps by which the County Constabulary progressed towards its long-delayed reorganization, it will be convenient to follow the method before adopted, when dealing with the somewhat similar march of events in the Metropolis, and to preface such description by a short account of the unreformed county police, thereby shewing how disastrous were the consequences of the faulty system in vogue, as revealed by the deplorable condition of rural England under its influence. The great source of information on this subject is the exhaustive report of the Royal Commission, appointed in 1839, to inquire as to the best means of establishing an efficient constabulary force in the counties of England and Wales. In the course of their enquiry (which was the most complete investigation of crime, its causes, and the means of its prevention, ever undertaken in this country), the Commissioners not only interrogated heads of business-houses, their commercial travellers and foremen, country magistrates, policemen, and coastguards, but examined thieves, receivers, and all kinds of gaol-birds.

The immediate result of the activity of the new metropolitan and municipal police forces was found to be, that habitual criminals had migrated in large numbers from London, and from those towns where an improved constabulary had superseded the old parish watch, and had begun to ply their trade in the unprotected districts. Country magistrates unanimously reported that the bulk of the more serious offences recently committed in their respective neighbourhoods was the work of strangers from the great towns. The superintendent of the Liverpool dock police stated that about a thousand well-known thieves, who had been evicted from the city, were now continuing their depredations in the suburbs and small towns near. Questioned on this subject, a prisoner confessed—"I considered that in London and Liverpool, or such places as have got the new police, there is little to be done, unless it be picking pockets; people there think that they are safe under the eye of the new police, and will take large sums of money in their pockets." Another prisoner, in corroboration, said "The most important obstructions that could be placed in the way of depredations is a more efficient police similar to that in London and Liverpool—very few robberies in the centre of Liverpool,—all in the outskirts, out of the police districts." A second cause that contributed to the migration of both thieves and receivers to the provinces was the extension of the railway and canal systems, which, besides facilitating the rapid movement of plunderers from place to place, exposed quantities of valuable merchandise on truck and [281]canal boat without protection. Merchants were indifferent to the fate of their goods when once a receipt had been obtained from the carriers; and they again, in common with the shipping agents, found it extremely difficult to put a stop to the petty thieving that went on, partly because the loss was generally undiscovered until the goods reached their destination (which as often as not was in a foreign country), and partly because the number of people through whose hands the property passed was so great, that the attempt to fix the responsibility on any individual would have been to incur a laborious and expensive system of checking and counter-checking that the value of the articles stolen did not seem to justify. Of all these petty thieves, the bargemen were the worst offenders, and the opportunities they met with, combined with the impunity they enjoyed, attracted many thieves to the calling; all over the country receivers of stolen property set up shop near the canals; burglars would bring their spoil by night to a pre-arranged rendezvous, and hand it over to the bargees, who took it aboard, concealed it under the cargo, and disposed of it at the fence's shop as occasion offered.

Much ingenuity was displayed in this traffic. For instance, an ex-bargeman convicted of theft explained to the Commissioners how he and his mates used to extract valuables from bales, casks, and boxes without risk of discovery, every trip they made. Silk could be withdrawn from the centre of a bale by means of a hook specially designed for the purpose; chests of tea were carefully opened, a few pounds [282]extracted, and the remainder made to occupy the original space by means of judicious damping. In the case of casks of wine or spirits, the following ingenious method was resorted to; first one of the hoops was removed, and two holes were bored on opposite sides of the cask, one for drawing off the liquid, the other for letting in air; when a considerable portion of the liquor had been taken, the cask was filled up with water, the holes were pegged up, and all traces covered up by replacing the hoop. Nor did canal-thieves confine themselves to pilfering from boats, but as they travelled the country, they slaughtered sheep, snared game, and milked farmers' cows.

The next matter investigated by the Commissioners was the lack of proper protection to travellers on the public highways. By this time highwaymen, the terror of the last century, had been practically suppressed, but footpads were more common than ever; countrymen returning from market used to make up parties, and wait for hours for company rather than go home alone, whilst after dark many a commercial traveller would go armed with a pistol, and accompanied by a dog, for fear of being robbed. More serious still were the revelations brought to light with regard to wrecking. It was proved that almost all the inhabitants of the coast were wreckers; children were brought up to consider the practice legitimate, and women prayed that the winter would bring a rich harvest. When the weather was stormy, hundreds of people would crowd to the beach, not with any thought of rescuing [283]the drowning, but only eager for plunder; as wreckage neared the shore men might be seen swimming out to be the first to touch any article that appeared to be of value, for by local tradition undisputed ownership was in this way acquired. Witnesses testified to all kinds of atrocities. A ship called "The Grecian" went to pieces off the Cheshire coast—the captain was drowned, and his body was found stripped naked by the wreckers, who, not content with his clothes, cut off one of his fingers to obtain possession of the ring. Even this act of savagery was surpassed at a village called Moreton, where it was proved that a woman had bitten off the ear-lobes from a female corpse for the sake of the earrings.

Mr Dowling, the Commissioner of the Liverpool police, stated that in Cheshire parish constables never interfered with wreckers, and on occasions when the borough police were employed on salvage duty they had to go armed to protect themselves against the hostility of the neighbouring villagers. In Cornwall, public opinion was so well disposed towards wreckers, and so superstitiously hostile to shipwrecked sailors, that the coastguard were frequently intimidated and forced to desist from their efforts to save life. It is related how, on one occasion, after communication had with much difficulty been established with a stranded ship by means of the rocket apparatus, the onlookers rushed down and cut the hawser when only one man had been saved, because they believed that if the crew was rescued, ill-luck would befall the district.

The Commissioners' summing-up on this part of [284]the subject was couched in the following words: "It is our duty to report, as the result of the extensive inquiries we have made, as to the mode in which the primary duties of a civilized community, in the protection of the persons and property of wayfarers and strangers, are performed, that the barbarous practices above described are not confined to particular districts, but prevail among the population of our coasts wherever wrecks occur...."

Another matter which occupied the attention of the Commission had reference to the lawlessness prevailing in the manufacturing districts. As is well known, the introduction of machinery, or, more correctly speaking, the quarrels and consequent cessation of work to which the innovation gave rise, brought much suffering to the wage earning classes. In 1826 the hand-weavers of Lancashire rose in rebellion, and the combinations entered into by the operatives in mines and factories were at first remarkable for the extreme violence of the methods employed, being signalised by an epidemic of machine-breaking in some counties, and by the crime of vitriol-throwing in others. The right of every man to sell his labour at his own price, or to cease work altogether if it pleased him to do so, was at this time recognised, and the legality of combination was no longer denied; but the organizers of labour were not willing to grant to the independent artisan the same measure of liberty that they demanded for themselves and for those whom they claimed to represent. The result of this attitude on the part of the leaders of trades-unionism was that cases of coercion, accompanied by [285]violence, were of common occurrence, and the need of an efficient police force to protect life and property, as well as to prevent intimidation, was very urgent. In this connection the Commissioners remark "some of the strongest corroborative evidence in favour of the efficiency of a well-organized constabulary or police force, might perhaps be found in the extreme bitterness of invective with which the parties implicated in illegal practices in these districts treat any proposition for its introduction, whilst they view with complacency any actual increase of the military force." The "illegal practices" above referred to had their origin, not only in differences between employers and employées, such as the rate of wages and hours of labour, but certain organizations, confident that they were stronger than the representatives of the law, presumed to take the law into their own hands, and to dictate terms right and left. At Sevenoaks, in Kent, a colony of journeymen paper-makers determined to pay no poor-rate, and terrorised the local constables when they came to levy distress. The authorities having sought the assistance of the Metropolitan police, a small party was dispatched from London, which, though savagely attacked, succeeded in arresting some of the rioters. On their return they proposed to take one of the local constables with them to identify the prisoners, but he was so alarmed at the consequences of incurring the vengeance of the paper-makers, that he tried to escape, and could only be induced to accompany the victorious policemen by counter threats of personal violence.

[286]

Scanty as was the protection afforded to the well-to-do, the chief sufferers under the parochial system were the very poor. Inability to pay for a substitute compelled a poor man, whatever his trade or employment, to serve in person, if chosen as constable; and it was seldom that the fees he could honestly earn in his office recouped him for the losses he was certain to sustain in his business. Again, if a labourer had anything stolen from his cottage, he had to put his hand in his pocket for half-a-crown, or more, before he could employ a parish-constable, and should there be no committal, all the expense of the investigation and subsequent proceedings fell on the man whose only offence had been that he had lost his property; and even when the offender was convicted it sometimes happened that the circumstances made it impossible for the magistrate to allow full expenses. The injustice of such a state of affairs is well illustrated by a case heard at Devizes in 1853, the details of which were as follows: a poor man had a pair of boots stolen from his barge, he followed the thief into Somersetshire, and after a long chase, caught him and handed him over to the nearest constable, who conducted the culprit back to Wiltshire, where at the ensuing Sessions he was convicted and sentenced. The constable's bill amounted to £4, 16s. 7d., made up as follows:—

To apprehending prisoner	£0 2 6
Maintaining do. two days	0 3 0
Guard-watching do. one night	0 2 6
	————
Carry forward,	£0 8 0
Brought forward,	£0 8 0[287]
Conveyance of prisoner at 9d. a mile, and allowance to Constable 8d. a mile (37 miles)	2 12 5

Three days' loss of time	0 15 0
Hire of conveyance, coach, and other fares	1 1 2
	————
Total	£4 16 7

but because the offender, a boy, was convicted under the Juvenile Offenders Act, which only authorized an allowance of forty shillings for expenses, there was a deficit of £2, 16s. 7d. to be made good by the man who had lost his boots.

The reluctance of the public to prosecute, which, as we have seen, was one of the many avenues of escape open to the criminal, was only to be expected, and was due rather to a defective system than to any lack of what is called public spirit. At a time when punishments were vindictive, men sympathized with the prisoner, and could with difficulty be induced to appear against him; this was especially the case when the community at large, and not any particular individual, had suffered injury. When the severity of the penal code was mitigated, it still remained unfashionable to prosecute, partly from force of habit, partly because the public which had no confidence in the police, would not willingly incur the trouble and danger of taking an active part in the administration of justice, but chiefly because the expense of putting the law in motion was prohibitive for all but the comparatively [288]wealthy. Well aware of their impunity, tramps would enter cottages at an hour when the owners were at work in the fields, steal the supper from the cupboard, and perhaps take a coat from behind the door, confident that poor people could do nothing to further the ends of justice as long as the first question asked by the parish constable was sure to be "Who is going to pay me?"

Even when thieves were caught red-handed, and delivered over to the constable, the informant was frequently tempted to think better of it, and either let the matter go by default or compound with the prisoner. In 1837, within a space of seven months, 201 persons, taken into custody for felony, were discharged without trial, simply because the parties concerned refused to prosecute, and out of this total as many as 53 were well-known thieves.

Under these circumstances it is not to be wondered at that from all parts of England suggestions poured in, urging the necessity of provision being made for the appointment of a public prosecutor, suggestions which were emphatically echoed in the report of the 1839 Commission. In Scotland, it may be mentioned, such an official, called the Procurator Fiscal, had existed for some time, with the most beneficial results, whilst in London, the Metropolitan police undertook similar work in the public interest.

Amongst many contributing causes which were answerable for the breakdown of the parochial system of police, the chief was undoubtedly the incompetency of its agents. Frequently a pauper [289]would be chosen constable, either with the idea of saving expense to the parish by keeping down the poor-rate, or from a misdirected impulse of charity, which prompted people to give the appointment to an old man who could earn his livelihood in no other way. Sometimes the parish constable would add the business of master of the village alehouse to that of policeman, a comfortable arrangement which, if not otherwise advantageous, at least produced perfect harmony between the representative of the law and the representative of the trade.

Justice, so called, was administered in a haphazard, and often in a ludicrous, manner. In one country town constables were instructed to arrest all vagrants, and after having their heads shaved at the local gaol, set them at liberty; in another district the magistrates ordered parish constables to tap with their staves the pockets of all labourers they might meet after dark, in order to break any pheasants' or partridges' eggs that might be concealed there; a Bedfordshire farmer who had given offence to a gang of poachers was shot in broad daylight on the public road, and in the view of several persons, but the assailant was not arrested, the constable excusing himself from acting on the plea that he did not think himself justified in apprehending anybody without a warrant. A return from the City of Lincoln, on the other hand, described how an over-officious parochial constable "brought two men in handcuffs to the police station at Lincoln for a trifling squabble and assault, which he did not [290]witness, and without any previous information or warrant."

Complaints against constables, on the score of their neglect to pursue criminals, came from all parts of the country. A return from a Monmouthshire village reported the escape of a murderer which was solely due to the refusal of the constable of the tything of Colgive to get out of bed at midnight, though "repeatedly and urgently called upon" to do so; and in another country parish, the constable, when summoned to quell a disturbance, sent word to say that he regretted that he was unable to come himself "but that he sent his staff by bearer." At Welchpool the wife of a shopkeeper poisoned her husband, and the same night eloped with the shop-assistant. The Coroner's inquest returned a verdict of wilful murder against the guilty couple, but no pursuit was made for several days, and then only after the magistrates and others, scandalised at such a miscarriage of justice, had got up a public subscription to defray the expenses of the constable's journey.

The apathy of those who were responsible for the policing of rural England produced its natural result; and, in the absence of adequate Government protection, people who were not content to submit quietly to be robbed by any scoundrel who preferred plunder to labour, made their own arrangements for self-protection. In 1839, there were upwards of five hundred voluntary associations for the apprehension of felons; of these associations some only concerned themselves with the financial side of the question, [291]and by a system of mutual assurance guaranteed compensation, in part at least, to any member of the society who had suffered loss by theft or arson; others took a more active part against depredators, and revived the ancient institution of Hue and Cry in a practical manner by binding themselves to make quick and fresh pursuit on horseback after any aggressor. During a parliamentary election at Maldon, one party was compelled to employ a bodyguard of professional boxers to protect its candidate from the attacks of political opponents, who, in their turn, retained the services of a band of gypsies, as a measure of retaliation. But perhaps the most irregular of all these associations was that established in the Isle of Ely, where the parishioners of Whittlesea kept a pack of blood-hounds for the purpose of hunting down sheep-stealers. After carefully considering the operations of these societies for self-protection, the Special Commissioners unanimously condemned such expedients, and stated, that in their opinion, "the fact that they had been found necessary was as serious an indictment as could be preferred against the rural police," and remarked, that the existence of such associations might, in after years, be cited as a proof that the community which employed them was relapsing into a state of barbarism.

The prostrate condition of English police under the parochial system should be sufficiently clear without the production of further evidence. What, however, is perhaps the most convincing proof, that [292]could be found, of the utter futility and unseemliness of the police arrangements in rural districts, is contained in the following plain statement from the magistrates of the Trant division of Sussex, on the subject of the lack of proper lock-ups for the temporary detention of prisoners. "In case," they complain, "a prisoner is remanded for further examination, there is no efficient place nearer than Lewes (23 miles) ... there are cages in several parishes but never used being unsafe ... for twenty years we have been compelled to hire a man, and handcuff him to the prisoner, and they are obliged to live at a public house.... Two incendiaries were each locked to men hired for the purpose, and kept at a serious expense ten days, separately in different houses." Some sixty years ago a comic engraving was published, which portrayed a prisoner handcuffed to his gaoler, undergoing a mock trial in the taproom of an alehouse for the amusement of the village tipplers. Such an incident may well have happened, at a time when it was no uncommon occurrence for a constable to confine his prisoner in a stable, or to chain him to a bedpost, until it might be convenient to remove him to a distant lock-up.

In concluding their comprehensive and interesting report, the Commissioners (Colonel Rowan, Mr Shaw Lefevre, and Mr Edwin Chadwick) strongly recommended the immediate establishment of a paid rural constabulary throughout England and Wales, with an organization similar to that of the Metropolitan police, and pointed out, that in order to lessen the expense of the proposed establishment, [293]the new constables might conveniently perform various civil and administrative services, in addition to their normal duties connected with the maintenance of the peace.

Shortly after the presentation of the report, an Act of Parliament, commonly called "The Permissive Act,"[206] was passed, enabling a majority of the Justices in Quarter Sessions, to raise and equip, at their discretion, a paid police for the protection of their county. Justices who decided to take advantage of the Act were empowered to appoint a chief-constable, and delegate to him the power of appointing, directing and disciplining a sufficient number of police constables, the expense of the force to be charged against the general county rate.[207] Adjoining shires were permitted to unite for the common purpose of policing the larger area; and if any county refused, as a whole, to avail itself of the facilities now afforded, any division of that county might maintain a separate police force; provision was also made for the voluntary amalgamation of existing borough forces with any country constabulary, that might thereafter be appointed in the immediate neighbourhood.

The permissive character of the "Rural Police Act" has often been adversely criticised, sometimes, perhaps, without due allowance being made for the difficulty of the problem which confronted the government. It cannot be denied that, judged by [294]its immediate results, the Act was largely a failure, and it is equally certain that its ill-success was consequent upon the free choice between adoption and rejection allowed to local magistrates; but it must be remembered that the power of the government in this matter was far from being unrestricted, the only possible alternatives before the authorities being, the policy of making a small beginning, and the policy of doing nothing at all.

Reference has already been made to the difficulty of securing satisfactory recruits for the metropolitan police, and the available supply had been still further reduced by the demands made upon it to satisfy the necessities of the boroughs. An endeavour to provide simultaneously the whole of England and Wales with efficient police-officers would have been to attempt the impracticable, whilst knowingly to admit inferior men into the ranks of the new constabulary would have been to condemn it irretrievably. Nor was the lack of suitable material the only reason why a cautious plan of campaign was necessary and inevitable; the same spirit of obstinate opposition which had been encountered and nearly overcome in London was, to some extent, apparent in the counties; country gentlemen, besides being indisposed to favour any innovation that threatened their personal supremacy so near home, were strongly opposed to any additional burden being thrown on the county rate. The press, without repeating the bitterness displayed in 1829, added its influence to that of the county magnates, and the idea that any reform of the rural police was at all necessary was [295]scouted by people who ought to have known better; the very men who a year before had testified to the increase of rural crime, now declaring that any interference with the existing machinery for its suppression would be disastrous. Amongst the many objections put forward, some were not very complimentary to the "great unpaid;" it was argued, for example, that the county justices were comparatively harmless so long as they wielded that blunt instrument, the parish constable, but should they be armed with a sharp weapon, such as the police-constable was admitted to be, no man could foresee the damage that would result.[208]

Whilst public opinion remained in ferment the Government was surely well advised to act with caution, by making the adoption of the Act dependent upon the consent of those whom it was designed to benefit. In this way much opposition was disarmed, and the care of the infant institution was entrusted only to those who voluntarily undertook it.

Between 1840 and 1856 the history of rural [296]police divides into two branches: in the counties which adopted the Permissive Act, the record is one of almost constant progress towards efficiency; in the counties which preferred to prolong the defective régime of the parish-constable, the story is largely one of stagnation, unnecessary friction, and weak-kneed experiment. Although these tendencies are so diverse, the migratory habit of criminals makes it impossible to follow the history of either to the exclusion of the other. No police system can rightly be considered without constant reference to neighbouring systems, because every improvement in the police of one district immediately increases the difficulties of every adjacent district. The result of the Permissive Act was precisely what might have been expected, and the situation may be summed up in the single phrase—crime follows impunity. The influences of pride and local jealousies proved powerful enough to prevent a complete recantation by those counties which had pinned their faith to the *status quo ante*, but they were not sufficiently potent to produce insensibility or indifference when the day of reckoning came. County magistrates, who in 1840 had refused to set their houses in order, were ready to embrace almost any expedient by the end of 1842. By this time they were only too glad to accept the services of police officers, trained in London or elsewhere, and to entrust them with the task of supervising the local constables. One of the chief reasons why parochial constables had become so useless, was because there was no one [297]to keep them up to their work. The office of High-Constable (finally abolished in 1869) had long been purely nominal, and Justices of the Peace could hardly be expected to devote much time or trouble to the unpleasant task of extracting service out of unwilling agents. In country towns where watchmen were employed, it was usually the constable's duty to oversee the watchman, but it was found by experience that the business was so indifferently performed that a plan, known as the "clock system" had, in many places, been introduced. This method of supervision consisted of a mechanical contrivance, in the shape of a clock with a revolving face: the watchmen were instructed to pull the chain attached to the clock every time they passed any of the machines during the night. In the morning, the constable would visit the clocks, and note the hours at which the chains had been pulled; but as a matter of fact the check on the watchmen was valueless, because subsequent inquiry showed that one man could easily attend to three or four clocks. In the more remote country districts watchmen were seldom or never employed, and no responsible person conceived it to be his particular business to supervise the comings or goings of the parish-constables.

Under these circumstances, an attempt was made in 1842 to infuse new life into the decrepit parochial system by an Act[209] of Parliament, which ordered Justices of the Peace to hold special sessions for appointing proper persons to act as parish constables, and which authorized the employment of new functionaries called Superintending Constables to have [298]the management of Lock-up Houses, and also the supervision of all the parish-constables within the Petty Sessional Division of the county for which they might be appointed—such superintending constables to receive a fixed salary out of the County Rates.

The Superintending Constable system was given a fair trial; most of the counties in England and Wales which refused to adopt the Permissive Act employing trained stipendiaries to look after their unpaid and amateurish parochial constables. That the compromise proved a comparative failure must be attributed not to the shortcomings of the officers selected, but to the impossibility of the task they were required to perform. Individually, superintending constables were often meritorious officers, and they proved so far useful that a substantial improvement was soon apparent in the police of nearly every county which employed them; but their exertions, however great, were doomed to failure because the very unpromising material they had to manipulate was proof in the long run against the limited powers they were allowed to exercise.

Without asserting that parish constables were altogether hopeless, it may be said without fear of contradiction that only the strictest discipline could have sufficed to render them efficient; but the sole punishment a superintending constable could inflict on a refractory subordinate was the very mild one of reporting him to the Justices, who, in their turn, were powerless to administer anything like adequate correction. To expect a parochial constabulary to learn efficiency voluntarily from a superintending [299]constable living in their midst, was as unreasonable as it would be to look for knowledge in a schoolroom where a scholar without authority is the teacher.

Whilst this want of control was the chief element of weakness, it was not the only fault of the system under consideration. For effectual action, responsibility should be centred if possible in the hands of one individual, or at all events not equally divided between a dozen or more participants; yet in counties where the system of superintending constables obtained, there was no uniformity or general plan, but the officer of each petty sessional division took his own line, and as long as he put in an appearance at the Sessions, and visited the various parishes of his district once a fortnight, no one interfered with him, or directed his method. It was the custom for the county to provide each superintending constable with a horse and cart, but, even with this convenience, the districts were frequently too large for any one man to supervise; in Kent, for example, a certain division contained as many as fifty-six different parishes, whilst in Northumberland the normal area of a single police district was about three hundred square miles.

Despite its obvious defects, the system was popular: not on account of any hidden virtue which it may perhaps have possessed, but simply because the small initial outlay required to start it made it look cheap: opposition to the alternative system, on the other hand, though it assumed many garbs, had its root and origin in the [300]false economy which hopes to avoid paying for the measure of security which it knows to be indispensable.

The pioneer county, as far as stipendiary police is concerned, was Cheshire, where a paid constabulary was already ten years old when the Permissive Act was passed.

At the time of the formation of the metropolitan police, Sir Robert Peel was anxious to make trial of a similar organization in the country. His efforts were successful in so far that he obtained the necessary parliamentary sanction[210] and induced the County Palatine of Chester to appoint an experimental force; once established, however, he was unable to exercise any control over its destinies, and the first rural police developed along lines never intended by its author.

The only point of similarity between the Metropolitan and the Cheshire Constabularies was that they were both stipendiary bodies; the county was divided into nine police districts, six of which were identical with existing Hundreds; each district was under the supervision of a High-Constable, assisted by from six to eight petty constables. The whole scheme, therefore, was conceived on a paltry scale; the petty constables were not selected with sufficient care, they were not graded, and they wore no uniform; responsibility was not vested in the hands of any one man, and internal jealousies rendered impossible that co-operation, which is so necessary to the efficiency of the whole.[211] One of the reasons [301]why Cheshire was selected as a trial ground, was because rural crime was more prevalent in that county than elsewhere; but although some lessons of value were acquired for future application, as a result of this experiment, it must be confessed that the Cheshire Constabulary were hardly more successful in preventing crime than the parish constables had been.

Among those counties which were wise enough to take immediate advantage of the Permissive Act, the lead was quickly taken by Essex, which had the good fortune to entrust the control of its rural police to a really brilliant chief-constable in the person of Captain M'Hardy, a retired naval officer, who had already done good work for the Coast-guard service. Taking "efficiency with economy" for his motto, Captain M'Hardy was able to achieve results which proved that a really well-managed force could be made self-supporting, or in other words that an efficient constabulary saves and earns as much as it costs. The strength of the rural police in Essex averaged about one constable to every fifteen hundred of the population, and the gross expenses, which included the erection and maintenance of suitable station-houses, were from the first considerable; yet the chief-constable claimed that the net annual cost of the whole establishment was only £80, 6s. 3d. This sum is surprisingly small, but not so incredible as, at first sight, it may appear. The figures (which are printed at length in an Appendix to the 2nd Report of the Select Committee appointed in 1853) were arrived at by placing on the debit side of the [302]account the gross amount expended for all police services, and on the credit side, the total savings and earnings effected by their agency. The largest credit taken was an item of five thousand pounds odd on account of the decrease of vagrancy, and the second largest, one of nearly four thousand pounds on account of the estimated increase in the value of land, calculated at the rate of only one penny per acre.[212]

The practical difference between the working of the parochial system and that of the rural police could find no better illustration than that afforded by a comparison of the extent of vagrancy respectively existing under the two systems. Formerly parish-constables served at a loss unless crime was plentiful, and their interest therefore lay towards the encouragement rather than in the prevention of offences. It is not suggested that parish constables, as a class, were in the habit of deliberately manufacturing crime, but instances not infrequently came to light which proved that such practices were not so exceptional as they ought to have been. We have it on the authority of the Vagrancy Commission, that a regular system of fraudulent collusion between constables and tramps was common as recently as the year 1820.[213] It appears that at this time parish constables were entitled to ten shillings for apprehending a vagrant, upon proof being shown that the [303]latter had either solicited or received money, and the fraud consisted in a compact between the two by which the constable first gave the vagrant a penny, and having arrested him as a beggar, claimed the reward, which was ultimately divided between the conspirators.

Under the rural police system such a state of affairs was impossible. Constables were paid a regular salary, and had no interest in crime except to prevent it by every means in their power: prevalence of crime in any district meant extra work and less chance of promotion for every policeman concerned.

Of the many excellent arrangements introduced by Captain M'Hardy, with a view to reducing the expense of the Essex constabulary, none was so successful as the plan of employing constables as assistant relieving officers for casuals. The resulting advantage was twofold. The prospect of having to interview a policeman acted as a moral check upon vagrancy, and the constable acquired in this way an extensive and first-hand acquaintance with the members of a fraternity professionally interesting to him. The success of this experiment, with which was associated the supervision of low lodging-houses, astonished even its strongest adherents; a comparison of the vagrancy returns for 1848 and 1849 (the year of the initiation of this policy) shewing a decrease amounting to ninety per cent. in the number of indoor, and to seventy-seven per cent. in the number of outdoor vagrants, the gross figures being 24,882 for 1848, and 2977 for the following year—this result was achieved, moreover, without relief being [304]refused, as far as could be discovered, to a single pauper who was really destitute.[214]

The Essex constabulary was also the first to undertake the supervision of Weights and Measures, thus saving the salaries previously paid to the old inspectors who were inefficient, and saving the pockets of labouring men who were the chief sufferers by short weight. The extent to which false measures used to be employed can only be conjectured; but it is a fact that, when in 1845 the rural police of Wiltshire took charge of this department, in no less than 14,942 instances were defective weights and measures discovered. Further savings were effected in Essex under the headings of, conveyance of prisoners, prevention of fire, excise duties, etc., etc., whilst private associations for the apprehension of felons died a natural death wherever the maintenance of the peace was entrusted to the new police.

The effect of the admirable force established in Essex was to compel the adjoining counties of Suffolk, Hertfordshire and Cambridgeshire reluctantly to follow suit, and in other parts of England and Wales rural police were gradually appointed. By May 1853, twenty-two counties had adopted the Permissive Act, seven counties had partly adopted it, and twenty-two counties (including two Ridings of Yorkshire) continued the parochial system, with or without Superintending Constables.

A return dated 1853 shews the progress that had been made—

- *For the whole County*—Bedford, Cambridge, Durham, Essex, Gloster, Hertford, Lancaster, Leicester, Norfolk, Northampton, Nottingham, Salop, Southampton, Stafford, Suffolk, Surrey, Wilts, Worcester, Cardigan, Carmarthen, Denbigh, Montgomery.
- *In parts only*—Cumberland, Dorset, Rutland, Sussex, Warwick, Westmoreland, York.
- *Counties not adopting the provisions of the Permissive Act* —Berks, Bucks, Chester, Cornwall, Derby, Devon, Hereford, Huntingdon, Kent, Lincoln, Monmouth, Northumberland, Oxford, Somerset, Anglesey, Brecon, Carnarvon, Glamorgan, Merioneth, Radnor, Flint, Pembroke.

Three years later the distribution was still much the same, only two counties having remodelled their police in the interval. Unfortunately there was little uniformity of system throughout the twenty-four police forces now established: some counties framed their regulations on those of the Royal Irish Constabulary; others adopted an independent attitude; Lancashire was unlucky; Cheshire was unique; and only Hampshire and Cambridgeshire were humble enough to take full advantage of the excellent model designed by Captain M'Hardy.

The confusion resulting from this patchwork arrangement was put an end to by the second great Rural Police Act, passed in 1856, "to render more effectual the police in Counties and Boroughs in England and Wales." This measure, commonly called the "Obligatory Act," enacted that where a Constabulary had not already been appointed for the whole of a County, the magistrates were forthwith [306]to cause such a force to be appointed for the whole or residue of that County, as the case might be; and further, that the police forces of all Boroughs containing five thousand inhabitants or less were to be consolidated with the police of the County wherein such Boroughs might be situated. An annual statement respecting crime in Counties was required to be transmitted by the magistrates (a similar statement for Boroughs to be rendered by the Watch Committees), to the Secretary of State for the Home Department, in order that an abstract of the same might be presented to Parliament. Provision was also made for the appointment of Inspectors of Constabulary, with authority to visit and enquire into the state and general efficiency of the police in the several Counties and Boroughs, and to report thereon to the Secretary of State. On a certificate from the Home Secretary that the police force of any County or Borough was efficient, a sum not exceeding one-fourth part of the total cost of pay and clothing for such police force was to be paid by the Treasury.[215]

The effect of this Statute was, for the first time, to provide every part of England and Wales with stipendiary police, thus completing the process which had been initiated at Bow Street more than a hundred years before. The Metropolitan Police Act, the Municipal Corporations Act, and the Permissive Act, valuable and indeed indispensable as they undoubtedly were, had been effective only in certain districts: delinquents, whom the activity of the metropolitan [307]police had driven out of London, found a home in other large towns; a second migration followed when the Boroughs got their police; and yet a third took place, as we have seen, after the partial introduction of rural constabularies. If it is true that the degree of impunity looked for has more to do with the amount of delinquency prevailing than the want of life's necessaries, or any other factor, it is not a matter for surprise that a large army of vagrant thieves continued to ply their trade as long as there remained twenty counties and scores of small towns where no interference with their illegal pursuits was to be anticipated, and to which they might return after a successful raid to safely dispose of their plunder.

The Obligatory Act tended to reduce crime in many ways, for not only did a criminal career become much less attractive after the last Alsatia had been closed, but the efficiency of all existing police bodies was enormously increased by the uniformity and co-operation between different units which naturally followed upon the compulsory adoption of one general system through the whole country. Local control was not interfered with by this Act, but a certain standard of excellence was set up and maintained by means of the government grant—the withholding of which as a punishment for inefficiency, took the place to some extent of the amercements once levied against districts whose police had been found wanting. And finally, the vexatious restrictions which prevented constables from acting outside the narrow limits of their constablewicks, were removed [308]by the clause which gave County constables the same powers in Boroughs as Borough Constables enjoyed in Counties, thus restoring (in a form improved by modern aids, such as the postal service and the electric telegraph) a power similar to that which our English police long ago possessed, of carrying the Hue and Cry from township to township, and from shire to shire "untill the offender be apprehended, or at the least untill he be thus pursued to the seaside."

[309]

CHAPTER XVI
CO-OPERATIVE POLICE AND THE SUPPRESSION OF RIOTS

When the new police was first introduced, the promoters of the scheme did not look beyond the creation of a local force, sufficient to protect life and property in the metropolis and its immediate neighbourhood. No doubt Peel intended that his police should serve as a model to other forces which he hoped to see established throughout the kingdom; but it was no part of his plan that the Metropolitan Police should be extended until the whole of England was policed by a homogeneous organization administered from a central bureau in London. Such a result, however, was at one time imminent, and would have become inevitable if the process had not been arrested by the timely reforms in County and Borough, described in the last chapter; reforms which, besides helping towards the general reduction of crime, prevented also the threatened centralization, by securing to provincial districts the control of their own police.

As the Metropolitan Police increased in numbers and efficiency, it began to lose its strictly local character, and to become a national police. Up to a certain point this was to the public advantage, but it would have been calamitous if the tendency had been [310]allowed to continue beyond that point. It is obvious, however, that after the failure of the Permissive Act in 1839, the retention of local control, so desirable on many grounds, was only rendered possible by making the abolition of the parochial system universally compulsory.

As a matter of fact, the powers of making additions to the Metropolitan District, acquired in 1839,[216] were only taken advantage of to a very small extent, and the growth of the Metropolitan Police was almost entirely confined within the limits originally assigned to it. In 1840 the Houses of Parliament and the London Docks were taken over; next came the Woolwich and Deptford Yards; Woolwich Arsenal, and Greenwich were incorporated in 1843; then the Tower of London, and finally the Royal Dockyards (Portsmouth, Devonport, Chatham, and Pembroke Dock) were policed by the Metropolitan force in 1860. The entire establishment, which in June 1830 was 3314 of all ranks, had risen to 5625 in 1852, and ten years afterwards a new division (X) was created to deal with the crowds which were expected to visit the second International Exhibition. In 1864 the total strength was 7113. Colonel Rowan resigned in 1850, and in 1856 the two Commissioners were replaced by one Commissioner (Sir R. Mayne) and two Assistant Commissioners.

At first no steps were taken to fill the gap caused by the disappearance of the Bow Street Runner, and the Popay incident discouraged the Commissioners [311]from venturing on what was felt to be dangerous ground. The lack of a detective service was a great source of weakness, and so in 1842 a new department, especially devoted to this very necessary branch of police work, was instituted by Sir James Graham, and attached to Scotland Yard.

A small staff was selected out of the uniform branch to form a nucleus. At first the department only consisted of three inspectors and nine sergeants; soon afterwards six constables were added, and gradually the numbers were increased until in 1878 the whole detective service was reorganized, and the Criminal Investigation Department created.

At the time when the Metropolitan force was the only efficient police in the kingdom, individual officers, it may be remembered, were often sent to the provinces, on loan or permanently, to assist in the formation of similar organizations in other parts of England; this of course was right and proper, and was attended by the best results. Subsequently, the practice arose of temporarily drafting large bodies of London policemen to keep the peace in distant districts wherever disturbances were feared, a course of action sound enough in theory perhaps, but seldom found effectual when put to the test of experience. An English mob quickly resents high-handed interference, and will not tolerate at the hands of strangers the same degree of repression it would quietly submit to from local peace officers.

Several examples might be given of the ill-success which has almost invariably attended the employment of London police in the provinces; but the [312]following is selected as a particularly well-defined instance. In the summer of 1839 a force of Metropolitan policemen, about ninety strong, were dispatched to Birmingham, to over-awe the turbulent crowds which, it was feared, might proceed to extremities if their demands were not complied with. When the police arrived in the town, a noisy public meeting was in progress at the Bull Ring, but no overt act of violence had as yet been committed. The Superintendent in charge of the constables peremptorily ordered the crowd to disperse; his summons was as positively disregarded, and within five minutes blows were exchanged. In the melée which followed, the police were worsted, and the situation was barely saved by the opportune appearance of the military. On the ensuing Monday evening, a second conflict took place, in which the policemen were victorious, though at the expense of an increase of bitterness on both sides. A spurious semblance of peace having thus been restored, fifty constables returned to London, and only forty were left to deal with any recrudescence of disorder; for this they had not long to wait, as an attempt to break up a public meeting, a few days later, was followed by the most serious consequences. After destroying some iron palisading which surrounded the Nelson Monument, the crowd, now animated by a worse temper than before, made weapons of part of the débris, and drove the small force of constables to take refuge in the police-yard. For the next hour and a half the town was at the mercy of the rioters, who, having begun by [313]smashing lamps and windows, ended by pillaging shops and warehouses.[217] Eventually the police charged the mob with drawn cutlasses, and, assisted by dragoons, got the upper hand; shortly afterwards the police were withdrawn, and the task of keeping order was entrusted to a strong levy of special constables locally enrolled, who succeeded in maintaining the peace where their more professional *confrères* had failed. There is little doubt but that these riots might have been avoided, or at least mitigated, had no strangers been introduced to quell them.[218]

An isolated fact seldom proves anything; but it will be allowed, without the production of additional evidence, that the Birmingham fiasco affords sufficient proof that the Metropolitan Police had not yet learnt the art of managing an angry crowd. There are, no doubt, many occasions on which it is desirable to transfer bodies of police from one place to another in order to concentrate the forces of law and order at some threatened or strategic point, but in so doing the danger to be apprehended from the resulting increase of local animus, ought to be taken into account, and adequately provided for.

[314]

The valuable, if not indispensable, nature of the services which may be rendered by Special Constables when directed towards the suppression of riots, already indicated at Birmingham in 1839, was more fully exemplified in 1848, when the Chartists assembled at Kennington Common, threatened to descend upon London. The fear that the Metropolis might be subjected to an access of anarchy similar to that which bestowed an evil notoriety on the Gordon Riots, gave rise to preparations for defence on an unprecedented scale. At this crisis not less than two hundred thousand citizens enrolled themselves as Special Constables; the Metropolitan Police were told off to guard the bridges; and all available troops were held in reserve, mostly in houses on the Middlesex side of the river. The Duke of Wellington took command of this huge police army, and so perfect were his arrangements that, without the display of a single redcoat, the rioters outside dared not advance to the attack, and their sympathisers within dared not make any diversion in their favour.

The whole subject of the policing of riotous and riotously disposed crowds is of the highest importance; but being a science in itself, its many aspects cannot be discussed in a book which only professes to tell briefly the story of police development in this country. At the same time, if we are to appreciate correctly the bearing of one fact upon another, if we hope to draw intelligent conclusions, it is impossible [315]to avoid altogether what may be called the semi-scientific side of the question. In order to estimate the efficiency of any police force, to decide, for example, whether its failures are due to faulty organization or to bad generalship,—it is not sufficient to have an acquaintance with a mass of facts, dates and figures, but a key is required to read the cipher, some guide is necessary to assist in arranging the known factors in the order of their relative importance.

An indifferently directed force may be capable of dealing in detail with isolated offenders; but the problem of pacifying a combination of peace breakers may induce a strain which will find out the faulty link in all but the most highly tempered organizations. Just as a concerted breach of the peace by a number of persons is disproportionately more serious than an independent breach by any individual, so also do police duties take a higher range as soon as it becomes necessary to concentrate the energies of a number of constables for the attainment of a common object. If he is to employ his constables to the best advantage, a superior officer of police must have some knowledge of the general laws that sway men when they are assembled together in great numbers, those "volcanic forces" which, in the words of an American writer, "lie smouldering in all ignorant masses."

Men have a gregarious instinct which, under the influence of excitement, induces them to herd together without any definite object and often at great inconvenience to themselves; the progress of the resulting congestion is normal until a certain [316]point is reached, the point at which entirely new forces begin to act. When this moment arrives, all self-control is repudiated, decent and orderly men become desperadoes, cowards are inspired by a senseless bravado, the calm reason of common-sense gives place to the insanity of licence, and unless the demoralising tendency is checked, a crowd rapidly reaches the level of its most degraded constituent. The explanation of these phenomena is probably to be found in an excessive spirit of emulation aroused under conditions of excitement, which makes a man feel that the responsibility for his actions is no longer to be borne by himself, but will be shared by the multitude in which he has merged his identity. It is the business of the police to exhaust every art in a sustained effort to prevent the ferment from reaching the critical stage, and to watch the crowd so narrowly that the first symptom of violence may instantly be suppressed. This can best be accomplished by local constables who are acquainted with the persons and names of individual members of the crowd, while it is of even greater moment that the constabulary should not be the first to give offence, or contribute to a breach of the peace by the use of exasperating language or aggressive action.

The problem before the policeman operating against a riotously disposed crowd is somewhat similar to that which confronts the soldier in the face of the enemy, and it was on this account that the Metropolitan force was given a semi-military organization. In some respects, however, the policeman's [317]task is the more difficult of the two, chiefly because he has to strive for peace whilst actually engaged in conflict; the soldier at least enjoys the advantage of knowing his own comrades, whereas the constable is often unable to distinguish friends from foes, and continually runs the risk of converting the former into the latter. Whilst the greatest possible latitude must be allowed to individual constables, the secret of success lies in mutual, not in independent action, and for mutual action to exist, there must be discipline and intelligent direction. When the use of force can no longer be delayed, the plan adopted by the officer in command should be easy of accomplishment, simple of comprehension, and its success should leave the law-breakers at a strategical disadvantage sufficiently obvious to convince them of the futility of further resistance. Nothing is so fatal as vacillation: partial success leads on a mob to the commission of fresh excesses, partial repression only aggravates it. It is far better to leave a crowd altogether alone, than to sustain even an apparent defeat. Force is no remedy unless it is unswervingly and unhesitatingly applied; and as it is comparatively immaterial in what direction repression is exercised so long as it is consistent and irresistible, it is usually good policy to divert the energies of the mob towards the line of least resistance. It is more efficacious, for example, to keep a crowd moving in some definite direction, than to dissipate the strength of the police in attempts to arrest ring-leaders, to seize banners or the like, which may degenerate into a series of disconnected single combats not uniformly [318]favourable to authority. Any apparently uncalled-for attack may convey the impression of wanton outrage, and so tend to defeat the object in view, by increasing that state of irritation and excitement which it is the principal duty of the police to allay. Many branches of police science which to-day are in the common knowledge were unheard of and unsuspected during the first half of the nineteenth century. This is particularly the case with regard to that part of the constable's duty which has to do with the management of crowds: before 1830 there were only two methods of dealing with a riotous mob, the first was to leave it severely alone, and the second was to allow a regiment of cavalry to trample it into submission. No government worthy of the name is justified in adopting a policy of non-interference at a time when the lives and property of law-abiding citizens are in preventible jeopardy, and the disastrous consequences that may follow upon the employment of the second method were sufficiently advertised (to cite two instances only) by the Bristol Riots and the so-called Peterloo Massacre.

London police and London crowds are now renowned all over the world, the former for the general excellence of their arrangements, and the latter for their almost invariable good humour. Perhaps the credit is not always fairly apportioned, for it is not too much to say that the good humour of the crowd is more often due to the admirable tact of the police than to any inherent virtue that exclusively resides in Londoners. At first the [319]police were hardly more successful in suppressing riots than the soldiers had been: in Birmingham as at Coldbath Fields, events shewed that the unpopularity of the new constabulary went far to neutralize the undoubted superiority naturally possessed by a civil, over a military, force for the purposes of peace maintenance. As time went on, and as police and public came to understand each other, riots became less frequent, and conflicts less bitter, until the harmony which now so happily exists was arrived at. If it is allowable to talk of a turning-point in a process which is gradual, this point was reached soon after the disturbances which commonly go by the name of the Sunday-Trading-Bill Riots. Though not accompanied by any loss of life, nor followed by those unsparing attacks on the conduct of the police that had embittered the Coldbath Fields controversy, the collision which took place in July 1855, between the Metropolitan Police and a mixed London crowd, were serious enough to stir up much of the old animosity, and to prove that, if the policeman was no longer an object of active dislike to his fellow-citizens, neither could he as yet lay claim to any great measure of popularity.

The disturbances in question arose out of the following circumstances. Lord Robert Grosvenor had introduced a bill, the object of which was to prevent all buying and selling within the City of London and metropolitan police district on Sundays. Popular feeling, which ran high against the measure, found expression in a variety of ways, some serious and some serio-comic. The point of view of the [320]masses was not badly summed up in these lines:

"Sublime decree, by which our souls to save

No Sunday tankards foam, no barbers shave,

And chins unmown, and throats unslaked display,

His Lordship's reverence for the Sabbath day."

Unfortunately the opponents of the obnoxious bill did not confine themselves to versification, but caused handbills to be circulated, announcing that on the 24th of June, an open-air meeting would be held in Hyde Park "to see how religiously the aristocracy observe the Sabbath, and how careful they are not to work their servants or their cattle on that day." The result of this manifesto was that, at the time mentioned, a mob assembled near the Serpentine, but the demonstration did not assume serious proportions, the crowd contenting themselves with hooting and jeering at those who were taking their afternoon ride or drive in the Park.

Throughout the following week, certain persons continued the agitation, and, by means of placards, summoned their sympathisers to meet them on the next Sunday in Hyde Park, where it was announced that "the open air concert and monster fête, under the patronage of the Leave-us-alone Club will be repeated." Another appeal was of a more personal nature and ran as follows, "Let us go to Church with Lord Robert Grosvenor next Sunday morning. We can attend his lordship in Park Lane at half past ten, go to Church with him, then go home to dinner, and be back in time to see our friends in [321]Hyde Park. Come in your best clothes, as his lordship is very particular."

These handbills and placards having been brought to his notice, Sir Richard Mayne replied by publishing a proclamation requesting well-disposed persons not to attend the proposed meeting, at the same time warning all concerned that steps would be taken by the police to prevent the meeting being held, and that, if necessary, force would be employed to maintain the peace.

Undeterred by this notice, thousands of people entered the Park on the afternoon of Sunday the 1st of July, drawn thither, some by curiosity, some for purposes of recreation, some with the fixed determination of resisting the police. Certain precautionary arrangements were made by the Chief Commissioner, and orders were issued to the effect that any persons shouting or frightening horses, or attempting to address the crowd, were to be cautioned as to the consequences of their action and required to desist, the police being instructed to remove, and if necessary take into custody, any who persistently refused to obey their orders.

As on the previous Sunday, the disturbances commenced with hooting and shouting, but the police who, in obedience to orders, were lying down on the grass, did not interfere; at about half past three, the crowd began to assume a more threatening attitude, and things began to look serious. A dense mob was gathered along the railings and across the carriage way, stones were thrown at carriages, some wooden hurdles were broken up, and the fragments [322]used as missiles, whilst the crowd continued to hoot, whistle and make discordant noises, with the object of frightening the horses.

The Superintendent in charge, thinking that the time for vigorous action had arrived, ordered the police to draw their truncheons and clear the roadway. Whilst this order was being carried out, a considerable number of people who did not give way with sufficient promptitude were struck and some knocked down. The mob now turned upon the police, making insulting remarks, throwing stones, and repeatedly attempting to break the line of constables, who retaliated by making short rushes and taking into custody all who offered resistance. Victory eventually rested with the police, but desultory fighting continued throughout the afternoon, and it was not until six o'clock in the evening that the commotion in the neighbourhood of the Drive subsided.

Whilst the main crowd was being dispersed, a mob some 400 strong, with cries of "Now to Lord Robert Grosvenor's," left the park, and proceeded to Park Street, and at the same moment another body made their way to the Magazine Barracks, where they amused themselves by throwing stones at a small party of Grenadiers stationed there. The sergeant in command sent to the police for assistance which was promptly rendered, and quiet was soon restored.

Meanwhile the constables in Park Street were endeavouring to persuade the crowd, who had gathered in force in front of Lord Robert's house, [323]to disperse quietly, but when their efforts proved of no avail, and when cries of "Chuck him out" and threats of violence were raised, the reserves previously stationed at Stanhope Gate were moved up, and the street cleared by force. In this encounter truncheons were again used, and numerous minor injuries inflicted, but only one arrest was made.

By nine o'clock the police were withdrawn, all disturbance being at an end. In the course of the day forty-nine policemen were reported hurt, and on the other side seventy-two persons were taken into custody and removed to Vine Street Police Station, ten of them being charged with felony, and the remaining sixty-two with riotous conduct or with assaults on the police.

Unfortunately the accommodation at Vine Street was altogether insufficient for such a large number of prisoners, the cells ordinarily in use were soon filled, and then recourse was had to an underground room, formerly the place of confinement attached to the old parish watch-house. Into this prison, which was dark and badly ventilated, were crowded forty-three persons, ten of whom were subsequently removed, but the remaining thirty-three had to spend the night (which happened to be unusually sultry), standing up, or lying on the damp floor as best they could. Many of the prisoners were respectable people, unused to dirt and discomfort, and their sufferings must have been considerable.

The Inspector in charge of the Vine Street Station, somewhat tardily communicating with Sir Richard Mayne, informed him of the overcrowded state of the cells, with the result that thirty-one prisoners out [324]of the original seventy-two were removed to neighbouring stations by order of the Chief Commissioner. In the course of the next two days, all the accused were brought before the magistrates, when twenty-nine, or nearly half the number, were discharged, the remainder being fined or sentenced to short terms of imprisonment.

The conduct of the police in Hyde Park, and the treatment of the prisoners at Vine Street, having given rise to serious allegations and to much adverse comment in the public press, the Government decided to hold an inquiry into the matter. Three Commissioners were appointed, and given full powers to investigate and report upon the occurrences of the 1st of July and the following days. In the course of the inquiry, several attempts were made to discredit Sir Richard Mayne; some accused him of slackness for not personally directing the police in the park, whilst others held that he was over-officious in not leaving the crowd alone altogether. The responsibility for the overcrowding at Vine Street was laid to his charge, and it was suggested that he failed in his duty, in that he did not go to the police station, and, by virtue of the powers vested in him as a Justice of the Peace, admit to bail those prisoners who were not charged with felony, and who might be able to find sufficient guarantee for their future appearance.

Of these charges, which were made by people who seemed to think that any stone was good enough to throw at the chief officer of police, the two first, when taken together, were mutually destructive, besides [325]being silly when considered separately; whilst the suggestion that Sir Richard Mayne ought to have admitted certain of the accused to bail, was not to the point, because it had been clearly laid down by Statute when the office was first created, that any exercise of the powers of a Justice by the Chief Commissioner of Police was to be strictly confined to his duties connected with the preservation of the peace.

The net result of the labours of Her Majesty's Commissioners was to establish, beyond a doubt, that certain constables had been guilty of unnecessary violence; that the Superintendent in charge, losing his head, or his temper, or both, had authorized stronger measures than the circumstances of the case warranted; and that blame attached to the authorities at Vine Street for the mismanagement which caused the detention of a far larger number of prisoners than there was accommodation for at that station. On the other hand, it was proved that the large majority of the police had acted with moderation and good temper throughout a long and trying day in spite of the continued attempts of the crowd to harass and annoy them; and that the measures adopted for the preservation of the peace had on the whole been successful, in so far that a mob many thousands strong, bent on mischief, had been effectually controlled and prevented from doing any material damage worth mentioning.

From the evidence as a whole, it is clear that the accusing witnesses (and they were very numerous,), must have been guilty of much exaggeration when describing the violence with which they said the [326]police had acted; since in a conflict lasting several hours, in which it was alleged the constabulary used their truncheons unmercifully, sparing neither age nor sex, no life was lost, no limb was broken, nor was any permanent injury inflicted. On the other hand, many witnesses voluntarily came forward to testify to the good behaviour of the police, not only on this particular occasion, but generally in all their dealings with the public.

The promptitude with which the inquiry was granted, and the thorough and impartial manner in which it was carried out, was attended by the happiest results, and did much to foster friendly relations in the future between police and public; the latter were reassured that Government would not tolerate, much less countenance, any excesses committed by the police, upon whom again it was impressed that even a disorderly mob must be treated with a certain amount of consideration, and that high-handed interference would lead to the punishment of the offending constables.

A minor improvement which originated from this inquiry may, in passing, be noticed. Hitherto a constable's number had been surrounded by a scroll of embroidery that made it difficult to decipher except at very close quarters, so that identification was often rendered impossible: to rectify this, the plain metal figures now worn by constables on collar and helmet were introduced.

The Sunday-Trading Bill riots were quite unimportant as riots, and yet their influence upon the future of the police was very great, because [327]the inquiry which followed illuminated a question that had been obscured by ignorance and prejudice, causing misconceptions to be removed on both sides, and a better understanding and mutual appreciation to be substituted, with the result that the metropolitan force soon began to be popular in quarters where it had previously been hated. The best proof of its efficiency, so far as the management of crowds is concerned, may be found in the fact that, during the first forty years of its existence, the peace was so well maintained, that the damage done to property by rioters was quite insignificant, and this without the intervention of the military; whilst in witness of the moderation of the methods employed by the police in the attainment of this result, it need only be stated, that in every conflict which occurred during the same period, the personal injuries sustained by the aggressors were invariably less severe than those suffered by the constables, though the latter were all men of exceptionally fine physique, and were armed with truncheons. In the course of the Reform riot which took place in Hyde Park in the year 1868, two hundred and sixty-five policemen were wounded out of a total of 1613 actually on duty, "and one Superintendent, two Inspectors, nine sergeants, and thirty-three constables were so severely injured as to be rendered unfit for duty, many for life," yet "the police behaved with the most admirable moderation and not a single case of unnecessary violence was proved against them."[219]

There is a saying that the strength of the Man [328]in Blue lies in the fact that he has the Man in Red behind him. This of course is superficially true, in so far that in the event of a riot or other disturbance, with which the local police is for any reason unable to cope, a sufficient number of troops will be called out to assist the civil arm. But the saying is not true if any suggestion of an offensive alliance between constabulary and soldiery is intended; nor is it true if it is meant to give the impression that there is a potentiality of physical force behind the policeman, which, under any circumstances whatever, could be exerted to coerce the nation at large.

The members of the English police are public servants in the fullest sense of the term; not servants of any individual, of any particular class or sect, but servants of the whole community—excepting only that part of it which in setting the law at defiance, has thereby become a public enemy. The strength of the Man in Blue, properly understood, lies in the fact that he has behind him the whole weight of public opinion; for he only wages war against the law-breaker, and in this contest can claim the goodwill of every loyal citizen. If a police constable is in need of assistance, he can call upon any bystander, and in the King's name demand his active co-operation; should the bystander refuse without being able to prove physical impossibility or lawful excuse, he can no longer be considered as a loyal citizen, but is guilty of an indictable offence and becomes liable to punishment.

The basis upon which our theory of police ultimately rests, is the assumption that every lawful [329]act performed by a police officer in the execution of his duty, has the sanction and approval of the great majority of his fellow-citizens; and under our constitution it would be impossible for any constabulary force to continue in existence, if its actions persistently ran counter to the expressed wishes of the people.

The actual continuance of the English police is therefore dependent upon the consent of the people; but this mere acquiescence is not enough. If the police are to be efficient, they must earn for themselves the respect and sympathy of all classes, they must be popular. It is only on the rarest occasions that a policeman is actually the eye-witness of a crime, nor in the nature of things is he likely to be in the confidence of the criminal. As a rule he must rely on information, and generally speaking the public is the only source from which the necessary knowledge can be obtained. If the public are hostile, the one source of information is closed, and the police are rendered powerless. This difficulty has often been experienced in Ireland, where, on several occasions, it has proved a practical impossibility to discover the authors of agrarian crime, even when all the facts were well known to dozens of people, simply because the whole neighbourhood had entered into a conspiracy of silence. Such a manœuvre instantly paralyzes the civil executive. In the olden days, when an offence had been committed and there was no culprit forthcoming, a fine was levied against the hundred or hundreds implicated, and justice was satisfied; in mediæval times, the "peine [330]forte et dure" was employed to elicit information; but since the abolition of torture no effectual method has been invented by means of which an unwilling witness can be forced to tell what he knows; in Ireland, especially, the inducements held out by Government, to tempt a man to speak, are of little avail against the terrorism that the other side can invoke by the mere whisper of the word "informer."

But there are other reasons, besides this important question of obtaining information, why a measure of popularity is of such extreme value to every police force. There are a thousand ways in which the members of an unpopular service can be embarrassed and thwarted. No matter how capable and painstaking a man may be, he cannot do himself justice, nor can the best results attend his labours, if his every act is questioned, and if at every turn he has to surmount some obstacle set up to annoy and discourage him. The constabulary has been described as "The great army of order that is always in the field"; the protracted campaign in which this army is engaged is under all circumstances extremely arduous, but it becomes doubly so when its operations have to be conducted in an enemy's country.

We demand intelligence, good personal character and great physical strength from those to whom we entrust the duties of peace maintenance; and if we are to obtain men of the right stamp, men, that is, who possess these qualifications, it is essential that the police service should be held in popular esteem, and that the position of a constable should be sufficiently well thought of, and sought after, to create a keen competition for the vacancies as they occur. It would never do to have to beat up recruits for the constabulary forces, and to fall back on the expedients that the military authorities have to resort to to fill the ranks, nor to enlist immature lads in the hope that some day they will grow into well-developed men.

From every point of view, then, popularity is of the utmost value to the police; and yet, from the very nature of their duties it is extremely difficult for them to win it. A policeman who will lend himself to the screening of crime, or who is conveniently blind on occasions, may quickly become the object of a worthless and fleeting popularity; but it is not the friendship of the publican nor the applause of the rabble that is desirable; what is wanted is the respect and approval of all good citizens.

Year by year, in spite of occasional set-backs, the English police have risen in the estimation of their fellow-countrymen until they have won for themselves a position in the minds of the people which for respect and regard combined is without a parallel in Europe. "Weak in numbers as the force is," wrote Mr Munro, the late Commissioner of Police for the Metropolis, "it would be found in practice altogether inadequate were it not strengthened, to an extent unknown, I believe, elsewhere, by the relations that exist between the police and public, and by the thorough recognition on the part of the citizens at large of the police as their friends and protectors. The police touch all classes of the public at many points beyond the performance of their sterner duties as representatives of the law, and they touch them in a friendly way.... The police in short, are not the representatives of an arbitrary and despotic power, directed against the rights or obtrusively interfering with the pleasures of law-abiding citizens: they are simply a disciplined body of men, specially engaged in protecting 'masses' as well as 'classes,' from any infringement of their rights on the part of those who are not law-abiding."

The wisdom of fostering cordial relations between the people and the civil defenders of their lives and properties seems so obvious, that it is a source of wonder that so little attention has been given to the study of how best to promote this desirable *entente cordiale*. Before the new police was instituted constables were merely despised; after the re-organization was completed they were generally feared and often hated; the fact that they won their way to popularity is to be attributed almost entirely to their own merits. At the beginning of the century Colquhoun, who was a long way in advance of his contemporaries in his conceptions of what a police force should be, wrote: "Everything that can heighten in any degree the respectability of the office of constable, adds to the security of the State, and to the safety of the life and property of every individual," but at the time only a very few people heeded what he said; and parish authorities persisted in the idea that it did not matter who or what a constable was so long as he was cheap, whilst in more recent years, politicians of a certain stamp, who ought to be alive to the fatal consequences of their action, have not scrupled to try and stir up bad blood between the constabulary and the uneducated section of the public, whenever it has suited their purposes to do so, though happily without much success.

If the co-operation of which we have been speaking is to be complete, it should rest on a more substantial basis than goodwill: it is not sufficient that private citizens should be well-disposed towards their allies, it is necessary also that they should be acquainted with the conditions that govern the mutual relationship. The sphere of police utility is seriously limited by reason of the ignorance which commonly prevails, both as to the executive powers that private persons can assume as citizens, and with respect to the functions that officials may exercise by virtue of their office. In his "History of the Criminal Law," Sir James Stephen thus explains the position. "The police in their different grades are no doubt officers appointed by law for the purpose of arresting criminals, but they possess for this purpose no powers that are not also possessed by private persons.... A policeman has no other right as to asking questions or compelling the attendance of witnesses than a private person has; in a word, with a few exceptions, he may be described as a person paid to perform as a matter of duty acts, which if he so minded, he might have done voluntarily."[220] The law on the subject is further defined [334]by another authority in these words. "If a constable be assaulted in the execution of his office, he need not go back to the wall, as private persons ought to do; and if, in the striving together, the constable kill the assailant, it is no felony; but if the constable be killed it shall be construed premeditated murder."[221] For all practical purposes, however, the only real difference that exists between the powers that are actively made use of by the police, and the latent powers that are vested in every British citizen, is this:—A police officer may arrest (without warrant) if he has a reasonable suspicion that a felony has taken place; a private person cannot arrest unless he has certain knowledge that a felony has actually been committed.

Within these limits, and according to our opportunities, the duty of each one of us is clear and inalienable, remaining the same to-day as it was in the time of Queen Elizabeth, when it was written "So that every English man is a sergeant to take the thiefe, and who sheweth negligence therein do not only incurre Evil opinion therefore, but hardly shall escape punishment."[222]

[335]

CHAPTER XVII
POLICE STATISTICS AND PENOLOGY

Attention has already been directed to the excessive zeal of the opponents of the "New Police"; but no mention has been made of those enthusiasts who looked for an instant millennium to follow upon the adoption of the measures they advocated. Yet there were many such who formed extravagant hopes too high for realization. It is seldom easy for the observer to arrive at a just estimate of the value of a new institution until his standpoint is far enough removed from the stress of the moment to secure him from the current partisanship which every novelty arouses. We, however, who have crossed the threshold of the twentieth century, can disregard the extreme views of both parties, and heedless of the outpourings of admirers and detractors alike, can gauge the issue by the light of ascertained results, supported by facts and figures. Judged by this standard, and viewed from the standpoint of to-day, the police reforms inaugurated between 1829 and 1856 will be found to justify all reasonably conceived expectations, disappointing as they no doubt appeared to over-sanguine extremists at the time.

[336]

Since the ideal standard of excellence aimed at by every properly constituted police force is the complete prevention of crime, and as there can be no record of offences prevented, it is obviously impossible to arrive at an entirely satisfactory conclusion as to the efficiency of police by means of any arithmetical process. At the same time it will be allowed that if, whilst population increases, recorded offences are a stationary, or better still if they are a diminishing quantity, there is at least strong presumptive evidence that the result is largely due to the efficiency of the established police. Unfortunately there is no infallible method of discovering the amount of criminality existing in the country at any given time; but, of all available statistics, the best for our purpose are certainly those, which give the annual total of commitments for indictable offences from 1834 until the present day. Before 1834 the records are not altogether trustworthy; but the Parliamentary Committee which sat in 1828, stated that in the ten years between 1811 and 1821, during which the average increase of population was about nineteen per cent., the average increase of commitments for the same period was no less than forty-eight per cent. There can therefore be no doubt that prior to the establishment of the new police the increase of crime was outstripping the increase of population; but taking only those figures which are generally acknowledged to be correct, we get the following interesting table.

[337]

Census Years.	Population.	Number of Commitments.	Proportion.
1841	15,914,148	27,760	174·6 per 100,000
1851	17,927,609	27,960	156·2 " "
1861	20,066,224	18,326	91·3 " "
1871	22,712,266	16,269	71·6 " "
1881	25,974,239	14,704	56·6 " "
1891	29,002,525	11,605	40·0 " "

Such is the remarkable result obtained by taking the whole number of indictable offences sent for trial at Assizes and Quarter Sessions in each Census-year since 1834, nor is there any reason to suppose that the process of amelioration has slackened to any appreciable extent during the last decade. When the Census returns for 1901 are published it will probably be found that the population of England and Wales now totals to about thirty-two millions; and assuming that the amount of crime committed during the current year is not abnormal, the number of commitments will work out at a little more than thirty for every hundred thousand inhabitants. That is to say, during the last sixty years, serious offences have decreased nearly sixty per cent. in actual volume, and some eighty per cent. if considered relatively to population—or in other words, between two-thirds and five-sixths of the type of crime, which sixty years ago brought men to trial, is now prevented. These figures, of course, deal with detected crime only: if it were possible to include all grave offences, irrespective of whether their authors were discovered or not, the results [338]would be even more striking, because owing to the increased activity on the part of the police, and to the greater readiness to prosecute on the part of the public, comparatively few serious crimes now remain mysteries for any length of time. Calculations based on the number of offences disposed of by Courts of Summary Jurisdiction are valueless if the object in view is to estimate the prevalence of crime, because not only are new minor offences continually being created (thus rendering such returns too intricate for purposes of ready comparison) but the inclusion of trivial breaches of the Licensing Acts, Education Acts, Vaccination Acts &c. reduces the plane of the enquiry from one which deals only with crimes to one which is mainly concerned with misdemeanours.

If we confine our attention, therefore, to the Commitment Returns, the most noteworthy feature which strikes us, is the drop between 1851 and 1861—the decade in which the Obligatory Act gave the *coup-de-grâce* to the parochial system, and for the first time covered the whole of England and Wales with a network of stipendiary police. At first sight it would appear that here was cause and effect, that is, that the signal improvement indicated by these statistics was primarily due to the Act of 1856; it is more likely, however, that the result must, in the main, be placed to the credit of the police reforms of the previous decade, for reasons which will presently appear.

In view of these eminently satisfactory figures, it [339]may well be asked how it came about that those persons, who most firmly believed that security was only to be attained through police instrumentality, were so grievously disappointed at the imaginary failure of their pet scheme. In order to find the answer to this question it will be necessary to probe a little deeper into the statistics, and to do so by the light of contemporary events. In the first place it is to be remarked that a closer inspection of the Commitment Returns reveals the fact that a reaction took place between 1860 and 1863, the figures for those years reading as follows:

1860 15,999

1861 18,326

1862 20,001

1863 20,818

This result was due, no doubt, to the combined effects of two distinct causes, one of which produced an actual growth of crime, whilst the other accounted for what was but an apparent increase of delinquency. If it is true that crime was more common than before, it is no less true that offences were more commonly detected, the apparent increase being the necessary result of the efficient action of the newly organized Constabularies, which, naturally enough, did not take full effect until the whole machine was in proper working order. Before preventive police can develop its maximum deterrent energy, it has to prove its title to respect by its success in the detection of crime; criminals do not search the Statutes at Large, nor judge of the efficiency of a policeman [340]from government statistics.[223] They take him as they find him, and learn to fear him only after they have acquired a practical familiarity with his activity, either by personal contact, or vicariously, through the misfortunes of acquaintances. The significance of the heavy Calendars in the early sixties, therefore, is largely discounted by the fact, that the accumulations of former years had to be dispersed, before entire responsibility for the amount of crime prevailing could be laid at the door of the new régime. With regard to the second reason for the despondency above referred to, it must be remembered that offences against property so outnumber other offences, that they entirely dominate all criminal statistics; whilst the public alarm occasioned by a single case of robbery involving personal injury to an individual, is infinitely greater than that caused by a whole series of depredations on property if unaccompanied by violence. In the quinquennial period (1857-1861), the number of persons for trial at Assizes and Quarter Sessions, charged with murder, attempted murder, manslaughter, felonious wounding, malicious wounding and assault, amounted to 1451; whilst in the next quinquennial period (1862-1867), the number of commitments for these offences had risen to 1712; and herein lay the [341]*raison d'etre* for the widespread alarm which, in 1862 and 1863 especially, may be said to have amounted to panic. Not only were such crimes more frequent than had formerly been the case, but they began to be marked by a degree of violence[224] which argued that a peculiarly desperate class of criminal was abroad; and such indeed was the actual state of affairs, occasioned by the temporary breakdown of the penal system and consequent upon the discontinuance of the practice of shipping the most dangerous criminals across the seas.

Before the abolition of transportation, the career of the criminal was generally brief unless he confined his attention to petty depredations, or unless he was particularly skilful in avoiding capture; a felon once caught was given little chance of repeating his offence. If he escaped the gallows he was as a rule removed from the scene of his temptations, never to return; and the labours of the police were far less arduous as long as distant colonies were content to absorb the dregs of our population, and as long as the press-gang claimed a large proportion of our vagabonds and neer-do-weels. Impressment, however, practically ceased in 1835; and Australasia soon grew weary of the refuse which we were yearly depositing on her shores. Between 1840 and 1845 as many as seventeen thousand convicts were sent to Van Diemen's Land alone, and in one [342]year more than four thousand felons were transported to Australia: the result was that the supply exceeded the demand, and the colonists, though not blind to the advantages of a moderate supply of free labour, began to protest warmly against the wholesale importation of such eminently undesirable neighbours. A large public meeting was held at Sydney in 1850, at which it was unanimously decided to petition Her Majesty to procure the immediate discontinuance of transportation; the British Government at once consented, and after 1852 no more convicts were sent to New South Wales, Tasmania, or South Australia.[225] Morally bound, as it was, to comply with the request of the Colonists, the government found itself impaled on the horns of a dilemma: about nine thousand persons actually under sentence of transportation lay awaiting disposal in the Hulks, and the number was steadily increasing. It was impossible to set them at liberty; there was no room in the English prisons; and there was nowhere to send them to except Western Australia, which, though still willing to annually receive a certain proportion, was unable to digest such an accumulation. The demoralization which infected the ordinary gaols was as nothing compared to that which pervaded the Hulks,—filthy derelict vessels crowded with unclean and abandoned mortals who were allowed absolutely [343]free intercourse with each other, and who were subjected to no supervision beyond that exercised by a sentry or two with loaded muskets.

In this emergency extra prison accommodation was hurriedly provided. Portsmouth prison was opened in 1852; Dartmoor (originally designed for the detention of French prisoners-of-war, but long disused) was converted into a convict establishment in 1855, and a new prison at Chatham was made ready in the year following. In this way the immediate necessity was partially relieved; but for the complete solution of the difficulty, a radical reform of the whole penal system had to be devised. Convicts who had been sentenced to transportation could not in common fairness be detained in English prisons for the whole period of their sentences, and there was no law which authorized any remission. Prisoners felt that they had a grievance, and mutinous outbreaks occurred at Dartmoor, Portland and Chatham.[226] Under these circumstances a "Penal Servitude Act"[227] was introduced, which provided that henceforward penal servitude was to be substituted for transportation as the punishment for all offences too serious to be met by simple imprisonment, yet not of sufficient enormity to deserve a sentence of fourteen years; at the same time it was notified that those persons, then in confinement, who had been condemned to transportation were to be released with a free pardon after the expiration of [344]from half to two-thirds of their original sentence. In 1857 another act was passed, authorizing the Secretary of State conditionally to discharge convicts undergoing penal servitude in England, before they had served their full term. This system, popularly known as the Ticket-of-leave system, was sound in theory, and whenever properly administered has proved both beneficial to prisoners and harmless to society. But when first inaugurated it produced the most disastrous consequences. Under present conditions a convict can only earn remission by good behaviour and constant industry, generally leaving the prison a better man than when he entered it, even if he is not entirely reformed; whilst under the old conditions, incarceration corrupted the novice in crime, and still further hardened the habitual offender. The last hulk was closed in 1857, and a few years afterwards the effect of the unavoidable policy of turning loose unreformed gaol-birds was fully experienced, and the sequel made apparent in the criminal statistics of the period.

According to the intention of its authors, adequate police supervision over those who had been conditionally liberated on license was an essential feature of the Ticket-of leave system, but this was not the interpretation adopted by the Home Office, for on behalf of that Department, evidence was given before the Select Committee of 1856 to the effect that "it was thought far better to give no directions whatever to the police on the subject, but to leave them (*i.e.* the license-holders) precisely in the situation of men who had served out the whole period of [345]their sentence." On every ticket-of-leave issued, the following conditions were endorsed:—"Notice—(1)—The power of revoking or altering the license of a convict will most certainly be exercised in case of his misconduct. (2)—If, therefore, he wishes to retain the privilege, which by his good behaviour under penal discipline he has obtained, he must prove by his subsequent conduct that he is really worthy of Her Majesty's clemency. (3)—To produce a forfeiture of the license, it is by no means necessary that the holder should be convicted of any new offence. If he associates with notoriously bad characters, leads an idle or dissolute life, or has no visible means of obtaining an honest livelihood, &c.—it will be assumed that he is about to relapse into crime, and he will be at once apprehended, and recommitted to prison under his original sentence."

These conditions, admirable in themselves, were not enforced and so were practically useless. Ticket-of-leave men almost invariably destroyed their licenses (which they were not compelled to keep), and if apprehended for a fresh offence, or on suspicion, stoutly denied that they had previously been convicted; nor was it easy for the authorities to prove the contrary in the absence of any proper system for the registration of convicts. The helplessness of the police in the matter may be measured by the fact that constables were instructed on no account to interfere with ticket-of-leave men, "nor when seen in public houses are they to be pointed out to the landlord, and required to leave, as in other cases of convicted thieves and suspected characters." It was [346]of course only just that convicts released on license should not have their comings and goings continually dogged by constables; but to elevate them into a privileged class, and to place them on a higher plane than "suspected characters" who had never been convicted, was, in the words of Sir Richard Mayne, "to give them opportunities to commit crime which they might not otherwise have." The police were not to blame for this state of things, for they only carried out the instructions of the Home Office, which, again, did not feel justified in interfering with liberated convicts unless authorized to do so by Act of Parliament. To shew how entirely the police authorities dissociated themselves from any responsibility for the supervision of licensees, it may be mentioned that, in his evidence before the Select Committee of 1856, the Chief Commissioner of Police for the Metropolis made the following confession. "It may appear strange for me to say so, but until a few months ago I never saw a ticket-of-leave, and did not know what was endorsed upon it:—it was no business of mine."[228]

Fortunately this state of affairs was not allowed to continue indefinitely. Various reforms, extending over a series of years, were successively taken in hand with the object of making penal servitude reformatory as well as retributive, of ensuring that convicts released on ticket-of-leave should remain under police supervision until the expiration of their sentences, of arresting the criminal career of juvenile law-breakers by means of reformatories and industrial [347]schools; and of protecting society, as far as possible, from the repeated ravages of incorrigible offenders, by instituting a system for the thorough identification and registration of criminals. The history of these reforms must be briefly sketched.

Of all the abuses which used to disgrace our penal establishments, the most disastrous in its results, was the promiscuous herding together of male with female, adult with juvenile, habitual with casual offenders, under conditions calculated to lower the tone of the whole prison community to the level of the most degraded inmate. The evils inseparable from unchecked association of felons in confinement were recognised even in the eighteenth century; and Bentham, Howard, and other reformers persistently urged the adoption of the "separate" system for all English prisons. Ultimately the Government was induced to make the experiment, and in 1821 Millbank Penitentiary was opened for the reception of prisoners. A long delay followed, and not until 1840 was the first stone of the next model prison laid at Pentonville. Both Millbank and Pentonville were constructed on the "radiating" principle which admits of the constant exercise of perfect supervision over all the prisoners, who are, however, confined in separate compartments. The expense of the new establishments, as well as a popular prejudice against solitary confinement due to its too rigorous enforcement in Pennsylvania, retarded progress, and although a few gaols of a modern type were here and there constructed, the large majority of those convicts who were not transported, were allowed to corrupt each [348]other in the old-fashioned local prisons. This policy of inaction continued until 1865, when the "Prison Act" was passed, which requires that every male prisoner shall be accommodated with a separate cell, and which insists on uniformity of treatment for all persons (except first-class misdemeanants and debtors) undergoing a sentence of two years' imprisonment or less.

We have already seen how the gradual discontinuance of transportation (1838-1867) and the abolition of the hulks (1857) caused "Public Works Prisons" to be established at Dartmoor, Chatham, etc. At these places, (where prisoners undergoing penal servitude are incarcerated) the plan of silent associated labour by day, with separate confinement by night, was adopted; and although no relaxation of discipline was allowed, the reform of the criminal, rather than his punishment, was aimed at. Under the modern system the convict spends the first nine months of his penal servitude at Pentonville, or in some other local prison, and during this period is kept to solitary hard labour of an irksome and unproductive description; he is then moved to one or other of the "Public Works Prisons," where his life at once becomes less monotonous. As long as his conduct merits advancement, he is passed through various stages, each more tolerable than the last; most of his work is now done in the open air and in the company of his fellows; and hope lightens his labour, for by constant industry and by an exact observance of the prison rules, he is allowed to earn a partial remission of his sentence, amounting to [349]about a quarter[229] of the whole term. Our penal system may not yet be perfect; but during the late reign prison life underwent a marvellous metamorphosis. Pest-houses have been transformed into sanatoriums where the patients have to submit to a healthy discipline beneficial to the mind as well as to the body; formerly gaol-fever, dirt, and bad food ruined the constitution, whilst evil communications corrupted the mind; now convicts leave their prison physically robust and often morally convalescent. This amelioration of the conditions to which prisoners are subjected has been accompanied, *pari passu*, by a steady decrease in the number of convicts in confinement. When Queen Victoria came to the throne, 43,000[230] of her subjects were convicts, at the present time they number less than 6000,[231] and this in spite of the fact that during the interval the population of these islands has just about doubled itself.

Whilst the reform of the adult and hardened convict is of very high import, the welfare of society is even more profoundly influenced by the result of its efforts directed towards the prevention of crime in the first instance; and the value of prevention (which by common consent is at all times higher than that of the best possible cure) may be said to bear an inverse ratio to the age of the individuals who are saved from committing themselves to a career of crime. The surest method of permanently reducing [350]the number of criminals lies in the comprehensive employment of agencies especially devoted to the prevention of juvenile delinquency. Anti-social habits formed in childhood are in after years only eradicated with the greatest difficulty, the criminal child too often being the father of the criminal man. During the latter half of the eighteenth, and early in the nineteenth century, the manufacture of juvenile criminals went on apace. Bow Street Runners on the look-out for blood-money were careful not to interfere with a promising youngster until he had actually committed a felony; parish constables would not trouble to pursue a culprit upon whose conviction only half expenses were allowed; and the reluctance of the general public to prosecute was especially pronounced when the offender was of tender years. Meanwhile scoundrels of the Fagin type, trading on the impunity enjoyed by child-thieves, grew rich on the plunder collected by their pupils, who, sooner or later, received the finishing touches to their criminal education in the public gaols at the public expense. The extent of the evils which resulted are incalculable; but competent experts were of opinion that nearly sixty per cent. of habitual offenders had been initiated into their dishonest career before they were fifteen years of age.[232]

Private philanthropy interested itself on behalf of the children long before the Government made any move in the matter. In the eighteenth century a Marine Society for sending lads to sea, and an [351]agricultural school for teaching farming, had been formed at Portsmouth and Redhill respectively, with the object of befriending boys who otherwise were in danger of lapsing into crime; but for many years these were the only agencies of the sort. The Ragged School movement, so warmly espoused by Lord Shaftesbury, took practical shape soon after the Queen's accession, in schools in Westminster, at Old Pye Street, and at Field Lane. The first industrial feeding-school was opened at Aberdeen in 1841; and it proved so successful that the idea was taken up throughout Scotland. Before long Manchester and other English towns followed the example set by the granite city. Excellent as were many of the schools established by private benevolence, they all laboured under two very formidable disadvantages:—they could not compel unwilling parents to send their children to be reformed, or to contribute anything towards their maintenance, and they could not legally detain their pupils any longer than they cared to stay.

The first public institution for the detention of juvenile criminals was opened at Parkhurst in 1838. Though called a reformatory, it was in effect a gaol, and hardly differed at all from other prisons except with regard to the age of its inmates. The exertions of Lord Shaftesbury and of Mr Adderley (Lord Norton) who strove to convince the nation of the fatal consequences of its apathy, were soon to be rewarded. A Select Committee of the House of Lords which sat in 1847, was followed by the Juvenile Offenders Act of the same year; in 1851 [352]and following years conferences, largely attended by people interested in the reformatory question, were held at Birmingham, with the object of discovering some better method of dealing with youthful criminals than that in vogue, and the whole subject was investigated at some length by Parliamentary Committees appointed in 1853 and 1854. The result of these deliberations took shape in the latter year when the "Reformatory School Act"[233] was passed, giving magistrates the option of committing offenders under sixteen years of age to reformatories, for a term not exceeding five years, in lieu of sentencing them to imprisonment, penal servitude, or transportation. The expense of the new reformatories was met, partly by Treasury contributions, partly by grants from the local authorities, and partly by compulsory subscriptions of not more than five shillings a week exacted from the parents or guardians of the offending children. The Act of 1854 was amended and improved by subsequent Acts passed in 1855 and 1856, but these early enactments[234] were open to the objection that they only applied to juveniles who had already been convicted of a serious offence, and left untouched a large class of children which, for one cause or another, always stands on the brink of criminality;—for no juvenile was eligible for admission into a reformatory unless he had previously been committed to prison for fourteen days.

This omission was repaired by the "Certified [353]Industrial School Act" passed in 1857,[235] and amended in 1861,[236] which provided that certain young persons, who had not been in gaol, might be sent to industrial schools under a magistrate's warrant, to be detained therein until they should attain the age of sixteen. The class of children to whom this Act applied were described as follows:—"Any child apparently under the age of fourteen years, found begging or receiving alms ... any child ... found wandering, and not having any home or settled place of abode, or any visible means of subsistence ... or being an orphan, or whose only surviving parent is in prison ... or who frequents the company of reputed thieves ... or whose mother has twice been convicted of crime ... or whose parents represent that they are unable to control him, ... or any child apparently under the age of twelve years who, having committed an offence punishable by imprisonment or some less punishment, ought nevertheless, in the opinion of the Justices, regard being had to his age, and to the circumstances of the case, to be sent to an Industrial School, &c."

In 1854 only twenty-nine children were sent to reformatories. Since that date, the numbers so committed gradually increased until 1881, in which year the maximum (6738) was reached. The decrease which has recently taken place may be chiefly attributed to the fact that magistrates now generally prefer the industrial to the reformatory school whenever possible, a method of dealing with [354]youthful offenders the wisdom of which has been vindicated by an accompanying diminution in the tale of juvenile crime.

The essential differences between Reformatories and Industrial Schools are, that no stigma attaches to any boy on account of his having been educated at the latter, and that whilst the discipline enforced at the former institutions is sufficiently severe for them to be considered as places of punishment, Industrial Schools are intended only to take the place of that parental control and training which the child cannot obtain at home. The principle of giving another chance to unfortunates who are rather sinned against than sinning lies at the root of the Industrial School movement; and there is no development of preventive police more in sympathy with the wisdom of the age than this. In recent years the same principle has, with excellent effect, been extended to embrace adult as well as juvenile offenders. The Summary Jurisdiction Act of 1879[237] (*i.e.* so much of it as permits the infliction of a fine instead of imprisonment) and the Probation of First Offenders Act of 1887,[238] are both, it may be noted, conceived in the same wise and merciful spirit. The latter measure especially, which was introduced by Sir Howard Vincent, has been instrumental in reclaiming to an honest life hundreds of prisoners "guilty of a first offence not the product of a criminal mind."[239] The latest Home Office returns go to prove that, in the large majority of instances [355]in which this humane policy has been applied, confidence has not been misplaced; for of the whole number of first offenders conditionally released upon recognizances,[240] to come up for judgment when called upon, only about ten per cent. have shown themselves unworthy of the leniency extended to them by relapsing into crime.

The tendency of recent penal legislation has been to discriminate as closely as possible between the casual and the habitual offender, reducing to the lowest limit, consistent with safety, the penalties exacted against the former, whilst placing every legitimate obstruction in the path of the latter, by making his punishments cumulative as long as he continues to offend, and by maintaining a vigilant supervision over his conduct whilst he is at large. This is one of the most important duties that modern police have to perform, and it is one which demands great tact combined with persistence from individual peace officers, as well as complete co-operation between all the allied police organizations throughout the country. Under the parochial system both these necessary qualifications were conspicuously absent, and if transportation had suddenly come to an end before the police reforms described in previous chapters had been taken in hand, the unchecked excesses of habitual criminals might have endangered the very foundations of English society.

[356]

It will be remembered that when the ticket-of-leave system was first introduced, considerable alarm was occasioned on account of the increase of crime; which, not altogether without reason, was generally attributed to the license-holders, who, unreformed by penal discipline, and consequently unfitted for unqualified liberty, were suddenly released in large numbers, without any adequate precautions being taken to control them. We have seen how the reorganization of the entire prison system gradually eliminated the causes which tended to make the ex-prisoner even more dangerous to society on the day of his discharge than he had been before conviction, and we have seen how by the introduction of an improved plan of giving marks for industry (which, however, were subject to forfeiture for ill-conduct), only those convicts were released before the expiration of their full sentence who had earned partial remission by virtue of consistent good behaviour. We now come to a consideration of the measures subsequently adopted for the proper supervision of these ticket-of-leave men.

The conditions endorsed on every license have already been given, but as the police were expressly ordered to take no notice of liberated convicts, unless they were actually engaged in criminal pursuits, but little practical value attached to the wording of the ticket. In 1864 some important changes were introduced by the 4th Section of the Penal Servitude Act of that year, which requires that:—

- I.—The holder shall preserve his license, and [357]produce it when called upon to do so by a Magistrate or police officer.
- II.—He shall abstain from any violation of the law.
- III.—He shall not habitually associate with notoriously bad characters, such as reputed thieves and prostitutes.
- IV.—He shall not lead an idle and dissolute life, nor be without visible means of obtaining an honest livelihood.[241]

The penalties for the non-observance of these requirements were as follows—(*a*) Any ticket-of-leave man, convicted of an indictable offence, *ipso-facto* forfeited his license, and this in addition to any punishment to which he might be sentenced upon indictment; (*b*) Any ticket-of-leave man proved to have transgressed the conditions of his license by an act not of itself punishable either upon indictment or upon summary conviction, nevertheless rendered himself liable to be summarily punished by imprisonment not exceeding three months. In 1871 the "Prevention of Crimes Act,"[242] amending "The Habitual Criminals Act" of 1869, extended the principle of keeping notoriously bad characters under observation, by enacting that persons twice convicted of certain crimes may be subjected to police supervision for not more than seven years after the expiration of the sentence imposed, provided that a previous conviction for an offence in the same category is proved at the time of the second conviction. Such persons are commonly called 'supervisees,' and they [358]come under the same conditions as license-holders. These conditions have since been modified by Acts of Parliament passed in 1869 and 1891, and they may now be summarized as follows. Both ticket-of-leave men and supervisees are required to report themselves within forty-eight hours after their arrival in any police district to the Chief-Officer of Police in that district, to report themselves once a month afterwards,[243] and to notify any change of address to the same authority; they are also expected to satisfy the police that they are earning their living by honest means.

A constable is justified in arresting without warrant any license-holder or supervisee whom he reasonably suspects of having committed an offence, or of having failed to comply with the above-mentioned conditions; and if it be found, after investigation by a competent magistrate, that such an offence has been committed or default made, the license-holder thereupon becomes liable to the forfeiture of his license, and the supervisee to imprisonment with or without hard labour for a period not exceeding one year, unless he can prove to the satisfaction of the proper authority "that being on a journey he tarried no longer ... than was reasonably necessary, or that he did his best to act in conformity with the law."[244]

In order that police supervision may be safe and effectual, it is of course necessary that the identification of habitual criminals should be certain and the registration of convicts complete. The present [359]system would have been fraught with the gravest dangers to public liberty had it been attempted at the time when there was no possibility of any more reliable record than that founded upon the memories of policemen and prison-warders; but since the introduction of photography, and especially since the recent adoption of the system of anthropometry which is associated with the names of M. Alphonse Bertillon and Mr Francis Galton, the chance of any miscarriage of justice, due to mistakes in identification, has been reduced to a minimum. Photography was first adapted to police purposes in 1854, when the governor of Bristol Gaol began to make daguerreotype pictures of the prisoners who passed through his hands; and gradually what was at first but the experimental hobby of an amateur developed into the officially recognised system. The "Prevention of Crimes" Act (1871) had directed that registers of all persons convicted of crime in England should be kept at Scotland Yard, but it was soon found by experience that a less voluminous record would be of greater practical value. Accordingly it was decided in 1877 that, in future, the registers (the compilation of which was at this time transferred from Scotland Yard to the Home Office) should contain only the descriptions of habitual criminals, officially so called. In 1880 a new department was opened at the Head-Quarters of the Metropolitan Police, called the Convict Supervision Office, which was largely occupied with the classification of offenders by means of books containing the photographs of habituals. These albums, together with a register [360]of distinctive marks, including a record of tattooed symbols and initials so universal amongst criminals, formed a regular rogues' gallery, and were instrumental in proving the identity of many inveterate delinquents who might otherwise have improperly participated in the leniency intended only for first offenders.

Some of the more energetic police forces in the provinces, also, prepared local registers; and something like a general scheme for tracing the antecedents of criminals was evolved by means of circular "Route Forms" (as descriptions of offenders whose identity was uncertain were technically called) which were forwarded in rotation from one police district to another, wherever the required information was likely to be forthcoming. The results obtained, however, hardly justified the expenditure of time and energy incurred in the process; accordingly in 1893 a Parliamentary Committee was appointed "to enquire into the best means available for identifying habitual criminals," and it was on the recommendation of this expert committee that the perfect anthropometric system of identification now employed was based.

Very briefly stated, the system is as follows. All persons convicted of crime against whom a previous criminal conviction has been proved, or who are subject to police supervision, are carefully measured before they are liberated, and the results tabulated on what are called card-registers. The parts of the body selected for measurement are those which in an adult are the least liable to alteration; the length and breadth of the head, and the length of the foot, for instance, being reliable indicia by [361]means of which thousands of individuals may readily be classified.

Whilst M. Bertillon's system of anthropometry is especially well adapted for purposes of classification, Mr Galton's finger-print method is preferable for purposes of identification. The minute lines which may be noticed on the skin covering the under side of the top joint of the human finger or thumb invariably display a well defined series of curved ridges, which, though never quite alike in different subjects, always approximate to one of four types, that is to say, they assume the form of an arch, a whorl, a right loop, or a left loop. The sum of the combinations which can be formed of these types and their modifications on the ten digits being a practically inexhaustible quantity, every human being carries on his finger-tips an infallible record of his personal identity. Accordingly the criminal is required to make signature by pressing with his thumb, fore, and middle fingers of both hands (previously smeared with printer's ink) on the reverse side of the card-register; whilst to make assurance trebly sure, the exact location and measurement of any distinctive marks that may be found are noted, and his photograph, both full-face and in profile, is added. When completed, the card-registers are filed in cabinets on an ingenious plan which enables the searcher to lay his hand on any particular "dossier" in the space of a very few minutes.[245]

The immense importance of having a comprehensive and accessible record of this nature can hardly be over-rated, for without its help it would be impossible to combat (with any chance of success) what is unquestionably the most dangerous development of contemporary criminality. It has recently been pointed out by Dr Anderson, of the Criminal Investigation Department, that despite the marked decrease of crime which we congratulate ourselves has been one of the most noteworthy features of the Victorian era, "the professional criminal is developing and becoming a serious public danger."[246] Since the abolition of transportation the company of criminals who are criminal by deliberate choice has been steadily increasing, and every mitigation of the penal code, every alleviation of prison existence, has helped to bring recruits to the profession. Frequent sentences of imprisonment will never deter the delinquent who is well acquainted with the inside of a gaol, as long as he can count on brief spells of exciting and luxurious liberty between whiles; moreover the tax on the police is excessive, for the habitual criminal may be trapped again and again, only to be released time after time to devise new and more elaborate attacks on a long-suffering society.[247]

A way will have to be discovered to eliminate this unexpected product of our penal system, and to this end various suggestions have been made. Some advocate life sentences for persistent offenders; others would make the restitution of the plunder, or at any rate a confession implicating the receiver of the stolen property, the only condition of release in cases of theft; but although authorities differ as to the exact course which ought to be pursued, all agree that the character of the criminal rather than the enormity of his offence should chiefly determine the question of the punishment administered. Whatever may be the nature of the plan of campaign eventually decided upon for the suppression of professional delinquency, the preliminary stage of the operations is necessarily the same, and consists in the preparation of a record containing an accurate and concise account of the antecedents and previous convictions of all habitual criminals.

There was a time when "abjuration of the realm" was considered a complete expiation for crime however heinous; but as the outer world became more civilised, and foreign parts more accessible, voluntary expatriation ceased to be the recognised alternative to punishment. The first result of the introduction of railways in this country (as far as the relation of crime to police is concerned) was to benefit the fraternity of thieves whose trade is essentially one that thrives best under nomadic conditions; subsequently, with the development of modern conveniences for travel, the police were again placed at a disadvantage, this time by the facility with which criminals, who are generally able to obtain at least a few hours' start, could find a safe refuge from their pursuers in some haven oversea—the modern equivalent for the mediæval sanctuary. There has ever been, and always will be, a ding-dong contest between the lawbreaker and the policeman, wherein the fortunes of the day favour first one side and then the other; for if the advantage that attaches to the opening gambit belongs to the criminal, his adversary is soon ready with an answer. The telegraph[248] beats the steamship, and the international system of police which now mutually provides for the surrender of fugitive offenders has restored the balance. The first extradition treaty in which Great Britain was interested was concluded with the United States of America in 1842, and the Extradition Acts of 1870 and 1873 now regulate the conduct of the English Government in its dealings with foreign powers in all that concerns this important department of police.[249]

In 1879, a reform long agitated for was inaugurated by the tardy appointment of a Public Prosecutor, who became responsible that the cause of justice is not injured through the non-prosecution of persons guilty of serious offences. The intervention of the Director of Public Prosecutions is seldom deemed necessary, but circumstances occasionally arise in which lack of funds, local sympathy with the criminal, or an attempt to compound a felony, may demand his active interference.[250] The "Pro[365]secution of Offences Act"[251] directs that Chief Officers of Police shall notify to the Director, that is to say to the Solicitor for the Treasury, such particulars of certain specified crimes committed within their districts as are described in the regulations[252] issued for the guidance of all concerned.

CHAPTER XVIII
DETECTIVE POLICE AND THE RIGHT OF PUBLIC MEETING

It is popularly believed that the least efficient department of English police is that which is concerned with the detection of crime, and our detective service is often compared with corresponding agencies abroad in order to point the moral that we should do well to imitate the methods of our neighbours. It is certainly true that our detectives are proportionally less numerous than their continental confrères, true also, that extraordinary facilities for successful police action such as are granted in foreign countries are here denied; but the familiar accusation that we maintain a clumsy gang of amateurs who are deficient in the finesse necessary to cope with the skilful forger or the accomplished cracksman, is either spitefully or ignorantly advanced. The self-constituted censors who are so ready to lament the alleged incompetence of our detectives would be the foremost to complain should a measure of State protection, equal to that enjoyed by foreign police functionaries, be conferred on any such agent at home. The traditional love of liberty which, in this country, [367]has always opposed espionage with so much resolution, is altogether admirable; but like everything else that is precious, it has to be purchased at a price, and in this case the price is the dangerous latitude conceded to "the powers that prey."

Before attempting to estimate the efficiency of the detective service, two considerations in particular ought to be weighed. One is that any institution which perforce must shun recognition and advertisement is little likely to be appraised at its true worth by the public. The other is that whilst the wealth of London attracts the best criminal talent of both hemispheres, its expanse renders the detection and pursuit of crime more than ordinarily difficult. In spite of this, and in spite also of the limitations imposed by national sentiment, the success achieved by the sleuth-hounds of the English police need not fear comparison, if fairly made, with that attained by any who are engaged in the same work elsewhere: it may be that tenacity of purpose and honesty of motive go a long way to compensate for any genius for artifice or power of disguise that the English detective lacks.

It must be confessed, however, that honesty has not invariably distinguished our thief-takers. The Bow Street Runners were often arrant humbugs besides being self-seeking knaves, nor were their successors always free from reproach. The small detective force established in 1842 was at first exclusively recruited from the uniform branch of the police, and generally speaking the custom then introduced has since been adhered to; for although [368]theoretically any suitable person is eligible for employment as a detective, the few outsiders who have been given a trial have almost without exception proved failures. It cannot be held that the ordinary point and beat duty is the best possible training for a career which demands an exceptional astuteness of intellect, nor that the routine discipline of a constabulary force is calculated to develop the reasoning faculties to any great extent. But although the system which finds favour to-day is in all probability far from being the best that could be devised, it has nevertheless much to commend it; the responsibilities that belong to the detective, and the temptations which surround him, are so exceptional that it would be extremely dangerous to entrust an unknown man with the former or to expose an untried man to the latter. A second reason why the existing method of selection is desirable is because anything that tends to promote a good understanding and complete co-operation between the uniform and the plain-clothes branches of the police makes for efficiency.

The perils to which society is exposed when clever criminals and dishonest police officers conspire together had been forcibly exemplified when the celebrated bank-frauds came to light early in the nineteenth century. But the point of elaboration to which so obvious a criminal manœuvre could be carried was not fully realised until 1877, when the details of what is commonly called the De Goncourt case were published to the world. Harry Benson and his confederate Kurr were a brace of criminals [369]with a real genius for high-class swindling, such as, fortunately for gullible human nature, is rarely met with. After netting immense sums of money by means of bogus betting agencies and other nefarious schemes, Benson conceived the idea of insuring his ill-gotten gains by approaching the very police-officers (Meiklejohn and Druscovitch) who were charged with the duty of tracking him down, and of corrupting them with subsidies until they became his creatures and confederates. Once the proffered premium had been accepted, there was no limit to the audacity of the subsequent proceedings. Telegrams from Paris addressed to Scotland Yard were intercepted and handed to Benson, who was forewarned by his pursuers of every move intended against him. When the partners were eventually arrested in Holland, a forged telegram, purporting to come from the English headquarters of police, was addressed to the Dutch authorities ordering the release of the prisoners; but the artifice failed and the culprits were escorted home, in the custody, strangely enough, of Druscovitch, whose dishonesty was still unsuspected. Convicted and committed to Millbank, Benson at once proceeded to "give away" the policemen he had suborned, with the result that four inspectors were arraigned on charges of conspiring to defeat the ends of justice, and of complicity with the frauds of their late employer: three out of the four were found guilty and sentenced to various terms of imprisonment, but the matter was not allowed to end there. In order to guard against any recurrence of such a scandalous breach of trust, the organization [370]of the whole detective department was overhauled, and its administration placed in other hands. The task of reorganization was entrusted to Mr Howard Vincent,[253] who devoted his energies towards raising the tone of the then discredited detective service. In 1878 what was practically a new department was formed at Scotland Yard under the title of "The Criminal Investigation Department," consisting of a chief superintendent and about thirty superior officers at headquarters, besides a local inspector assisted by from six to fifteen detectives in each of the town divisions—the whole under the control of the Director of Criminal Investigations,[254] who takes charge of all the criminal business of the Metropolis, and whose assistance, sometimes indispensable, is often solicited by the chiefs of rural and urban constabularies throughout the country.

The numerical strength of the detective force has been considerably augmented since its reorganization in 1878 (in 1895 it consisted of 472 officers), and its rôle increasingly tends to grow in importance. In 1880 the newly established Convict Supervision Office was brought into close association with the Criminal Investigation Department, and the constant vigilance that has to be maintained over foreign anarchists domiciled in England, as well as [371]the necessity for frequent correspondence with the American and Continental police, preliminary to the extraditing of fugitive offenders, causes the department to wear the aspect of an international bureau for the unravelment of crime. The detective branch of the City of London police, on the other hand, makes a speciality of the investigation of commercial frauds, a vast field of possible enterprise, not the less extensive for the fact that the area policed by the City force is but a single square mile.

It would have been worse than useless to have increased the detective staff unless at the same time care had been taken to safeguard the public from the risk of a repetition of abuses similar to those revealed in the course of the de Goncourt case, and this made the problem of reform a difficult one. It is impossible to devise a method of selection by means of which every black sheep who may seek admission is infallibly recognised and excluded, nor is it easy adequately to supervise confidential agents without interfering with their work; but it may safely be said that since the reorganization of the department, a high standard of honesty has been found to be not incompatible with professional zeal and proficiency. No policeman who is thorough in his work can please all parties, and some thirteen or fourteen years ago a series of ill-natured attacks were directed against both branches of the Metropolitan Police. Constables and detectives were accused of exceeding their authority and of levying blackmail, but the [372]allegations, which were somewhat recklessly supported by prominent illwishers and busybodies, could not be substantiated when the charges came to be investigated by the proper authority.[255]

The intense hostility with which Peel's reforms were at first greeted, besides being the cause of much inconvenience at the time, was also the parent of many posthumous difficulties, that continued to embarrass the police authorities long after the original quarrel was dead and buried. It will be remembered that the two main contentions, often repeated by the hostile party in 1829 and after, were to the effect that the liberty of the subject was in grave danger at the hands of an unconstitutional "gendarmerie," armed with mysterious powers of domiciliary espionage, and that the expense to the ratepayers of maintaining these tyrants would be ruinous. Rather than give a handle to his adversaries, who were sure to acclaim every plain-clothes policeman as a Government spy intriguing against innocent citizens, the author of modern police was forced to dispense with the invaluable assistance of a detective staff; and in order to disprove the forecasts of opponents who prophesied financial disaster, he was compelled to fix the constable's wage at a very low figure. Enough has been said as to the manner in which the original lack of a detective department has gradually been remedied, and although space does not admit of anything like a full account being given of the various phases through which the financial problem has passed, a subject so vital to the well-being of police cannot be altogether ignored.

[373]

Police expenditure is of two kinds: there is the weekly wage-bill, and there are the working (including administrative) expenses. Under the old system, although little was spent in actual pay, large sums were scandalously muddled away in rewards, fees and allowances; when the new constabularies superseded the old parochial bodies, much public money had to be sunk in the acquisition of sites, and in the erection of suitable station-houses, cells and offices; and the upkeep of these establishments, as well as the incidental working expenses connected with them, were on a generous scale. As, therefore, only a very limited income was available for the whole service, and as interest had to be paid on the original outlay, the balance that remained was only sufficient to permit of a low rate of remuneration for the rank and file. Watchmen had been so miserably underpaid in the past that the increased wage offered to the first policemen appeared, when compared with the old tariff, to be considerable, if hardly dazzling. As a matter of fact, regard being had to the type of man required and to the responsibilities thrust upon him, the salary was far too small, and furthermore there was so little margin in hand after distribution that it was financially impossible to set aside any portion of the general income to form a pension fund for long and meritorious service. All available cash had to be devoted to the provision of a weekly wage to attract a sufficiency of recruits.

The risks that a constable has to face, the long night work and the constant exposure to all weathers that are his lot, and which eventually impair even [374]the strongest constitutions, make it especially incumbent on his employers to provide adequately for him when he is worn out. Quite apart, however, from this moral obligation (which cannot honourably be evaded) the existence of a well-conceived and well-administered superannuation scheme has a most important bearing on the stability of any police force—deferred salary contingently due to his employées being a most valuable hostage, for the satisfactory completion of the contract undertaken by them, in the hands of the paymaster. Moreover if a man has in prospect a respectable pension on retirement, he is not tempted improperly to devote himself to the acquisition of a sum of money for his future maintenance, nor, of course, has he any inducement to stay on in the service, blocking the promotion of those below him, after he is past his work.

At first the percentage of resignations amongst young constables was extremely high: men of some few years' service, wearying of a life of discipline, or finding the duties they had to perform more irksome than they had anticipated, resigned without hesitation a position which they had no particular inducement to retain. This constant leakage was considerably reduced by the creation of a superannuation fund by Act of Parliament[256] in 1839, and since that year, policemen, whatever their grade, have contributed [375]some two and a half per cent. of their salaries[257] towards their retiring pensions. The money raised for this purpose was so lavishly spent that by 1849 the fund was insolvent, and seven years later it was bankrupt. This necessitated further legislation, and by a Statute passed in 1856[258] authority was obtained to make good the deficiency out of the rates. Thenceforward the administration of the fund was the reverse of generous; and in 1862 it was promulgated that pensions on the higher scale, for service of more than fifteen and less than twenty years, were not to be granted under any circumstances whatever, and that in order to qualify for the maximum pension policemen had to serve a full term of twenty-eight years, notwithstanding the fact that expert opinion had unanimously declared that twenty-five years spent in outdoor police work incapacitates the ordinary man. Irritation at the financial legerdemain which obscured the true position of the superannuation fund, and dissatisfaction with the current rates of pay, caused widespread discontent that culminated in 1872 in an outbreak of insubordination amongst the Metropolitan police, many of whom refused to go on duty until their grievances were redressed. The ringleaders of what was very nearly a mutiny were prosecuted, and others less guilty were dismissed the force; but investigation shewed that the hardships complained of were none the less real because certain ill-advised malcontents had adopted a suicidal policy [376]in order to gain an immediate hearing. After the excitement caused by this unfortunate occurrence had subsided, a compromise was arrived at, removing some of the more pressing grievances; but it was only a compromise, and beneath the surface an undercurrent of justifiable discontent still remained. In 1881 the Home Secretary (Sir W. Harcourt), addressing a representative gathering of the Metropolitan police, said he hoped that at an early period it would be his grateful office to add to their comfort and content "by supplying a defect which has long been felt, in placing on a fixed and satisfactory footing, not only in London, but throughout the country, the superannuation and pension of those who have spent the best days of their lives in the service of their countrymen."[259]

The hopes of the Home Secretary, like those of the constabulary, were however not yet to be realised; and it was not until 1890 that anything like a satisfactory solution of the vexed question of police superannuation was arrived at. By the "Police Act,"[260] passed on the 14th of August of that year, policemen who have completed twenty-five years approved (*i.e.* diligent and faithful) service become entitled, without a medical certificate, to retire and receive a pension for life, whilst fair provision is made for those who at any time are certified as incapacitated for further service. The Act also defines the conditions under which pensions or gratuities may be granted to the widows and [377]children of deceased officers, deals with the forfeiture and suspension of pensions, directs how the fund is to be invested, and, in short, fully propounds the law which governs the whole field of police superannuation.

Although the police forces of England are now in possession of a charter which has enormously improved their prospects, and in spite of the further concessions recently granted, it cannot yet be said that they are well-content with their financial position; nor is their point of view unreasonable. They only ask that their work should be estimated on a present-day valuation, and paid for accordingly; they naturally object to be underpaid because their predecessors were half-starved. Moreover, enforced residence in respectable quarters in some particular locality where rents may be high, regulations which debar policemen from earning extra money in their spare time, and other conditions peculiar to their calling, unite to form a strong case in favour of a more generous scale of remuneration being granted in the future than that considered necessary in the past.

This is not the place to discuss the precise rate of wages that a constable should receive, nor to suggest any scheme by which funds might be raised to meet increased expenditure under this heading. But it may be remarked without impropriety, that the more the public take their share of the police duties which as good citizens they ought not to shirk, and the stronger the support, be it moral or physical, that they extend to their deputies, the less need will [378]there be for the maintenance of an ever increasing army of constables, until the time arrives when, with a falling police rate, it becomes possible to forget precedent, and to remunerate our peace officers in accordance with their deserts.

In 1889 one thousand men were added to the metropolitan force. There is little doubt that the expense entailed by this increase might have been saved if, after the West-End Riots, the public had been politic enough to back its own side instead of playing into the hands of its enemies by adding to the difficulties that the police had to contend with already. The difficulties referred to arose out of the following circumstances.

Early in 1886 London was the scene of a sudden riotous outbreak as serious as it was unexpected. Remarkable from many points of view, it is especially to be remembered on account of the utter failure of the police authorities to cope with it, and especially to be regretted because it was the first of a series of incidents which for many months disturbed the cordial good-will and co-operation between police and public that had been so carefully built up and encouraged through many a year.

A meeting having been advertised to take place in Trafalgar Square on the 8th of February under the auspices of the London United Workmen's Committee, the organizers (who were a respectable body of men desirous only of ventilating their grievances in a legitimate and orderly manner), having reason to fear that certain of the Social Democrats were bent on creating a disturbance, [379]approached the Chief Commissioner with a request that the police might assist them in their efforts to prevent a breach of the peace. Under these circumstances Sir Edmund Henderson decided to have a much larger force in reserve than was usual, and gave orders that whilst only sixty-six constables were to be detailed for duty in Trafalgar Square itself, a force of five hundred and sixty-three police of all ranks was to be held in reserve in the immediate neighbourhood. As soon as the crowd began to assemble it was remarked by some of the most experienced police officers present that a rougher element than usual predominated, but, on the whole, the proceedings in the Square were not of an alarming character, and nothing worse than inflammatory speeches, accompanied by the usual horse-play, took place. Shortly before four o'clock the meeting began to break up, and on this occasion, contrary to all police experience, which was to the effect that crowds invariably return by the same routes that they come by, a compact body some three thousand strong poured out of the Square, and started off in a westerly direction. Rapidly traversing Pall Mall, where several windows were broken, the mob proceeded up St James' Street and down Piccadilly, doing considerable damage by the way. On arriving at Hyde Park, the bulk of the crowd called a halt and speeches were made, but the smaller and more lawless section, finding that no police force offered any resistance to their disorderly career, continued along S. Audley Street into Oxford [380]Street, smashing windows, looting shops, and insulting all whom they met. Eventually, at about five o'clock, a small body of police (only sixteen in number) confronted the mob at the end of Marlborough Lane, and after several vigorous charges, succeeded in dispersing the rioters.

It may well be asked how it came about that for the space of an hour a gang of roughs, which in the end was so easily disposed of, was permitted to riot with impunity through some of the richest thoroughfares of London, in defiance of the considerable force of constables on duty, and in spite of the fact that two regiments of cavalry were within ten minutes ride of the scene. The only possible explanation is to be found in the lamentable want of foresight exhibited on this occasion by the authorities responsible for the police arrangements, combined with the singular lack of initiative and resource shewn by the subordinate officers throughout the day. A cursory glance at the conditions prevailing in Trafalgar Square reveals in a moment the reasons for the defeat of the police; it is at once apparent that their failure must not be attributed to any physical cause whatever. The police force on duty was quite large enough; and the units of which it was composed were sufficiently well endowed with muscle, nerve and morale, to have kept in order a crowd twice as violent and many times more numerous than the one actually opposed to it; the collapse of authority was due to defects of organization, to bad strategy, and to tactical blundering. If a small body of mounted police had been present—if scouts had been instructed to watch the outskirts of the crowd to ascertain and [381]report upon the routes of dispersal—if the officer in command had taken up a prominent position known beforehand to his subordinates—if a system of circulating information rapidly and with accuracy had been adopted—if a single one of these obvious precautions had been taken, the West End Riots would not have occurred, and the crop of difficulties which blocked the path of the Metropolitan Police during the next two years would have been avoided.

On the 9th February another assemblage of roughs took place in Trafalgar Square, and fears that further riots would ensue took possession of the West End; but the police were equal to the emergency, and the meeting was dispersed without difficulty. Wednesday the 10th, however, was a day of serious apprehension; London was wrapped in a dense black fog, and the rumour gained credence that 50,000 desperate men from the riverside suburbs were concentrating prior to an organized attempt to loot the capital. The Bank of England retained its military guard; the Bond Street jewellers and other shopkeepers suspended business and barricaded their windows. Half London waited in hourly expectancy of hearing the shouts of the attacking columns through the fog.

It was clearly the business of the police authorities to satisfy themselves as to the truth or falsity of these rumours, and in the latter case to do all in their power to restore confidence. The course they actually pursued was to send out notices broadcast advising householders to take all precautions necessary for their own safety. This action of the authorities [382]only served to heighten the general alarm, people naturally assuming that it amounted to an official confirmation of the sensational stories that were everywhere current. The state of uncertainty and alarm continued through the night, but when, on the following morning, it became known that the whole story had had no foundation in fact, all the various emotions of the past three days gave place to a unanimous feeling of indignation against the police.

The value of the property destroyed and stolen by the mob, whilst the machinery for keeping the peace was thus temporarily out of gear, was comparatively trivial, and probably fell short of the £7000 paid as compensation; a far more serious factor was the loss of prestige that befell the police. The importance of the Trafalgar Square riots of '86 depends, not so much upon the damage done to Club-house windows and tradesmen's shop-fronts, as upon the fact that this was the first occasion since the institution of the modern police that the mob had succeeded in getting the upper hand of any considerable body of constables. Regrettable incidents had occurred in many of the tussles that had taken place since the first conflict at Coldbath Fields in '33; but on every occasion victory had in the end decisively rested with the peace officers, so that it came to be generally believed that it was useless to resist them. This was the very lesson that the chiefs of the police had been at such pains to impress upon the disorderly section of the public ever since the commencement of the new establishment; and [383]the success they had achieved in this direction had proved greatly to the advantage of the rate-payers, who had to support, in consequence, a much smaller force than would otherwise have been necessary. The policeman managing a hostile crowd, or keeping order in a slum peopled by thieves, is in much the same position as a solitary European holding his own amongst a swarm of Asiatics. Take away his prestige, and that same moment he ceases to be an object of respect, and becomes an object of contempt. The rough and the criminal do not fear the prowess of the individual policeman, they fear the organization behind him—take that away, and the constable becomes merely a big man armed with nothing more formidable than a wooden truncheon.

The result of this temporary and partial breakdown of the organization was that the whole force suffered a double loss; the general public, no longer feeling the old confidence in the power of the police to protect them, withheld to some extent their moral support; whilst the criminal public, assuring themselves that their old belief in the invincibility of the police was groundless, began to threaten where they used to cringe.

It was providential that the enemies of order and good government failed to take full advantage of a moment so auspicious for their designs. The weak places of the defence were exposed for an instant, but the breaches were rapidly repaired and strengthened: in allowing this opportunity to pass, the anarchists and revolutionists, who as a rule are not slow to advertise their existence, missed a [384]chance that is not likely to be offered a second time.

A good deal of inflammatory language was indulged in, but the attacks were ill-timed and unimportant. A large meeting of Socialists, followed by riotous proceedings, took place at Birmingham; but any serious consequences that might have resulted, were averted by a timely display of strength. London was allowed time to recover itself, and it was not until the 21st of February that a mass meeting held in Hyde Park, and attended by some 50,000 people, gave cause for alarm. Fortunately the dangerous classes were not conspicuously represented, and the violently disposed minority was effectually controlled by the police, who, smarting perhaps, under their recent reverse, handled the crowd with some roughness. A week later, rioting of a more serious character broke out in Manchester, to be repeated on a larger scale on March 18th; the local police, however, supported by soldiers, were successful in their efforts to restore order on both occasions.

At the time of the West End riots Parliament was not sitting, and the public indignation found expression in the columns of the newspapers, where a vigorous campaign was commenced, directed partly against the Home Office, and partly against the police authorities. This chorus of irresponsible criticism was to some extent silenced by the prompt action of the Home Secretary (Mr Childers), who immediately appointed a committee, on which he himself sat as chairman, to investigate the conduct [385]of the police. The report, which was issued on the 22nd of Feb. '86, impartially reviewed all the circumstances of the case, and pointed out the mistakes that had been made in the police arrangements. The committee found, amongst other defects, that the chain of responsibility in the force was very imperfect, and called attention to the remarkable fact that, although Standing Police Orders to regulate the conduct of constables at peaceable public meetings had long been issued, no regulations for the management of unruly mobs had ever been published. The report, (upon the authority of which the foregoing remarks on the Trafalgar Square arrangements are based) concluded with a strong expression of opinion as to the desirability of investigating without delay the administration and organization of the Metropolitan Police Force, and the Home Secretary promised to give immediate effect to the recommendations of the Committee by instituting an exhaustive inquiry into the question, with a view to making the necessary changes.

The resignation of Sir Edmund Henderson, which took place on the 20th of February, was perhaps inevitable under the circumstances; but much regret was felt and expressed throughout the force when it became known that the Chief, who for seventeen years had watched over the security of London, and under whose rule the police had earned a high reputation for efficiency, was about to leave Scotland Yard.

During his tenure of office the peace had been so [386]well maintained, and the police mechanism had worked so smoothly, that his experience had taught him to under-estimate the dangers that lurk below the surface in all large crowds, and to over-estimate the preparedness of the men under his command to deal with any possible outbreak. As he knew them, London crowds were well behaved, and London police were equal to any emergency.

The place vacated by the resignation of Sir Edmund Henderson was offered to Sir Charles Warren, a well-known officer of Engineers, whose talent for administration had been proved in Bechuanaland and elsewhere, and who now relinquished the Governorship of the Red Sea Littoral to take up the Chief Commissionership of the Metropolitan Police. The task entrusted to the new chief was definite if not easy. Before all things he had to restore the prestige which had suffered so severely on the day when the mob gained the upper hand, and he had to demonstrate, cost what it might, that the police could not again be defied with impunity.

After the occurrences of February 1886, there was a truce lasting some eighteen months during which the peace was successfully maintained in spite of the persistent hostility evinced by a large section of the public. But in the autumn of 1887, disorderly assemblages of the unemployed, led by demagogues, encouraged by foolish agitators, and reinforced with [387]the scum of London, became so frequent and intolerable,[261] that Sir Charles Warren had to make a bold move in the interests of order, by altogether forbidding the use of Trafalgar Square as a place of public meeting. His action was endorsed by the Secretary of State, but only in such a half-hearted fashion that the forces of disorder, confident that they were the masters of the situation, determined to fight it out. Accordingly both parties prepared for battle. On the one side some six or seven thousand special constables were sworn in, and a large military force was held in reserve; on the other, defiance was openly preached, and adherents were canvassed. When on Sunday the 13th of November the mob began to assemble, they found that the Square and its approaches were already held; but, undeterred by the force opposed to them, and in no mood to return quietly to their homes, the ring-leaders, after a short parley, tried to break through the police cordon. In the course of the protracted struggle which ensued, several minor casualties occurred on either side, and although the crowd resolutely returned to the attack time after time, in the end the police were successful all along the line; the square was cleared without loss of life or injury to property, and the ability of the police to carry out the orders of the Government was satisfactorily demonstrated. Subsequently other attempts were made to reopen the question; but the result was the same. The next phase was [388]the repetition of the familiar and easily disproved charges as to the alleged violence of the constables, many persons, who had attacked the police for their failure in 1886, now joining in the chorus anathematising their successes of the following year.

The entire responsibility for the instructions upon which the police had acted, belonged, of course, to the Government; and on the reopening of Parliament the focus of the agitation was transferred to Westminster, where the whole question as to the legal power of constabulary forces to prevent open-air meetings was debated at some length. In demanding an enquiry into the right of public meeting, Sir Charles Russell insisted that such a right existed by virtue of long-sanctioned custom, and contended that the Executive was not justified in vetoing any assembly that was not of itself illegal. The Home Secretary replied regretting the events of "Bloody Sunday," which he described as lamentable and distressing, but he denied that any right of public meeting, as such, was recognised by English law, and concluded by saying that "this series of meetings had exhausted the police, terrified the public, and made the veto necessary." Sir Henry James held that, whilst the purely legal side of the question was comparatively immaterial, the maintenance of the peace and considerations of the public safety were all-important; and urged that it was the duty of Government to employ such police measures as might be found necessary to prevent the undoubted liberties of the many from being interfered with by the intolerable whims of the few, even if the latter [389]happened to be legally within their rights.[262] The common-sense point of view enunciated by Sir Henry James found general acceptance, both in the House of Commons and throughout the country; Sir Charles Russell's motion was rejected, and the public began to rally to the support of the police.

CHAPTER XIX
CONCLUSION

From the time when Rural Constabulary forces were instituted in 1839, until the date of the creation of County Councils fifty years later, the police authority throughout rural England had been the County Justices of the Peace in Quarter Sessions, to which body alone, in the several counties, was each Chief-Constable answerable, provided that he conformed to the general regulations laid down by the Secretary of State. During this period various changes, in addition to those of a more important nature already mentioned, were brought about, having for their object the better management of the police, or the more convenient administration of justice. In 1846 County Courts for the hearing of civil suits involving minor issues were established in the different shires; and, by the gradual enlargement of the jurisdiction exercised by these tribunals, the higher courts have, to a corresponding extent, been relieved of much petty business to the advantage of larger interests. In 1869 the office of High-Constable was formally abolished, any powers that he had anciently exercised having long since dwindled almost to the vanishing point. At first the Treasury contribution towards the expenses of the rural police had been strictly [391]limited and quite inadequate in amount; but in 1875 the old limitation was suspended, first for one year, then for another, and finally indefinitely, until it became the rule for the public Treasury to provide half the cost for pay and clothing of all provincial police forces that, at the end of each year, are returned as efficient by the Home Office on the recommendation of the Government Inspector of Constabulary.

Following upon the Municipal Corporations Act of 1835,[263] some fifty Acts of Parliament, relating wholly or in part to municipal government, received the royal assent, and this at the rate of more than one a year; in August 1882 the mass of legislative amendments that resulted was consolidated and reduced to one Statute.[264] Amongst other police enactments, the formation of a separate constabulary, distinct from the county force, in any borough containing less than twenty thousand inhabitants, was hereby prohibited; but the control of local police forces already established was for the present confirmed to the existing Watch Committees, whatever might be the population of the borough concerned, and at the same time authority to enforce certain sanitary laws (*e.g.* The Public Health Acts of 1873 and 1875) was conferred on the Town Councils.

Six years later more important changes, affecting the police of counties as well as that of boroughs, were introduced by the Local Government Act of 1888,[265] which transferred the control of the rural [392]police from the Justices of the Peace in Quarter Sessions to an annually appointed committee (called the Standing Joint Committee) composed of a certain number of County Councillors, selected by and from the members of the new councils, and of an equal number of Justices chosen by Quarter Sessions. The effect of this Statute was not simply to substitute one consultative body for another, for to the Standing Joint Committee was also conveyed all that authority over the county police which had hitherto been enjoyed by Justices out of Session, the important proviso being added, however, that "nothing in this Act shall affect the powers, duties, and liabilities of Justices as Conservators of the Peace, or the obligation of the Chief Constable or other Constables to obey their lawful orders given in that behalf."[266]

Although local government in township, hundred and shire is as old as the Constitution itself, the birthday of the modern county councils in 1888 is from the historian's point of view an event of the first importance, for it deprived the county magistracy of a prerogative which for more than five hundred years had been steadily growing in completeness, by suddenly transferring the destinies of the rural police to a body that owed the half of its authority to the popular vote of the shire. From the standpoint of the practical politician, on the other hand, the change has so far proved but an incident; and, for all the effect it has produced on the actual efficiency and on the daily routine of the police forces concerned, it [393]has passed almost unnoticed. Standing Joint Committees have accepted and carried on the traditions which they inherited; and the administration of the county police remains much the same to-day as it was when the entire control was vested in the county magistrates, who, no longer overweighted by a mass of general—as distinguished from judicial—business, are now free to devote themselves to their proper duties as conservators of the peace.

By the first Municipal Corporations Act, any borough so disposed was allowed a separate police force on the understanding that, in the case of towns containing less than five thousand inhabitants, all expense connected with the maintenance of such forces should be borne by the borough availing itself of the privilege. In 1888, this power of choice was restricted, and all boroughs, which at the last census failed to show a population of 10,000, were amalgamated for police purposes with the county to which they belonged; if, however, any borough entitled to have its own police prefers amalgamation, it is permitted to contract with the Standing Joint Committee of the county in which it is situated for the establishment of a consolidated constabulary under the general disposition and government of the Chief Constable of that county, the powers of the Watch Committee remaining in abeyance as long as the contract lasts. A larger measure of autonomy was secured by the Local Government Act to certain boroughs, called County-Boroughs, being those which were either counties in themselves before the passing of the Act, or had [394]an estimated population of at least 50,000 on the 1st of June 1888. As, however, the police of a County-Borough is for all practical purposes on the same basis as one maintained by any other town, that controls a separate constabulary, it is unnecessary further to enlarge upon this part of the subject. It is sufficient to state that in 1899 one hundred and twenty-four English and Welsh boroughs possessed independent police forces, and that out of this number sixty-one were county-boroughs.

At the present time there are only two portions of the United Kingdom that do not manage their own police. Ireland is one and London is the other. Ireland is not allowed the privilege for reasons with which we are not here concerned, but which have been succinctly put by a politician who is not ill-disposed towards that country, "If Kerry was treated as Northumberland," said he, "Kerry must control her police, and if Kerry controlled her police, there was an end of law and order."[267] The case of London is altogether different: when the Local Government Act readjusted the command exercised by the various local authorities over their county and borough police forces, the Metropolitan area was especially exempted from provisions that applied elsewhere. A County of London, carved out of the counties of Middlesex, Surrey and Kent, was called into being on the 1st of January 1889, but its area did not coincide with the Metropolitan Police District, nor was the London County Council [395]given any voice in the management of London's constabulary.

This anomalous position of the Metropolitan Police, governed as it is by a Chief Commissioner appointed by the Home Office and independent of municipal control, has ever since been a subject for controversy amongst local politicians. Members of the progressive party have held that the control of the police ought to be transferred from the Government to the London County Council; and, in support of the desired change, argue that as the ratepayers find the money they should have a voice in its expenditure; they contend that it is an insult to London that she alone amongst the great towns of England is debarred from the management of her own constabulary. At first sight it would appear reasonable to extend to London the same measure of self-government in police matters that provincial towns enjoy; but the answer of those who are content with the present arrangement is that the Metropolitan Police is an Imperial rather than a local force—provincial towns and districts have only provincial interests to guard, London has responsibilities as wide as the Empire; and however public-spirited local authorities may be, the danger will always remain that they may be induced to prefer local to national interests. The Houses of Parliament, the British Museum, public offices and foreign embassies happen to be in London, but they are not local institutions: the head-quarters of the Criminal Investigation Department is no more inseparable from Scotland Yard [396]than is parliament from Westminster: London is the focus of crime and it is convenient that it should also be the head-quarters of the machinery for its prevention, but that is no reason why the principal detective agency of England should be subordinated to Spring Gardens influences. The inhabitants of Canterbury might as well aspire to the control of the National Church on the strength of their pride of See, as Londoners insist that the Metropolis must bear the responsibilities of the National Police. It is repeated that the ratepayers of London pay for the Metropolitan force; but this is only partly true. It would be more correct to say that they pay half the bill, and, in return, they obtain the protection they pay for, the Imperial Treasury providing the balance.[268]

It has been suggested that a fair compromise might be found in a division of the responsibility, by giving the London County Council control over a moiety of the force for local purposes, and transferring to that body the authority to license hackney-carriages, pedlars and lodging houses together with the management of street traffic, &c., &c., whilst retaining a separate police establishment for imperial purposes; but there is little doubt that such a change would only lead to friction, and might conceivably bring about a recrudescence of that jealousy which was the bane of the old parochial system.

[397]

The whole question is complicated by the independent position that the City of London has been allowed to retain. From many points of view it would be advantageous to concentrate the entire police of the metropolis under one and the same administration, and to some amalgamation seems desirable for the sake of uniformity, if for no better reason; but regularity in our institutions is not in itself a great end to strive for, and it would be prodigal of labour to tinker with our going concerns merely to eliminate deviations from the normal. Against amalgamation much can be urged. The city wishes to retain its ancient privilege of policing itself, and as long as it maintains an efficient force entirely at its own expense, the government is not likely to interfere. The matter is largely one of finance. Under the existing arrangements, three-quarters of the total cost of the City police is raised in the city by a local police rate, and the remaining quarter is subscribed by the Corporation out of its revenue; if, however, the control was transferred to the Chief Commissioner of the Metropolitan Police, the city would only have to pay five-ninths of the total cost instead of the whole amount as at present—or putting it in another light, amalgamation would cost the Imperial Treasury more than fifty thousand pounds a year, which sum is the price that the city now pays for the privilege of managing its own police. A second objection to amalgamation is that the Justice Rooms at Mansion House and Guildhall are presided over by magistrates who are experts in commercial jurisdiction, and consequently the usefulness of these courts would be to some extent impaired if they became ordinary metropolitan police courts.

Modern police in the City of London dates from 1839, in which year, it will be remembered, the Corporation awoke to the necessity of reorganization, and so escaped the consolidating process that had already absorbed all the other independent and semi-independent police establishments within the 688 square miles that surround Charing Cross. Since then the advisability of fusing together the two London police forces has often been debated, and after the death of Sir Richard Mayne in 1869 the threatened amalgamation would have become a *fait accompli* had the Government been ready to acquiesce in the suggestion made by the Corporation that the City Commissioner should be promoted to the command of the proposed combination. In 1894 the Royal Commission on the Unification of London reported in favour of bringing the whole of the police of the metropolis under one administration; but its advice has not yet been acted upon, nor is there any immediate prospect of its recommendations being carried into effect. If, however, the City authorities should at any time fail to keep up the high standard of police that they have hitherto maintained they would certainly lose their historic privilege of police independence, and the knowledge of this fact contributes to the undoubted efficiency of the force they control. At the present day both the metropolitan and city forces rightly consider themselves *corps d'elite*, and a proper rivalry exists between them, which is at once creditable in itself and advantageous to the public interest. We have said that the ultimate authority over the city police rests with the Corporation. It may however be remarked that the appointment of any person has to be ratified by the Crown before he is confirmed in the Commissionership, and that practically speaking the powers possessed by the Corporation are exercised by proxy. To a Police Committee consisting of some eighty members selected by the Common Council is delegated everything that concerns the pay, allowances, and financial business of the force; whilst all questions touching the discipline and disposal of the men under his command are referred to the Commissioner, who is thus supreme in his own department.

One of the clauses in Peel's Act had disfranchised the new police by denying to constables the right to vote for the election of a Member of Parliament for the district comprised in the metropolitan police area: with the growth of other forces this disability was correspondingly extended, and all over the country policemen were debarred from taking their part in parliamentary elections. For the moment the prohibition was in all probability a wise one; elections were then very turbulent affairs, public opinion was already aflame with excitement over the impending parliamentary reforms, and men could only speculate upon the future behaviour of the as-yet-untried constabulary. Even if it had been possible to guarantee that the police would maintain a perfectly correct attitude, prudence would still have counselled the advisability of dissociating the guardians of the peace from the factious interests of electioneering. The public were so suspicious, and Peel's scheme had so many opponents, that in every political contest the losers would to a certainty have attributed the result to the sinister influence of the bogey-man in blue. When, however, both popular prejudice and popular excitement had subsided, there was no longer sufficient cause for the disfranchisement of a numerous and important class of public servants who had proved themselves worthy of all trust; but the original prohibition still held good, to the great disadvantage of the police service. This continued for nearly half a century, that is until 1887, when the "Police Disabilities Removal Act" of that year for the first time gave the parliamentary suffrage to all properly qualified police officers who comply with certain regulations made for the joint convenience of police and public.[269] Six years later constables became entitled to vote, if qualified, at School Board, Municipal and other elections; but in no case are they allowed to canvass, any attempt to influence an elector rendering the offender liable to a penalty of £10.

The wisdom of enfranchising the police has been amply proved by the result, for on no occasion since their admission to the suffrage has it been as much as suggested that they make an improper use of the privilege. Although English police of the twentieth century is a very different thing from [401]Anglo-Saxon police of the tenth century, there is a potent characteristic which is common to both; that is to say, the modern system rests, as the ancient one did, on the sure foundation of mutual reliance. We may rely upon it that the law-abiding character of the British nation is largely due to the rarity with which espionage as a method of control has been employed in these islands, just as the trustworthiness of our English Constabularies is largely the outcome of the confidence that we repose in the wisdom and integrity of our peace-officers. We are well served by our police because we have wisely made them personally responsible for their actions. The constable suffers equally with the non-official citizen for any illegal action he may commit; the law protects him only in the performance of acts authorized by the law; nor can he divest himself of responsibility by pleading the orders of his superior officer, if those orders should chance to be illegal. This personal responsibility is not only a curb to excessive zeal, it is also a spur to legitimate activity. "When," says Sir Arthur Helps, "a man can do anything well, and is entrusted to do it, he has generally an impulse to action which is as strong and abiding as can be found amongst human motives, and which will even surpass the love of gain."

To teach the value of self-reliance is one of the most important duties that a Chief-Constable has to perform, and the efficiency of the force under his command will largely depend upon the manner in which he has imbued individual constables with the [402]lesson. To this end the military model of organization and discipline must not be too closely followed; soldiers generally act in masses and but rarely on their own responsibility, whilst policemen do nine-tenths of their work as individuals. The main object of discipline in the army is to make a man obey orders from force of habit on occasions when his natural instinct would impel him to think only of his personal safety, advantage, or honour; the principal end to be attained in the education of the constable is that he should know his duty, and do it with circumspection and self-control, generally on his own initiative and frequently in opposition to the sympathies of the crowd.

Police discipline has been described by Sir Howard Vincent as "the obedience and respect to lawful authority which distinguishes an organized body from a rabble"[270] and Sir Henry Hawkins (Lord Brampton) has insisted upon the necessity of absolute obedience being rendered by constables to all in authority over them, "Such obedience and observance," he said, "I regard as essential to the existence of a police force."[271] All who have had any experience of dealing with large bodies of men will endorse every word of these pronouncements. First obey orders and, if necessary, complain afterwards, is a rule upon the application of which depends the life and well-being of every properly-disciplined body; at the same time it should not be forgotten that the too-strict enforcement of a rigid [403]type of discipline neither conduces to the value of a police force nor to the advantage of the public. Periodically since 1829 alarmists have repeated the formula that "the era of dragooning has dawned"; on every occasion hitherto the cry has proved as groundless as that of the proverbial shepherd-boy, but, in order to make quite sure that the fable shall for us have no actual counterpart, it is politic to remember that a watchdog which is not kept under proper control may become as dangerous as any wolf. In Continental Europe this danger has not, as we think, been sufficiently guarded against: the police functionary is there entrusted with powers that render him to some extent independent of the ordinary law of the land, for he cannot be prosecuted for malfeasance unless special permission has first been obtained from the Government, and this permission is only granted under very exceptional circumstances.

Occasion has already been taken to remark that the freedom enjoyed by the Press of this country is an invaluable safeguard against police tyranny, that the public Press in fact polices the constabulary. This, however, is only one of the many police functions that modern journalism performs. When a serious crime is committed the newspapers raise a Hue and Cry so far-reaching and persistent that soon every tavern discusses the news, every village harbours a potential detective. Whenever a criminal is caught and convicted the deterrent value of the punishment served out to him is increased a thousand-fold by the publicity given by the Press to the award of the [404]judge. In former days capital punishment was publicly inflicted with the mistaken idea that in this way was the maximum deterrent effect of the death penalty assured[272]; now, not only is what was a brutalizing spectacle decently veiled from the public gaze, but in place of the depraved thousands who formerly used to witness the "turning off" of each poor wretch, normal millions read, and it is to be hoped inwardly digest, the lesson that these tragedies are meant to convey. The Press also acts most effectually as a modern substitute for the pillory. The knowledge that an account of his offence will figure in the morning's police intelligence for all his friends to read, is far more likely to prevent a man (who lays claim to even a shred of respectability) from committing himself, than is any fine that the police magistrate might impose. Nor is the efficacy of the Press as an auxiliary agent of police confined to its success as a deterrent—newspapers advertise the bankrupt's loss of credit, expose the tricks of the swindler, ruin the trade of the impostor, and chastise many an offender whom the law cannot reach. Finally, a free Press, being a guarantee for public liberty, acts as a seton for the escape of evil humours which, if confined, might become a source of danger to the Commonwealth; for as Bentham has said, "a people sure of its rights, enjoys them with moderation and tranquillity."[273]

[405]

In his introduction to the "Criminal Statistics for 1898," recently published by the Home Office, Mr C. E. Troup, of that Department, says that the general conclusions to be drawn from a study of the comparative tables which form part of the statistical returns, may be summed up as follows—"That the actual number of crimes brought into the courts has diminished appreciably during the last thirty years; that, if the increase of population is taken into account, the decrease in crime becomes very marked; that, if we also take into account the increase of the police forces and the greater efficiency in the means of investigating and punishing crime, we may conclude that the decrease in crime is even greater than the figures shew; and finally, if we take into account the fact that habitual criminals are now for the most part imprisoned only for short periods and have much more frequent opportunities than formerly of committing offences, we must hold that the number of criminals has diminished in an even greater ratio than the number of crimes."[274]

It is of course impossible to estimate with any degree of accuracy to what extent this diminution of crime and this increased security of recent years are due to the exertions of our modern constabularies; enough has been said to make it abundantly clear that the amelioration is real, and that it is progressive in its tendency, but the difficulty is to apportion the credit justly between the various agencies that have contributed to the result. There is no doubt [406]that the spread of education and the labours of religious and philanthropic bodies have done much to civilise the masses; it is certain also that an improved prison system and a reformed penal code have reacted beneficially on the criminal classes; but if we believe in the teachings of history we shall put our trust in no combination of influences directed towards the maintenance of the peace that does not at least include a good preventive police-force. If Lombroso's theories are correct, even if some men are born criminal beyond all hope of human redemption, these are only reasons for redoubling our police precautions: the delinquent who is a delinquent from his cradle is the more dangerous on that account, and to the congenital criminal must be denied the opportunity for mischief. But such freaks are rare and the normal criminal is anything but a creature of impulse; his calculations may not be shrewd but they are undoubtedly deliberate. "Abandon fait larron!" When poverty or the want of life's necessaries lead to theft, or where native cruelty and love of bloodshed give rise to deeds of violence, police, however efficient, can effect but little in the way of prevention; but it is the almost unanimous opinion of those best qualified to judge that the bulk of the offences committed in this country are perpetrated by those who enter upon a criminal career because it appears to them that it is easy and profitable, and because they think that it will enable them to obtain luxuries that lie beyond the reach of their industrious and honest companions. It is obvious, therefore, that an effective police, by making [407]the profession of dishonesty difficult and precarious, can remove the principal incentive that makes men criminal.

The circle of police employment is constantly widening, and many of the functions delegated to the Constabulary by Parliament and by local authorities have not been so much as touched upon in this book, which, in a small compass, has endeavoured to trace the main features of police development in England through a great number of years. It is to be hoped, however, that the tendency to load police officers with duties heavier and more diverse than they have to perform already will not go on increasing. It is difficult to fix the precise limits within which it is proper that they should act; but it is certain that by indefinitely multiplying their duties we run a twofold risk, viz., that of rendering the work of police constables so complex and varied that men of average talent and education will be unable to perform it thoroughly, and further of undermining the popularity of the force by exhibiting its members before the eyes of the people as universally interfering and censorious. It is, of course, right and proper that the policeman should endeavour to prevent the commission of any act that he knows to be illegal, at all times and in all places; but it is generally advisable to employ functionaries who do not belong to the police for purposes not closely connected with the maintenance of the peace, whenever the employment of outsiders is equally effectual: it is more convenient, for instance, that game-keepers should protect the rights of owners on sporting estates, and [408]that custom-house officials should examine portmanteaux, than that such duties should be performed by constables. His Majesty's Coastguard, the Inspectors of Mines and Factories, and other persons appointed by Societies for the prevention of cruelty to animals, and for the suppression of mendicity, etc., relieve the police of much work by carrying out the various parts assigned to them by Government or by private enterprise; it is worth considering whether it would not be more profitable to delegate to functionaries, other than constables; all duties connected with the inspection of weights and measures, the enforcement of sanitary laws, the protection of arsenals and dockyards, and with the maintenance of order on racecourses. A force specially devoted to the last mentioned object is desirable on many grounds. In the first place the knowledge that such a body would possess of the welshers, cardsharpers, and pickpockets who travel about from one race-meeting to another, and with whom the different local police forces are unable to cope, would put an end to a great deal of the crime which is at present unchecked and undetected; and in the second place, it would no longer be necessary to withdraw large bodies of police from their proper duties for the protection of race-goers. On the occasion of the riot at Featherstone in 1893, the calling out of the Military, and the loss of life which followed, was largely attributable to the concentration at Doncaster of all the available Yorkshire constables, an unfortunate arrangement which bared the rest of the county of its regular protectors, and encouraged the rioters to proceed to lengths they would not otherwise have attempted.

Although it will hardly be denied that our police discharge their office conscientiously, courteously and courageously, the general public has shewn itself somewhat slow to acknowledge the debt which it owes to the men who undertake what is by common consent a thankless task; who armed with no extraordinary powers, and protected by no elaborate exemptions, perform arduous duties on behalf of their fellow-countrymen, for little reward, and at considerable personal risk. Perhaps it may not be presumptuous to hope that the foregoing pages, by adding their quota to the scanty sources of information on the subject, may cause a corresponding increase in the tribute of public goodwill, that has been so well earned, and so long awaited, by the police forces of England.

THE END

FOOTNOTES:

[1] *Fraser's Magazine*, No. xvi. p. 169.

[2] Evidence of Mr Murray, a magistrate at Union Hall, before the Parliamentary Committee of 1834.

[3] Report of Police Commissioners, 1839.

[4] See Stubb's "Constitutional History," end of para. 60.

[5] In the reign of Edward VI. the well-known legal maxim, "The King never dies," was first enunciated; since which time it has been held that there can be no break in the continuity of kingship; that is to say, that the accession of each succeeding monarch and the decease of his predecessor are simultaneous.

[6] Chron. Ang. S., *ad ann.*, 1135.

[7] "Thane" is here used in the loose and popular sense to signify the resident owner of considerable territorial possessions.

[8] Headborough, Borsholder, and Chief-Frankpledge are three words which describe the same functionary. The latter of Norman, and the two former of Saxon origin. Borsholder = Borhes-ealder—Borhes (often written Borough as in "Headborough"), meaning Pledge or Surety. It is probable that the connection between Borough signifying "Town" and Borough the correlative of Plegium, is merely an accidental coincidence.

[9] It is difficult to avoid the confusion which arises from the use of the word "Hundred." Here the police-hundreds (probably introduced for the first time into England by Edgar) are referred to. The statement does not necessarily imply that the grouping of families into Tythings, and of Tythings into Hundreds took place before county areas were subdivided into smaller areas called Hundreds. It may be remarked, however, that an uninhabited Hundred (and there must have been many such if the whole kingdom was divided in this way) can have had no police significance.

[10] See Note on the Liability of the Hundred, p. 180, chap. ix. post.

[11] Burn I. p. 671.

[12] Edgar, Secular Ordinance, c. 6.

[13] Writing at the end of the eighteenth century Jeremy Bentham declared: "This is the great problem of penal legislation—(i.) To reduce all the *evil* of offences, as far as possible, to that kind which can be cured by a pecuniary compensation. (ii.) To throw the expense of this cure upon the authors of the evil, or in their default, upon the public."

[14] In addition to the "Trinoda necessitas" which besides compelling a man to serve in the Militia, also claimed his services for the repair of bridges, and for the up-keep of the national fortifications.

[15] See "Spelman's Glossary," *sub verbo* "Fredus."

[16] *Ll. Aelf.* 40; *Ll. Ethelb.* 34.

[17] The germ of trial by jury.

[18] Gneist. "History of the English Constitution."

[19] Coke. 2 Instit. 73.

[20] Bede H. E., II. xvi.

[21] It is probable that the *scir-gerefa* was originally elected by the freeholders in the folkmoot: the Norman Sheriff, on the other hand, was invariably appointed by the Crown direct.

[22] This fine was called the "Murdrum."

[23] Bacon's "Office of Constables."

[24] (Magna Carta, Section 20). King John also promised as follows: "We will not make men justiciaries, constables, sheriffs or bailiffs, unless they understand the law of the land, and are well disposed to observe it."

[25] Second Great Charter of Henry III.

[26] "Chronicle of Dunstable," vol. i. p. 155.

[27] *Dictum de Kenilworth*, sect. 14, Stubb's "Select Charters."

[28] 10 Geo. II. c. 22, and 14 Geo. III. c. 90.

[29] 13 Edw. I., *Statuta civitatis* London.

[30] 23 Edw. III., sect. i. c. 7.

[31] "Commissioners' Report," 1839.

[32] From form of oath administered by Hubert, Archbishop of Canterbury ("History of Vagrants," by Ribton Turner).

[33] See Chitty's "Office and Duties of Constables": Coke 3 Inst. 116, 117; and 2 Hale P. C. 102.

[34] See "Statute of Northampton."

[35] 3 Edw. I. cap. 34.

[36] Coroners are first heard of in the directions given to the itinerant Justices by Richard I. in 1194, when four of these officers were assigned to each county.

[37] 4 Edw. I. Stat. 2.

[38] "History of Vagrants."

[39] Fitzherbert, Dalton, Burn, etc.

[40] The edict of Hubert Walter.

[41] Rot. Pat. 14 Edw. I. m. 25.

[42] Rot. Pat. 10 Edw. I. m. 8.

[43] Stephens' "Hist. of the Crim. Law," i. 112.

[44] 2 Edw. III., c. 3.

[45] Rot. Parl. 6 Edw. III.

[46] 34 Edw. III., c. i.

[47] 36 Edw. III., c. 12.

[48] 1 Edw. IV., c. 2. See Reeves' "Hist." vol. iii. p. 9.

[49] Burn's "Justice," v. 302, 25th edition.

[50] See also in this connection Carter's "English Legal History," p. 93.

[51] I. Hale's Sum. 96.

[52] Hist. Ram. Gale. vol. iii. 416, 417.

[53] Extended to other towns in 1427. By 6 Henry VI. c. 3 Justices are to discharge in counties the same duties as are performed in towns by Mayors and Bailiffs.

[54] 2 Hen. V. c. 1.

[55] 4 Hen. VII. c. 13.

[56] *Cf.* Koenig.

[57] Viscount—"an arbitrary title of honour, without a shadow of office pertaining to it" (Blackstone).

[58] Coke viii. 43.

[59] 13 & 14 Car. ii. c. 12.

[60] Selden Society, vol. vi. p. 35.

[61] Secular Dooms, Cap. 81.

[62] All evil customs of forests and warrens, and of foresters and warreners, sheriffs and their officers, waterbanks and their keepers, shall immediately be inquired into by twelve knights of the same county, upon oath, who shall be chosen by the good men of the same county; and within forty days after the inquisition is made, they shall be quite destroyed by them, never to be restored.—*Magna Carta.*

[63] Spelman's Glossary *in verbo* "foresta."

[64] Manwood, "Treatise of the Forest Laws," 4th ed., p. 143.

[65] Vert included trees, underwood and turf; venison comprised the hart, the hind, the hare, the boar and the wolf, which were beasts of forest—the buck, the doe, the fox and the marten, which were beasts of chase—the rabbit, pheasant, partridge, quail, mallard, heron, etc., which were beasts or fowls of warren. So sacred was the stag that should one be found dead an inquest had to be held, and a verdict as to the cause of death taken. (See Low and Pulling's "Dictionary of English History," under Forests.)

[66] It was a universal principle of Early English Law that no defence was valid if the culprit was caught red-handed, he was *ipso facto* convicted. (See Carter's "English Legal History," p. 175.)

[67] Assisa et Consuetudines Forestae, anno 6, Edward I.

[68] Coke Inst., iii., p. 294. This is according to Coke, who derives "Mayneer" from the Latin *Manus*. Manwood, on the other hand, has the phrase "taken in the manner," using manner in the sense of "*maniére.*"

[69] Coke Inst., iii. 289 *seq.*

[70] Coke Inst., iii. 294.

[71] Although the authenticity of this document is denied, there is good reason to suppose that, as far as the following enumeration of forest officers is concerned, its accuracy may be trusted.

[72] Manwood, p. 163.

[73] Manwood, p. 78.

[74] Forest Law, as once administered, was perhaps the worst example of class legislation ever known to the English Constitution—it was a deliberate violation of the rights of the many for the gratification of the few—the same act which was venial in the gentleman became unpardonable when committed by the villein. For example, a common man who slew a deer was guilty of felony and might be capitally convicted, whereas a nobleman riding through the King's Forest was allowed to kill a stag or two for his refreshment, on the understanding that he did so in the sight of a ranger, or if no ranger was present, provided that someone blew a horn for him, "that he seem not to steal the deer" (9 Henry III.).

[75] Dalton, cap. 60, fol. 141.

[76] "Town Life in the Fifteenth Century," Mrs J. R. Green, vol. i. chapter iv.

[77] "Liber Albus," p. 312.

[78] "Liber Albus," p. 315.

[79] Hist. MSS. Com., ix. 174.

[80] 51 Hen. III., stat. 6.

[81] 12 Edw. ii. c. 6.

[82] See Final Report of H. M. Commissioners appointed to enquire into the operation and administration of the Laws relating to the sale of intoxicating liquors, chap. xvi. p. 21.

[83] The King could tax foreign merchants resident in England without having to obtain the consent of Parliament.

[84] The test was usually a verse out of the 51st Psalm—commonly called the "neck verse."

[85] 7 & 8 Geo. iv. c. 28; and see Carter's Eng. Leg. Hist., pp. 202, 203.

[86] 6 Edw. I., c. 9.

[87] 22 Edw. IV.

[88] 3 Henry VII., c. 1.

[89] 34 & 35 Hen. VIII., c. 26 (Wales).

[90] "Tables of population," says Bentham, "in which are described the dwelling-place, the age, the sex, the profession, etc.... of individuals, are the first materials of a good police" (Bentham's "Principles of Penal Law," chap. xii.).

[91] The story of young Edward amongst the vagabonds has recently been told with great charm and pathos by one of the most popular writers of the day. Mark Twain's "The Prince and the Pauper" may not be history, but that it presents a truthful picture of the sufferings of vagrants in the sixteenth century cannot be doubted.

[92] Slaves might be bought, sold, or bequeathed by will, like any other chattel.

[93] 1 Edw. VI.

[94] 3 & 4 Edw. VI., c. 5.

[95] The command of the Militia was transferred from the Lords-Lieutenant of counties to the Crown in the year 1871 ("The Army Book for the British Empire," p. 373).

[96] To this there was one exception, viz., that foreigners were not allowed to keep inns "unless they have report from the parts whence they come, or find safe pledges" (Statute).

[97] 5 & 6 Edw. VI., c. 25.

[98] 27 Elizabeth, Private Acts.

[99] Ordinance, 27 Eliz.

[100] "The Commonwealth of England," Sir Thomas Smith, Ed., 1598, bk. ii. chap. 21.

[101] 5 Eliz., c. iv. sect. 7.

[102] See p. 302, chap. xv., post.

[103] 14 Eliz., c. v. sect. 2.

[104] 39 and 40 Eliz., c. iv.

[105] 43 Eliz. c. 2.

[106] 27 Eliz. c. 13.

[107] 39 Elizabeth, c. 25.

[108] See the Introduction to "Prothero's Select Charters," sect. v.

[109] Rymer's "Foedera," xvi. p. 279.

[110] Prothero's "Select Charters," p. 187.

[111] "Measure for Measure," act ii. scene 1.

[112] Strype's "Annals," 1824, Edn., vol. iv. p. 405.

[113] iii James 4.

[114] See Somers' "Tracts," edited by Scott, vol. ii. p. 266.

[115] 1 Jac. I., cap. vii. sects. 3 and 4.

[116] 7 & 8 Jac. I., cap. iv.

[117] I. Jac. i. cap. 31.

[118] This statute, which gave such extraordinary powers to constables, only remained in force for twelve months. (See article "The office of Constable," by H. B. Simpson, "English Historical Review," vol. x.)

[119] See Proclamations, etc., of Charles I. Bodleian, z. i. 17 Jur.

[120] I. Car. i. cap. 16.

[121] 3 Car. i. cap. 4.

[122] Lib. Albo, fol. 41, b, c, d, e; 23 Henry vi.

[123] "Minshæi Emendatio," ad ann. 1626.

[124] See Note on Liability of the Hundred, chap. ix. post.

[125] 4 & 5 Phil. Mary, cap. 2 and 3.

[126] For a full and interesting account of *Cromwell's Major-Generals*, see an article under that title by D. W. Rannie in the "English Historical Review," No. 10.

[127] See Professor Gardiner's "History of the Commonwealth and Protectorate, 1649-1660," vol. iii.

[128] An Excise duty on liquor had recently (1643) been introduced by the Long Parliament.

[129] Scobell, part i. p. 129; part ii. p. 320.

[130] D'Argenson, lieutenant of police, declared that "there were more irregularities and debaucheries committed in Paris during the Easter fortnight, when the theatres were shut, than during the four months of the season during which they were open" ("Memoirs de Pollnitz," vol. iii.).

[131] Macaulay's "History of England," 1889 Edn., p. 178.

[132] 13 and 14 Car. ii. c. 2.

[133] The number of such vehicles was strictly limited. In London no more than 400 were allowed.

[134] 14 Car. ii. c. 12, sect. 15. The statute also provides for the appointment of special constables in times of emergency.

[135] 15 Car. ii. c. 1.

[136] From "The duty and Office of High Constable, &c." by W. Brown, a clerk of the Court of Common Pleas. Lond. 1677, pp. 26 and 27.

[137] 13 and 14 Car. ii. c. 12 § 22.

[138] Worthies of England, p. 216.

[139] 13 Car. ii. c. 22.

[140] 4 William and Mary, c. viii.

[141] 6 Geo. i., cap. 25, sect. 8.

[142] "Le Blanc's Letters," vol. ii., 1737.

[143] "The Town Rakes," Brit. Mus., (816—m—19)/74.

[144] 1 Geo. i., stat. 2, § 5.

[145] 10 Geo. ii. c. 22.

[146] 8 Geo. ii. c. 16.

[147] 12 Geo. ii. c. 16.

[148] Ann Reg., 1763.

[149] See Gent. Mag., 1761, p. 475; 1780, p. 1446, and Laurence's "Life of Fielding."

[150] Of the several Statutes dealing with police passed during the reign of George II., the most valuable and important is the 24 Geo. ii., c. 44, which enacts that action cannot be brought against a constable for anything done by him in obedience to a Justice's warrant, unless the Justice who signed the warrant is made a joint-defendant with the constable; and which directs that if action is brought jointly against the Justice and the constable, then the jury shall find for the latter, provided that they are satisfied that he acted strictly in accordance with the terms of the warrant that he pleads in justification. When making an arrest a constable should, if required, shew the warrant which is his authority, but he need not allow it to leave his hand.

[151] 29 Geo. ii., c. 25.

[152] 31 Geo. ii., c. 17.

[153] 14 Geo. iii. c. 90.

[154] Wedderburn.

[155] This was the first occasion on which the word "police" was officially made use of in the British Isles.

[156] Irish Statutes, 26 Geo. iii., c. 24.

[157] 33 Geo. iii., c. 4.

[158] By 29 Car. ii. c. 7, § 7 it was enacted that no liability attached to the Hundred if a man be robbed whilst travelling on a Sunday—"for he should not travel on the Lord's Day, nor ought the Hundred to watch on that day of rest." Nevertheless it was ordained that Hue and Cry should be raised against a known offender, despite the non-liability of the Hundred, in order that depredators should not take advantage of the omission.

Actions against the Hundred had to be brought within three months from the date of the damage, and there was no liability for deeds done in the night-time—if, however, there was just sufficient light to see a man's face, liability might be proved, whatever the hour. No charge against the Hundred held good for any robbery done in a man's house, "because every man's house is his castle, which he ought to defend; and if any one be robbed in his house it shall be esteemed his own fault" (Dalton, c. 84); and with regard to liability on account of murder and robbery committed in the daytime, see "Year Book of the Exchequer," (16 Edward I.)

[159] 42 Geo. iii., c. 76.

[160] Between 1822 and 1828, the increase was about 38 per cent.

[161] It has been calculated that at this time there were as many as fifty fraudulent mints in the metropolis alone.

[162] In the hope of suppressing the seditious spirit so rife at this period, six coercive measures generally known as the "Six Acts" were rushed through both Houses of Parliament in a special autumn session of 1819. These Acts sought to preserve the peace by placing restrictions on the press, by forbidding the training of unauthorized persons in the use of arms, by empowering Justices of the Peace to search for and confiscate weapons, and by other repressive measures of a similar nature.

[163] "The policy of a legislator who punishes every offence with death, is like the pusillanimous terror of a child who crushes the insect he dares not look at."—Bentham, "Principles of the Penal Code," Part iv. Cap. xxii.

[164] "The more the certainty of punishment can be augmented, the more it may be diminished in amount."—Bentham, "Principles of the Penal Code." Rule viii.

[165] The ethical point of view is well put by Henry Fielding, who said, "Nor in plain truth will the utmost severity to offenders be justifiable, unless we take every possible means of preventing the offence."

[166] In a letter addressed to *The Times* of November 14th, 1849—Charles Dickens, himself an eye-witness of one of these brutalising exhibitions, wrote—"I am solemnly convinced that nothing that ingenuity could devise to be done in this city, in the same compass of time, could work such ruin as one public execution, and I stand astounded and appalled by the wickedness it exhibits."

[167] As early as 1597, by an act passed in the 39th year of Queen Elizabeth's reign—Quarter Sessions were empowered to inflict transportation, but at first the law could not be enforced because there was no place to which convicts could be shipped. A number of royalists were transported to Barbadoes after its capitulation in 1651, but this was only a temporary measure.

[168] 4 Geo. i. c. 2.

[169] 8 Geo. iii. c. 15.

[170] Escott's "England," 1885 Edn., p. 240.

[171] 7 & 8 Geo. IV., c. 18.

[172] It is impossible to say how far Bentham was influenced by Beccaria; the two men arrived at similar conclusions, but their methods were essentially different. Beccaria's great work, "Dei Delitti e delle Pene," was first published (anonymously) in 1764, and Bentham's "Rationale of Punishments and Rewards" was written eleven years later.

[173] In 1800 six women were publicly flogged till the blood ran down their backs for hedge-pulling.

[174] 9 Geo. iv. c. 61.

[175] See "Encyclopædia of the Laws of England" under Licensing Acts.

[176] 7 and 8 Geo. iv. c. 31.

[177] 2 Geo. iv. and 1 Will. iv. c. 70.

[178] "Mysteries of Police and Crime," Griffiths, p. 66.

[179] A River Police Office, with three Justices assigned to it, was authorised by 39 and 40 Geo. iii. c. 88.

[180] None of this applies to the "City of London" proper, which still retains its independent position, as far as its police is concerned.

[181] 10 Geo. iv. c. 44.

[182] 10 Geo. iv. c. 45.

[183] The official designation of the Chiefs of the Metropolitan Police was changed from "Justice" to "Commissioner" in the year 1839. The change was one of title only, and the

Police commissioners were still Justices of the Peace by virtue of their office. To prevent confusion the word "Commissioner" is henceforward employed in this book.

[184] "Sir Robert Peel," by C. S. Parker.

[185] Bentham defines the "Lettre de Cachet" as "an order to punish, without any proof, for a fact against which there is no law."—(Principles of Penal Law, chap. xxi. part 3).

[186] In the year 1820 the Spanish government suppressed some of the leading newspapers for daring to adversely criticise the police of Madrid, and at the same time it was currently believed in England that Italian police officials employed the torture to procure evidence against persons suspected of political offences.

[187] Hansard, vol. i. p. 271; and see Ann. Reg. 1830 Chron., p. 185.

[188] See article by Sir C. Warren, *Murray's Magazine*, Nov. 1888.

[189] See Report of Parliamentary Committee, 1838.

[190] 10 Geo. iv. c. 45.

[191] 3 Will. iv. c. 19.

[192] 6 & 7 Will. iv. c. 50.

[193] Peel wished to include the City of London in the Metropolitan Police Area, but in a private letter to a friend frankly confessed that he dared not meddle with it.—("Life of Sir Robert Peel," C. S. Parker).

[194] 2 & 3 Vict. c. 47.

[195] See 2 & 3 Vict. 47-71 & 93.

[196] See "The Police of the Metropolis," by Sir C. Warren—*Murray's Magazine*, Nov. 1888. On the 15th April 1829, Peel informed the House of Commons that crime was then far more prevalent in the metropolis than in the country—one person out of every 383 persons having, on the average, been committed in London, whilst in the provinces the proportion was only one in 822.

[197] 1st Report Constabulary Commissioners, 1839, page 13.

[198] 3 & 4 Will. iv. c. 90.

[199] This "Lighting and Watching Act" still remains the authority for the appointment of firemen, who may be "additional constables," and who, "shall, during the time they shall be on duty, use their utmost endeavours to prevent any mischief by fire." (3 & 4 Will. iv. c. 90, s. 41.)

[200] 5 & 6 Will. iv. c. 76.

[201] 13 and 14 Car. ii. c. 12.

[202] 1 and 2 Will. iv. c. 41.

[203] 5 and 6 Will. iv. c. 76.

[204] 1 and 2 Vic. c. 41.

[205] Bicknell's "Police Manual," p. 58.

[206] 2 & 3 Vict., c. 93.

[207] In 1840 the Act was amended, and a separate Police rate levied, by 3 & 4 Vict., c. 38.

[208] In the year 1842, the Criminal Jurisdiction of Courts of Quarter Sessions, which hitherto had been competent to deal with all offences except treason, was limited by 5 & 6 Vict. c. 38, which removes murder, capital felony and some other offences from the cognizance of the Justices. In the metropolis, at the same time, much criminal business was transferred from Justices of the Peace to Stipendiary Magistrates. This was due rather to the increase of commitments consequent upon an improved police, than to any implied incompetence of the Courts. In 1896 Quarter Sessions were again empowered to try Burglary cases (59 & 60 Vict. c. 57), and a further extension, or rather restoration, of the powers exercised by Justices in Quarter Sessions is understood to be now (1901) under consideration.

[209] 5 & 6 Vic. c. 109—amended by 13 & 14 Vic. c. 20.

[210] 10 Geo. iv. c. 97.

[211] See 1st Report 1853 Select Committee, p. 137.

[212] Those landowners who gave evidence before the Select Committee in 1853 were almost unanimous in their testimony that the value of property had increased in counties where rural police forces had been established.—See second Report, 1853 Committee, §§ 2770, 2792, and 2793.

[213] See ante p. 102, Chapter VI.

[214] See Second Report 1853 Committee, pp. 151, 152.

[215] 19 & 20 Vic., c. 69.

[216] 2 & 3 Vict., c. 47.

[217] In the course of these riots £50,000 worth of damage was done.

[218] After these riots the General Convention of Chartists issued a proclamation declaring "that a flagrant, wanton, and unjust outrage has been made upon the people of Birmingham, by a bloodthirsty and unconstitutional force from London, acting under the authority of men who wished to keep the people in degradation."—"Annals of Our Times, 1839." See also "Chronicles of Crime," Camden Pelham.

[219] *Quarterly Review*, No. 257, 1870.

[220] Sir James Fitzjames Stephen's "A History of the Criminal Law of England," vol. i. chap. xiv.

[221] Hale, Sum. 36, 37—I Hale, 457.

[222] From "The Commonwealth of England," by Sir Thomas Smith, 1589 edition.

[223] The County and Borough Police Act of 1856 required Rural Police Forces to furnish annual returns of all crimes committed, persons apprehended, and subsequent criminal proceedings in their respective districts, on forms of return supplied by Sir George Gray. From the materials thus supplied were the Criminal Statistics prepared until 1892, when an improved method of compilation was introduced by the "Police Returns Act" of that year—(55 and 56 Vict. c. 38).

[224] There were eighty-two cases of garrotting in London between June and December 1862; nor was the increased prevalence of crime confined to the Metropolis—most of the larger towns (especially Liverpool) suffered in the same way.

[225] Transportation to New South Wales and S. Australia ceased in 1850, to Van Diemen's Land in 1852; the last batch of convicts was sent to Western Australia in 1867.

[226] The Chatham mutiny occurred in 1861, some years after the "Penal Servitude Act" had become law, but it was due to very similar causes to those which had occasioned the earlier outbreaks.

[227] 16 and 17 Vict. c. 99.

[228] Select Committee on Transportation 1856, Para. 1824.

[229] In the case of women convicts remission to the extent of one-third or thereabouts can be earned.

[230] 50,000 is nearer the mark. There were 43,000 in Australasia alone.

[231] Speech by Sir H. Fowler, *The Times*, Jan. 15, 1901.

[232] See the article on Reformatories by Sir E. Du Cane in "Chambers' Encyclopædia."

[233] 17 & 18 Vict. c. 86.

[234] 18 & 19 Vict. c. 87, and 19 & 20 Vict. c. 109.

[235] 20 & 21 Vict. c. 48.

[236] 24 & 25 Vict. c. 113.

[237] 42 & 43 Vict. c. 49.

[238] 50 & 51 Vict. c. 25.

[239] "Police Code," pp. 80 and 81.

[240] These recognizances may be with, or without, sureties; and the obligation "to keep the peace" and "to be of good behaviour" continues during such period as the Court may direct. *Cf.* p. 49, chapter iii. ante, with reference to the powers conferred on Justices of the Peace by 34 Edw. iii. c. 1.

[241] Bicknell's Police Manual, p. 244.

[242] 34 and 35 Vict. c. 112.

[243] Female holders of licenses are not required to report themselves once a month.

[244] See Bicknell's Police Manual, p. 245.

[245] A complete description of the system as employed in England may be found in a pamphlet entitled "The Identification of Habitual Criminals," published by *The Police Review*.

[246] See "Our absurd system of punishing crime," by Dr Robert Anderson, in *The Nineteenth Century and After* for February 1901.

[247] See also a letter of Mr Justice Wills on the same subject, in *The Times*, 21st Feb. 1901.

[248] The electric telegraph was first adapted to police purposes in 1841.

[249] See Kirchner's "Law and practice relative to Fugitive Offenders."

[250] 42 & 43 Vict. c. 22.

[251] 47 & 48 Vict. cap. 58.

[252] These Regulations were revised by Sir Richard Webster (Lord Alverstone), Lord Herschell, and the Right Hon. Hugh Childers in 1886, and may be found on page 250 of Bicknell's Police Manual.

[253] Now Colonel Sir Howard Vincent, M.P., the compiler of "The Police Code," and a well-known authority on police questions.

[254] In 1884 the office of Director of Criminal Investigation was abolished, and the duties formerly appertaining to the office have since then been performed by an additional Assistant-Commissioner, appointed for the purpose; but the system remains practically the same as when it was first introduced in 1878.

[255] See *The Times*, 6th Feb. 1888.

[256] 2 & 3 Vict. c. 47, s. 22.

[257] In addition to the authorized deductions made from the pay of constables, all monies arising from fines imposed on constables, or for assaults on constables, from the sale of old police clothing, from pedlars and chimney sweeps' certificates, from fines imposed by a Court of Summary Jurisdiction, for offences under the Licensing Acts 1872-74, and from certain other sources, are now carried to the Pension Fund (see Police Act, 53 & 54 Vict. c. 45).

[258] 20 & 21 Vict. c. 64, s. 15.

[259] See "The Story of Police Pensions," by J. Munro.—*New Review*, vol. iii.

[260] 53 and 54 Vict. c. 45 (a).

[261] Disorderly meetings took place on the 17th, 18th, 19th, and 23rd Oct. '87; on the last of these occasions some two thousand rioters were guilty of brawling in Westminster Abbey.

[262] There is an interesting article on the "Right of Public Meeting," by Professor Dicey, in *The Contemporary Review*, April 1889. See "Annual Register," 1888.

[263] 5 & 6 Will. iv. c. 76.

[264] 45 & 46 Vict. c. 50.

[265] 51 & 52 Vict. c. 41, &c.

[266] See L.G.A., Section 9, para. 3.

[267] Speech by Mr Morley at Newcastle, 21st of June 1886.

[268] See article in the *Contemporary Review*, vol. lv. (Year 1889), by H. Evans, who therein pointed out that "the Treasury Grant to the Metropolitan Police Fund bears a higher proportion to the rateable value, than is the case with the contributions to the County and Borough Police."

[269] See section 2, 50 Vict. c. 9.

[270] Police Code, under "Discipline."

[271] From "An Address to Police Constables on their Duties," by Sir Henry Hawkins, printed in "The Police Code."

[272] Contrasting public with private executions, Henry Fielding remarked in favour of the latter, that, "the criminal dies only in the presence of his enemies, without the cordial of public approval to flatter his ambition."

[273] J. Bentham, "Principles of the Penal Law," chapter xxi.

[274] "Judicial Statistics England and Wales." Part I.—Introduction, page 25.

INDEX

- A
- Aberdeen, 351
- Abjuration of the Realm, 35, 363
- Admiralty, Court of, 62
- Agisters, 68
- Alehouse Act, The, 222
- Alien Act, The, 175
- Alfred the Great, 3, 10, 13
- Alverstone, Lord, 365
- Amercements, 19
- America, 208, 209, 364, 371
- Anderson, Dr Robert, 362
- Anglesey, 305
- Anglo-Saxon Police, 8, 14, 232, 401
- Anthropometry, 359, 361
- Appeal, 91
- Assize of Arms, the, 26, 27, 28
- Australia, 210, 341, 342
- Aylesbury, 72

- B
- Bacon, Lord, 17, 84, 113
- Bail, 50, 324
- Barbadoes, 129, 208
- Barkstead, Colonel, 128, 130
- Bath, 269
- Basket Justices, 115
- Beccaria, 219
- Bedel, 75
- Bedfordshire, 45, 126, 304
- Benefit of Clergy, 89, 222
- Bentham, J., xiii., 6, 94, 204, 205, 217, 218, 219, 223, 247, 347, 404
- Berkshire, 45, 105, 126, 305
- Bermuda, 209
- Bertillon, M. Alphonse, 359
- Birmingham, 252, 260, 273, 312, 313, 352, 384
- Blackstone, 56, 71, 85
- Blood-money, 140, 211
- Bonaventors, 115
- Bootless crimes, 11
- Borsholder, 4
- Bow Street, 156, 157, 191, 227, 263
- Bow Street Runners, 157, 191, 196, 265, 350, 367
- Brampton, Lord, 402
- Bravadors, 115
- Brecon, 305
- Bristol Riots, 272, 277, 318
- Buckinghamshire, 45, 126, 305
- Bullock-hunting, 197

- Burleigh, Lord, 100
- Burn, 5, 49

- C
- Camberwell, 253, 254
- Cambridge, 90, 274
- Cambridgeshire, 45, 126, 304
- Canterbury, 77, 396
- Canute, 63
- Capital Punishment, 204, 207, 404
- Card registers, 360
- Cardiganshire, 305
- Carmarthenshire, 305
- Carnarvonshire, 305
- Carta de foresta, 67
- Census Returns, 337
- Charles I., 119
- —— II., 131, 133, 136, 180, 208
- "Charlies," 133, 183, 184, 245
- Chartists, 313, 314
- Chateaubriand, 246
- Chatham, 343
- Cheshire, 30, 126, 283, 300, 305
- Chief Constable, 113, 122, 390, 392, 400
- Childers, Mr, 384
- Churchwardens, 104, 179
- City Marshalls, 187
- City of London Police, 6, 30, 32, 53, 186, 231, 263, 267, 397, 398
- Civil War, 124, 276
- Clarendon, Assize of, 25
- Clerks of the Peace, 53
- Coastguard, 283, 408
- Coke, Lord, 13, 35, 58
- Colchester, 34
- Coldbath Fields, 256, 319, 382
- Colquhoun, Dr, vii., 177, 181, 204, 218, 219, 220, 223, 332
- Colthrop, Sir H., 121
- Commissioners of Police, 234, 235, 242, 250, 256, 263, 285
- Commissioners of Sewers, 133
- Commitment Returns, 338, 339
- Commons, House of, 47, 52
- Constable, the, 43, 55, 56, &c.
- Conservators of the Peace, 19, 44, 392
- Convicts, 349
- Convict Supervision office, 136, 359, 370
- Cornwall, Earl of, 45
- Cornwall, 96, 126, 305
- Coroners, 37, 38, 91, 275
- Council of the North, 94, 137
- County Boroughs, 393
- County Councils, 390, 392

- County Courts, 390
- County, Power of the, 8, 45
- Courts, Ecclesiastical, 62
- Courts Leet, 17, 18, 40, 41, 54, 102, 122, 134
- Coventry, 270
- Criminal Investigation Department, 311, 370, 395
- Criminal Statistics, 340, 405
- Cromwell, Oliver, 125, 127, 131
- Cromwell, Thomas, 94
- Cumberland, 126, 138, 305
- Curfew Bell, 16, 31

- D
- Dartmoor, 343
- Decennary Police, 9, 18, 24, 75
- Decennier, 121
- De Goncourt Case, 368, 371
- Denbigh, 305
- Denville, Sir Gosselin, 39
- Derbyshire, 126, 305
- Detective Police, 311, 366
- Devonshire, 126, 305
- Dickens, Charles, 207
- Dictum de Kenilworth, 24
- Director of Public Prosecutions, 364
- —— Criminal Investigation, 370
- Dorsetshire, 126, 305
- Drawlatches, 29
- Dublin Police Act, 169
- Duelling, 202
- Durham, 126, 304

- E
- Edgar, 1, 6
- Edward I., 24, 30, 31, 36, 44, 60
- —— II., 39
- —— III., 26, 43, 46, 47, 60, 74
- —— IV., 51
- —— VI., 2, 46, 94, 96
- —— VII., 57
- Essex, 45, 104, 126, 301, 303, 304
- Expeditation, 66
- Extradition Acts, 364

- F
- Fielding, Henry, 141, 155, 158, 191, 207, 218, 220, 404
- Fielding, Sir John, 156, 157, 161, 167, 218
- Fightwitt, 6
- Flash-houses, 193
- Flintshire, 305
- Ford, Sir Richard, 194, 224

- Foresters, 68
- Forest Law, 62, 63, 69, 70, 119
- Frankpledge, 4, 15, 20, 42, 77, 121
- French Revolution, The, 246
- Frithbrec, 6

- G
- Galton, Mr Francis, 359
- Garrotting, 341
- George I., 147
- —— II., 151
- Glamorganshire, 305
- Gloucester, 304
- Gloucestershire, 126
- Gneist, 13
- Gordon Riots, 165, 167, 174, 314, 277
- Graham, Sir J., 311
- Gray, Sir G., 340
- Griffiths, Major, 215
- Grithbryce, 6
- Grosvenor, Lord R., 319, 322
- Gypsies, 10, 90, 109

- H
- Habitual Criminals Act, 357
- Habitual offenders, 355, 359, 405
- Hampshire, 126, 304
- Harcourt, Sir W., 376
- Headboroughs, 4, 8, 57, 178, 211
- Helps, Sir A., 401
- Henderson, Sir E., 379, 385, 386
- Henry I., 2
- —— II., 18, 63, 68
- —— III., 20, 23, 55
- —— IV., 54
- —— V., 54
- —— VII., 54, 82, 89
- —— VIII., 93, 137
- Herefordshire, 45, 126, 305
- Hertfordshire, 126, 139, 304
- Hext, Mr, 108
- High Constable, 55, 110, 113, 114, 122, 150, 151, 177, 390
- High Steward, 100, 160
- Highwaymen, 139, 143, 195, 282
- Home Office, 190, 221, 232, 275, 344, 346
- Howard, John, 217, 347
- Hue and Cry, 5, 27, 33, 34, 35, 36, 46, 59, 67, 83, 89, 104, 111, 123, 151, 179, 180, 189, 240, 291, 308, 403
- Hulks, the, 342
- Hull, 270
- Hundred, the, 4, 5, 105, 179

- —— liability of, 5, 122, 180
- Huntingdonshire, 45, 126, 305
- Hyde Park, 320, 324, 327, 384

- I
- Identification of Criminals, 347, 358, 359
- Industrial Schools, 353
- Inhabitant Watch, the, 150
- Inlaugh, 121
- Inspectors of Constabulary, 306, 391
- Ireland, 169, 329, 330, 394
- Irish Constabulary, Royal, 169, 305

- J
- James I., 115
- —— II., 248
- James, Sir H., 388
- John, King, 19, 20
- Judicium Pillorie, 79
- Jury of Annoyances, 159
- Justice of Assize, 125
- Justices Itinerant, 19
- Justices of the Peace, 43, 44, 51, 59, 93, 97, 101, 107, 116, 125, 144, 147, 232, 234, 275, 392
- Justices of the Quorum, 93
- —— Gaol Delivery, 93
- Justice Seat, Court of the, 64, 66
- Juvenile Offenders Act, 287, 351

- K
- Kent, 44, 45, 57, 126, 233, 285, 299, 305, 394
- Kerry, 394
- King's Bench, Court of, 58
- King's Highway, the, 3
- King's Peace, the, 1, 2, 62, 124

- L
- Labourers, Statute of, 60, 108
- Lambard, 8, 54, 56, 181
- Lancashire, 126, 284, 304, 305
- La Reynie, 246
- Leet. *See* Courts
- Leicestershire, 16, 126, 304
- Lepers, 31, 73
- Lettre de Cachet, 247
- Lewes, 292
- Liber albus, 80
- Licensing Acts, 97, 101, 338, 375
- Lighting and Watching Act, 274
- Lincoln, 34, 289
- Lincolnshire, 45, 126, 289, 305
- Little-goes, 197

- Liverpool, 271, 272, 280, 283, 341
- Livery Companies, 88
- Local Government Act, 391, 393, 394
- Lombroso, 406
- London, 6, 30, 32, 53, 73, 76, 78, 80, 125, 126, 132, 140, 144, 150, 165, 171, 182, 229, 243, 248, 252, 274, 280, 309, 318, 378, 384, 386, 395
- London County Council, 394, 395, 396
- London Docks, 310
- Lords-Lieutenant, 97, 278
- Lords-Marchers, 93
- Lords of the Manor, 17, 51, 134
- Lushington, Sir F., 191
- Lynch Law, 149

- M
- Mad Parliament, the, 23
- Maegbote, 10
- Magna Carta, 19, 63
- Mainprise, 50
- Major-Generals, 127, 129, 130
- Manbote, 10
- Manchester, 272, 351, 384
- Mansion-House, 152, 189, 397
- Manwood, 64, 69
- Marching Watch, the, 31
- Marine Society, the, 350
- Marlborough, Statute of, 20
- Martial Law, ix., 106, 107
- Mayne, Sir R., 234, 242, 253, 310, 321, 324, 325, 346, 398
- Mayneer, 65
- M'Hardy, Captain, 301, 303, 305
- Melbourne, Lord, 256, 259
- Merioneth, 305
- Metropolitan Police, 229, 232, 236, 238, 258, 260, 267, 288, 309, 312, 385, 395
- Metropolitan Police area, 260, 263, 268, 394
- Metropolitan Police District, 237, 394
- Middlesex, 45, 57, 100, 126, 170, 195, 196, 233, 394
- Middlesex Justices Act, 171, 172, 173, 176, 189, 190
- Militia, the, 7, 55, 97, 127, 152, 153, 167, 174
- Millbank, 347, 369
- Minsheu, 121, 123
- Mohocks, 144, 146, 277
- Monmouthshire, 126, 290, 305
- Montgomery, 305
- More, Sir Thomas, 92, 158
- Moss-troopers, 137, 138
- Municipal Corporations Act, 274, 277, 306, 391, 393
- Munro, Mr, 331, 376
- Murdrum, The, 16
- Mutual Security, 15, 17

- N
- "New Police," the, 335
- Newcastle, Duke of, 158
- Newgate, 78, 121, 150, 167, 215, 216
- New South Wales, 209, 210
- Norfolk, 45, 96, 126, 304
- Norman police, 14
- Northampton, Assize of, 18, 25
- Northamptonshire, 45, 126, 304
- Northumberland, 126, 138, 299, 305, 394
- Norton, Lord, 351
- Nottinghamshire, 126, 129, 304
- Norwich, 39

- O
- Obligatory Act, The, 305, 307, 338
- Ordeals, 12
- Oxford plague regulations, 118
- Oxford, Provisions of, 23, 24
- Oxford University, 90, 274
- Oxfordshire, 45, 126, 305

- P
- Parkhurst, 351
- Parliamentary Commissions, viii., 26, 160, 162, 199, 201, 221, 227, 228, 230, 234, 244, 255, 259, 261, 336, 344, 352, 360
- Parochial System of Police, 176, 182, 211, 237, 291, 355, 396
- Passports, 102, 135
- Patrol, Foot, 156, 194, 226, 233
- —— Horse, 156, 194, 224, 233, 263, 264
- Peace Guilds, 6
- Peace of the Church, 62
- —— of the Sea, 62
- Peace Wardens, 44
- Peel, Sir R., 227, 228, 230, 243, 245, 251, 256, 262, 309, 372, 399
- "Peine forte et dure," 330
- Pembrokeshire, 305
- Penal Code, the, 204
- Penal Servitude Act, 343, 356
- Pennsylvania, 347
- Pentonville, 347, 348
- Permissive Act, the, 293, 296, 298, 301, 396, 310
- "Peterloo Massacre," 314
- Petty Constable, Oath of, 114
- Photography, 359
- Pie-poudre, Court of, 270
- Pillory, the, 78, 79, 222
- Plague, The, 117, 118, 132, 133
- Police Act, the, 376
- —— franchise, 399
- —— Disabilities Removal Act, 400

- —— Pensions, 376
- —— Returns Act, 340
- —— Supervision, 357
- Poor Laws, 103
- Popay, 253, 256, 310
- Portland, 343
- Portsmouth, 271, 343, 351
- Posse Comitatus, the, 8, 39, 45, 54, 276
- Præpositus, the, 14, 56
- Press, the, 250, 403
- Press gang, the, 341
- Presentment, 40, 59, 239
- Prevention of Crimes Act, 357, 359
- Primarii, 68
- Prison Act, the, 348
- Prisons, 78, 149, 215
- Probation of First Offenders Act, 354
- Procurator Fiscal, 288
- Prosecution of Offences Act, 365
- Public Health Acts, 391
- —— Meeting, Right of, 388
- —— offices, 191, 264
- —— prosecutor, 109, 223
- —— works prisons, 348
- Purlieu, 66

- Q
- Quarter Sessions, 48, 112, 136, 151, 222, 293, 295, 337, 340, 390, 392
- Quarterors, 115
- Queen Anne, 144, 145, 146
- Queen Elizabeth, 99, 103, 105, 137, 159, 334
- Queen Victoria, vii., 277, 349

- R
- Radnorshire, 305
- Ragged Schools, 351
- Rainsforth, Mr F., 161
- Rangers, 68
- Recognizances, 355
- Reformatories, 350, 353, 354
- Reformatory School Act, 352
- Regard, Court of, 64, 66
- Regarders, 68
- Richard I., 19, 44
- —— II., 46, 48, 50, 53
- Riot Act, the, 96, 147, 258
- Riotous Assemblies, 314
- Riots, 202
- —— see Bristol
- —— see Gordon
- —— Featherstone, 408

- —— Hyde Park, 320
- —— Reform, 327
- —— Chartist, 314
- —— Sunday Trading Bill, 319
- —— West End, 317, 381
- Roaring Boys, 115
- Roberdsmen, 29
- Robin Redbreasts, 194
- Romilly, Sir S., 205, 206, 218, 219
- "Route forms," 360
- "Round-houses," 162
- Rowan, Colonel, 234, 253, 257, 258, 259, 292, 310
- Royal Society, the, 133
- Rural Police, 102, 182, 279, 295
- Rural Police Act, 293, 305
- Russell, Sir C., 388
- Rutland, 45, 126, 305

- S
- Sanctuary, 35, 115
- Sartines, 247
- Sayer, John, 193, 198
- Scavengers, 75
- Scotland, 93, 288
- Scotland Yard, 233, 237, 262, 263, 266, 311, 359, 395
- Searchers, 101, 117
- Shaftesbury, Lord, 351
- Shakespeare, 108
- Sheriffs, 7, 14, 16, 36, 40, 44, 45, 97, 119, 276
- Shropshire, 30, 126, 304
- Sidmouth, Lord, 224, 227
- Six Acts, the, 202
- Smith, Sir T., 102, 334
- Somersetshire, 108, 126, 286, 305
- Southwark, 74, 121
- Special Constables, 134, 176, 276, 314, 377, 387
- Staffordshire, 126, 304
- Standing Joint Committees, 392, 393
- Statistics, Police, 337, 339
- Stephen, Sir J., 333
- Stipendiary Magistrates, 173
- —— Police, 306, 338
- Stocks, the, 72, 77
- Street-keepers, 188, 240
- Stubbs, Dr, 1, 24, 25
- Suffield, Lord, 214
- Suffolk, 45, 126, 304
- Summary Jurisdiction Act, 354
- —— Courts of, 338
- Summons of the Array, 7
- Superannuation, 374

- Superintending Constables, 297
- Supervisees, 357
- Surety of the Peace, 50
- —— the Good Behaviour, 50
- Surrey, 45, 126, 233, 304, 394
- Sussex, 34, 126, 305
- Swanimote, Court of, 64, 66
- Sydney, 342

- T
- Tasmania, 342
- Thames Police, 176, 189, 223, 263, 266
- Thane, 3, 50
- Ticket-of-leave, 344, 345, 356
- Tine-men, 68
- Tourn, Court of the, 15, 18, 40
- Townsend, James, 170, 193, 194, 204, 212
- Trade Guilds, 84, 86
- "Trading Justices," 115, 169, 170
- Trafalgar Square, 378, 381, 387
- Trained Bands, the, 152, 248
- Transportation, 158, 208, 210, 341, 343
- Trinoda necessitas, 7
- Troup, Mr C. E., 405
- Tumbril (see Pillory)
- Tyburn, 141, 149, 158, 159
- Tyburn-ticket, 213, 214
- Tyler, Wat, 61
- Tything, the, 3, 4, 5, 120
- Tythingmen, 56, 57, 114, 125, 179, 180

- U
- Unification of London, 398

- V
- Vaccination Acts, 338
- Vagrancy, 33, 92, 102, 116, 221, 302
- Verderers, 65, 68
- Vert, 65
- Vicecomes, 14, 15, 18, 56
- Vincent, Sir Howard, 354, 370, 402
- Vine Street Station, 323, 324, 325

- W
- Wales, 92, 126
- Wapentakes, 179
- Warren, Sir C., 260, 272, 386, 387
- Warwickshire, 45, 126, 305
- Watch Committees, 81, 275, 306, 391, 393
- Watch and Ward, 21, 26, 27, 33, 71, 122, 183, 189
- Weights and Measures, 86, 304, 408

- Wellington, Duke of, 220, 243, 245, 314
- Westminster, 99, 100, 126, 128, 144, 160, 162, 163, 188, 198
- Westminster, Statute of, 159
- Westmoreland, 30, 126, 305
- Whitefriars, 115, 132
- Wild, Jonathan, 141, 143
- Willford, Sir T., 107
- William I., 2, 15
- —— III., 248
- —— IV., 251, 274
- Wiltshire, 126, 286, 304, 305
- Winchester, Statute of, 24, 25, 26, 29, 30, 32, 33, 36, 39, 42, 55, 71, 79, 112, 122, 151
- Wite, 11
- Woodmote Court, 64, 66
- Worcestershire, 305
- Wrecking, 283

- Y
- Yeomanry, 97
- "Yoongmen," 68
- Yorkshire, 39, 126, 305, 408

TURNBULL AND SPEARS, PRINTERS, EDINBURGH.

Transcriber's Notes

Obvious punctuation errors repaired.

p. 83 When property cansisted only of timber, replaced with
When property consisted only of timber,

www.ingramcontent.com/pod-product-compliance
Lightning Source LLC
Chambersburg PA
CBHW051804170526
45167CB00005B/1872